New Context for Learning

New Context for Learning

Edited by

Dr. G. VISVANATHAN

Professor, Department of Education,
Annamalai University, TN

Dr.S.K.PANNEER SELVAM

Assistant Professor, Department of Education
Bharathidasan University, T.N

RANDOM PUBLICATIONS

NEW DELHI (INDIA)

New Context for Learning

ISBN 978-93-5111-752-0

Published in 2015 in India by
RANDOM PUBLICATIONS
4376-A/4B, Gali Murari Lal, Ansari Road
New Delhi-110 002
Phone : +9111-43580356, 011-43142548, 011-23289044
e-mail : sales@randompublications.com
info@randompublications.com
randomexports@gmail.com

Reprinted 2021

Type Setting by : Shah Computer Graphics, Delhi-110094
Digitally Printed at: Replika Press Pvt. Ltd.

Contents

9

10

11

14

15

16

29

30

31

32

35

36

37

38

1

Attitude of College Students Towards Internet

Introduction

Internet is a useful tool for all in a technologically advanced world. Internet use for education is very important. It is now in practice to teach school to college to get more out of it. To make proper use of Internet in schools, colleges and universities there is a need to understand the attitudes of students toward the use of it. And it must be ensured that resources are being used in college legally and if there are problems, then problem areas must first strike and then put the necessary measures to overcome the problem. For the student's attitude toward Internet applications, university administration should know that the purposes for which students are using it as entertainment and sports, for academic purposes, correspondence and business and social purposes, etc. Now a day, all schools, colleges and universities are using Internet technology. With the help of this, schools, colleges and universities, teachers are valuable teaching tool. The study used an attitudes inventory to identify attitudes associated with gender issues of arts and science college students. Analyses of the findings indicate that contrary to earlier studies on these issues neither male nor female in this group reflected concern about the attitude towards internet. As like as neither urban nor rural group reflected about the attitude towards internet. The results carry implications for both general education and teacher education. Educators and trainers should re-examine their behaviors as they make decisions regarding career choices, on-the-job training opportunities and job placement.

The Internet is a useful tool for all in a technologically sophisticated world. The Internet is also widely used in education. The use of Internet for education is very important. It is now being used to teach in schools and colleges to get more out of it. The Internet offers more information than the largest libraries in the world. Using the Internet in universities has a positive value. Many universities around the world are also using Internet for educational purposes for easy and effective teaching. The Internet has become an essential part in educational institutions since it plays a vital role in meeting information and communication needs of students, teachers and institutions. Teachers are being invited to give their teaching materials and other support resources available through the Internet. Students use the Internet to communicate not only with colleagues, but also with their instructors. Students and teachers can communicate with each other with the help of internet. It has an easy access to all information on the latest research reports from anywhere in the world. It helps researchers, teachers, students and institutions to disseminate information to more viewers worldwide through websites. Teachers get useful information about their classes and also download useful and latest information on the subject. A teacher may ask students to find a topic and related research on the Internet. The Internet is also used to replace the traditional classroom lecture. The instructor can place course notes on web pages, create recordings video of a live conference for presentation to the Internet or can use combinations of these ideas.

As today's society is becoming more and more dependent on new technology, increasing attention is given to Internet literacy, which in the current information age is no less significant as was reading, writing and calculus in the 19th - 20th centuries. Internet literacy becomes an essential precondition for successful socialization and professional career. For this reason, education being an important factor in society development, it plays an essential role in addressing the issue of literacy and in particular computer literacy. Technology is the main support for the students learning developments now-a-days. With shifting from the teacher-centered instruction to child-centered instruction, the role, activities, attitudes, reflections of the students become more important concern to overlook the effectiveness of technology in instruction. Internet is the main technology support as a tool for effective learning and teaching process. As a technological tool, it provides the equal standards, opportunities and easy path for the successful understanding and also meaningful learning for students. In order to be reflective, recommend on the usage of Internet and facilities, there should be examination of the thoughts, attitudes of students towards Internet. Regarding the meaning of attitudes, different researchers gave different but somehow related definitions of the word. Aiken described attitudes as "learned predispositions to respond positively or negatively to certain objects, situations, concepts, or persons". Attitude is an inner psychic state influencing behavior. Therefore, it can be understand an inner state from actions and words. For instance, one might presume that a person actively avoiding a computer has a negative attitude towards it. Attitude is not an inborn, instinct phenomenon; it mainly depends upon person's experience and its impact in a new situation. Consequently, attitudes are formed in the process of experience and their change is possible due to the internal and external factors. Obviously the quality of computer literacy is closely related to one of the major attitudes components is motivation. If a student is absolutely motiveless to work with computer, the learning result will not be optimal. A motivated computer user, even under unfavorable conditions, willingly works with Internet. This article deals with the study of students' attitudes towards Internet using methods.

Significance of the Study

As we are living in the era of modern technology, therefore, there must to address the future needs and requirement of students. The future planning is the jurisdiction of policy making institutions and departments such as planning commission, policy institute, etc. The present study will enable future policy makers to provide Internet facilities to future generations. The study reveals that Internet is playing pivotal role in educational projects and especially for research. It is easier to search through internet as compare to sit in the library and collect information. The present study will send a strong message to publishers and writers to shift from their attention from hard binding books to soft copies of their finding and make available on the Internet so that more people can get access to this invaluable information. A wast majority of the student is using Internet in their educational life. The Internet use will encourage our younger generations to make use of modern technologies to accomplish their ambition. The present study will encourage those students who do not use Internet because of security and reasons to use internet and compete. The study will further contribute to create awareness among older age people who are afraid of both Internet. They should be provided training so that they can also use Internet. Now, the learning process has been done through online, namely 'online learning'. Already the new generation students come across the M-learning, it is the learning process which helps the learner to know about the subject he wants to learn with the help of the latest technology, the Internet. Hence, the online learning has the significance part. The students must know the way of learning from the Internet. There is a significant role of Internet in society and schools. It is discussable about bringing to educational change through Internet developments. Internet provides work speed, work efficiency, work power and removal of human error from work activities. With these brief facilities, it is understandable that Internet and higher information technology effect the students' learning and studying. It is questionable how effectively affect and what are the attitudes of students toward Internet role in education.

Contribution and Conclusion

This article was conducted on the students' attitude toward Internet applications. The research objective is to identify factors influencing student Internet use. Information was gathered through the questionnaires on students using the Internet. It finds that the Internet is an essential knowledge for students and teachers. Mostly the respondents are from computer and economics courses. Students use the Internet primarily for educational and research purposes and benefits instead of playing a positive role and participation in society. However, it provides extensive information on the required assignments, and thus covers many dimensions' that meet educational needs. Students find the Internet more informative as compared to teachers. The majority of students feel comfortable using the Internet. Respondents enjoy collecting more information than written material. Two third respondents overwhelmed with Internet found in the studies. Additionally, the results indicate that most respondents are satisfied that Internet access is more in college than at home and most of those participants said the Internet is slow at home. Students must realize that the Internet is a medium. It is recommended that students should not waste their time on useless activities. Basic Internet tools may be introduced to students in their early stages of education. The benefits of Internet should be disseminated to all students. Institutions should provide better infrastructure to facilitate students. Universities should organize courses that build up internal capacity of students require to use Internet in efficient and effective way. The courses organized by University should highlight the use of Internet research techniques and course materials should be situated on the Web to facilitate access by students. As a final note, studying attitudes toward Internet among students are critical for the successful implementation of information technology in the classroom. Findings of such studies will determine the proper direction toward the success of technology incorporation in the classroom. Additionally the instilling of positive attitude toward Internet will assist the nation to achieve its goal of an information literate society who is able to keep abreast with the latest technology development. In addition to this, students need a Internet education to get efficient studies in order to get related knowledge. At these conclusions, by following new trends and tendency to use Internet in order to help future success of students is necessary. By these reasons, teacher and student should accept that Internet has a great influence on educational context.

References

1. Aydn, C. H. (2001). Uses of Internet in Turkey, *Educational technology research & development*, v.49,Washington. ISSN: 10421629.
2. Aiken, L. R. (1980). Attitude measurement and research. In D.A. Payne (Ed.), Recent developments in affective measurement. San Francisco:Jossey-Bass.
3. Anderson, C.A. (1983). Computer literacy: Rationale, definition and practices. Pa per presented at a satellite teleconference on microcomputers in education. ERIC ED228983.
4. Chickering, A.W., & Gamson, Z. F. (1991). Applying the seven principles for good practice in undergraduate education. *New Directions for Teaching and Learning*, 47, 63-69.
5. Iakushina, E.V. (2002). Adolescents on the Internet: A specific charter of information interaction. *Russian Education and Society*, 44, 81-95.
6. Risinger, F. (1998). Global education and the World Wide Web. *Social Education*, 62, 276-277.
7. Selwyn, N. (1999). Students' attitudes towards computers in sixteen to nineteen education. *Education and Information Technology*, 4(2), 129-141.
8. Thompson, R. L., Higgins, C. A., & Howell, J. M. (1991). Personal computing: toward a conceptual model of utilization. *MIS Quarterly*, 15, 125–143.

2

A Conductive Teaching and Learning Environment for the Future Community

Introduction

Pedagogy, in its contemporary usage, is a perspective that envisions effective teaching "as a process, not a technique". Pedagogy situates effective teaching more as "two-way communication than a mode of one-way transmission or delivery" of information to students. A teacher candidate, then, practices approaches to teaching and learning that builds relationships with and among students and "prioritizes the constitution of learning over the execution of teaching". This is congruent with research that finds achievement is improved through active student participation in the learning process (Gallego et al., 2001). Hence, it is imperative that a teacher candidate create instructional conditions where students are actively engaged in learning. National standards "clearly favor teachers who emphasize advanced content, deep understanding, reasoning, and applications over a strong focus on just basic skills and facts...[and] leans more toward constructivist teaching than toward direct instruction". In essence, then, an evaluator of a teacher candidate is focused on the effects of teaching on students that result in active learning of subject matter content (see Floden, 2001). Effective teaching encourages student interaction within an academically rigorous curriculum. Based on cognitive research, Resnick and the Institute for Learning note, "For classroom talk to promote learning it must be accountable—to the learning community, to accurate and appropriate knowledge, and to rigorous thinking". This requires a learning environment that promotes student application of their intelligence. Additionally, research on effective teaching also supports a learning environment that: Provides clear learning expectations. Pedagogy, in its contemporary usage, is a perspective that envisions effective teaching "as a process, not a technique". Pedagogy situates effective teaching more as "two-way communication than a mode of one-way transmission or delivery" of information to students. A teacher candidate, then, practices approaches to teaching and learning that builds relationships with and among students and "prioritizes the constitution of learning over the execution of teaching". This is congruent with research that finds achievement is improved through active student participation in the learning process. Hence, it is imperative that a teacher candidate create instructional conditions where students are actively engaged in learning. National standards "clearly favor teachers who emphasize advanced content, deep understanding, reasoning, and applications over a strong focus on just basic skills and facts...[and] leans more toward constructivist teaching than toward direct instruction". In essence, then, an evaluator of a teacher candidate is focused on the effects of teaching on students that result in active learning of subject matter content. Effective teaching encourages student interaction within an academically rigorous curriculum. Based on cognitive research, Resnick and the Institute for Learning note, "For classroom talk to promote learning it must be accountable-to the learning community, to accurate and appropriate knowledge, and to rigorous thinking". This requires a learning environment that promotes student application of their intelligence. Additionally, research on effective teaching also supports a learning environment that: Provides clear learning expectations. Uses fair and credible assessments of student learning. Models and analyzes complex thinking. Recognizes authentic accomplishment by every student. Teaches students to self-monitor their learning.

Teacher candidate's instructional planning includes pedagogical approaches designed to engage students intellectually with subject matter content. Research indicates that teachers who use pedagogical approaches that focus on authentic assessment of student learning can improve "academic performance at all grade levels". Furthermore, pedagogy directly connected to authentic assessment "can be distributed equitably to students from all social backgrounds with reasonably equitable benefits"

Effective Teaching

Effective teaching is congruent with what is often referred to as "best practices." Daniels and Bizar (1998), for example, describe "six basic structures that help to create Best Practice classrooms...[and] inherently give students a real voice and meaningful choices" in their learning community. These teaching and learning structures include integrative units, small group activities, representing-to-learn, classroom workshop, authentic experience, and reflective assessment. As examples of effective teaching strategies, the following are descriptions of these six structures: *Integrative units* are evident in instructional plans and teaching when a teacher candidate crosses "subject boundaries, translating models from one field into another, importing ideas from other subjects, designing cross-curricular investigations, and developing rich thematic units that involve students in long-term, deep, sophisticated inquiry". *Small group activities* exist in "classrooms with effective sub-groups are usually well structured places where students follow carefully developed norms and routines, and where working together is not a disruptive departure but rather business as usual". This best practice is generally referred to as cooperative learning. Within such activities student collaboration with one another "is the mainstay of these classrooms".

Representing-to-learn refers to learning activities that provide students an opportunity to both construct meaning of content being learned and share this learning with others. A teacher candidate can help students understand new material by selecting "examples and metaphors that illuminate new ideas and skills, connecting new content to students' knowledge, interests, and a school's culture" (Danielson, 1996). Students in a *classroom workshop* "choose individual or small group topics for investigation, inquiry, and research" (Daniels & Bizar, 1998). This best practice approach differs from a teacher presentation and places value on teacher modeling where students work "with real materials...[and] become active, responsible, self-motivating, and self-evaluating learners, while the teacher [serves] as model, coach, and collaborator". *Authentic experience* makes meaningful connections to "real world" activities.

The National Academy of Science states, "Inquiry into authentic questions generated from student experiences....Teachers focus inquiry predominately on real phenomena... where students are given investigations or guided toward fashioning investigations that are demanding but within their capabilities" (Daniels & Bizar, 1998). Authentic experience, therefore, is developmentally appropriate and linked to "real issues that people face in the world" in a manner that helps students make connections "to the importance of what they are learning".

Reflective assessment nurtures student reflection, goal-setting, and self-assessment of learning. The concepts contained in the following section on "Learning Targets and Assessment" address this best practice for effective teaching.

These six structures are not intended as an exhaustive list and are only meant to provide a teacher candidate with examples of what is entailed in effective teaching practices that can promote student achievement.

Learning Targets and Assessment

Lessons designed and implemented around developmentally and grade appropriate EALRs demonstrate that a teacher candidate is fulfilling the state's expectation on what the focus of the school curriculum should be. EALRs and their respective frameworks form the basis of learning targets. Stiggins (2001) explains that "*a target* defines academic success, what we want students to know and be able to do". Types of targets vary according to the academic goals of a particular content-area that is being learned. Stiggins describes five types or categories of targets: *Knowledge*—mastery of substantive subject matter content, where mastery includes both knowing and understanding it; *Reasoning*—the ability to use that knowledge and understanding to figure out things and to solve problems; *Performance Skills*—the development of proficiency in doing something where it is the process that is important, such as playing a musical instrument, reading aloud, speaking in a second language, or using psychomotor skills; *Products*—the ability to create tangible products, such as term papers, science fair models, and art products, that meet certain standards of quality and that present concrete evidence of academic proficiency; and *Dispositions*—the development of certain kinds of feelings, such as attitudes, interests, and motivational intentions.

For effective student learning, an instructional plan must provide learning targets that are capable of assessment. To be valid and meaningful, assessments must be aligned with learning targets. To measure student learning and determine if a unit of instruction has had a positive impact on student learning, pre-assessment data must be gathered. At the conclusion of instruction, a comparison of pre-assessment and post-assessment data can provide an indication of the degree to which student learning has occurred.

Stiggins (2001) describes four assessment methods that can be matched with the above described learning target categories. The assessment methods are: *Selected response*: "includes all of the objectively scored paper and pencil test formats". *Essay*: "Respondents are provided with an exercise (or set of exercises) that calls for them to prepare an original written answer....Evidence of achievement is seen in the conceptual substance of the response (i.e., ideas expressed and the manner in which they are tied together)".

Performance: "Respondents actually carry out a specified activity under the watchful eye of an evaluator, who observes their performance and makes judgments as to the quality of achievement demonstrated".

Personal communication: "includes questions posed and answered during instruction, interviews, conferences, conversations, and listening during class discussions and oral examinations. The examiner listens to responses and either (1) judges them right or wrong if correctness is the criterion, or (2) makes subjective judgments according to some continuum of quality". A critical tasks for a teacher candidate "is to identify and choose the most efficient" assessment method that appropriately relates to the identified learning target for a specific learning context. Student motivation in learning is increased when students are aware of learning targets and assessment expectations throughout an instructional unit. A teacher candidate needs to be explicit about both learning targets and assessment methods so that students learn how they can engage in assessments that measure their own learning relative to learning targets. For classroom assessment to accelerate student learning and be successful, it must be student centered so that both students and parents can observe improvements in learning (Stiggins, 2001).

Engaging Low Status/Historically Marginalized Students

A teacher candidate must create learning experiences that enable all students to have valid academic accomplishments, especially for those students who historically score below their peers on measures of academic achievement. Whereas more than 90% of Washington teachers and teacher candidates are white and middle-class, student demographics indicate growing racial, economic, and cultural diversity in our public school classrooms as well as the larger society. Research indicates that teachers need to recognize this difference in order to begin closing the achievement gap for those students habitually assigned "low status" and inferior academic competence (Cohen, 1994; Dilworth & Brown, 2001). In a review of related research, the Learning First Alliance (2001), an organization of which OSPI and WACTE are members, explains that "failure to support the academic achievement of students is related to students' disengagement from school". A review of recent court decisions finds that "the constitutional criterion for an adequate education tends to emphasize opportunity" (Rebell, 2002). Low-status students are among those who lack opportunities to receive the equitable benefits of pedagogical approaches designed to help students acquire meaningful and engaging academic content that can help them meet state learning standards. "Low status" students include individuals whose academic rights have been historically marginalized by institutions and people in privileged positions. This discrimination continues to be experienced by many students of color, immigrant children, and students from low-income families (Banks, 2001). Based on her extensive research, Cohen (1994) found: Examples of status characteristics are race, social class, sex, reading ability, and attractiveness. Attached to these status characteristics are general expectations for competence. High status individuals are expected to be more competent than low status individuals across a wide range of tasks that are viewed as important....Since in our culture people of color are generally expected to be less competent on intellectual tasks than whites, these racist expectations came into play in the innocent.

Cohen further observed that low status students working, for example, in small learning groups "often don't have access to the task...and don't talk as much as other students. Often when they do talk, their ideas are ignored by the rest of the group".

When the low status/ historically marginalized student become disengaged in learning, teachers often see this as a discipline problem rather than a status problem that needs teacher intervention and support in order that such students can demonstrate academic competence (Adams & Hamm, 1998; McEwan, 2000). As one possible solution, research finds that effectively mediated "cooperative learning promotes students' enjoyment of school and interpersonal relations, development of social skills, sense of the classroom as community, and academic achievement" (Learning First Alliance, 2001).

Teacher candidates are expected to plan instruction that includes strategies to engage low status/historically marginalized students. Plans must be explicit as to how instruction will develop critical thinking and problem solving skills of all students, including those considered low status/historically marginalized. If, when a teacher candidate is observed, these particular students are rarely engaged in learning opportunities or do not receive teacher support to demonstrate academic competence, the teacher candidate will be rated "below standard." One way in which a teacher candidate can be "at standard" for this category of students is by creating learning opportunities for students to work both individually and in different groups, including heterogeneous groups that builds and recognizes academic competence in subject matter content. Thus, a teacher candidate is expected to have students engaged in learning community activities that foster their active inquiry, collaboration, and supportive interactions.

Conclusion

As research and the sad experience of children being academically left behind indicates, a new, inclusive way of approaching teaching and learning is necessary. The collaboration between Wacte and Ospi provides a performance-based approach to addressing this problem. Higher education and Ospi, however, cannot do this task alone. As higher education, Ospi, and the State Board work together in providing qualified beginning teachers, public school teachers, administrators, school boards, legislators, families, communities, and tribal councils must also join in a paradigm shift that is beneficial and effective for all children.

References

1. Evertson, C.M., & Randolph, C.H. (1999). Perspectives on classroom management in learning-centered classrooms. In H.C. Waxman & H.J. Walberg (Eds.), *New directions for teaching practice and research* (pp. 249-268). Berkeley, CA: McCutchan Publishing.
2. Floden, R. (2001). Research on effects of teaching. In V. Richardson (Ed.), *Handbook of research on teaching* (4th ed.) (pp. 3-16). Washington, DC: American Educational Research Association.
3. Irvine, J.J. (2001). The critical elements of culturally responsive pedagogy: A synthesis of the research. In J.J. Irvine, B.J. Armento, V.E. Causey, J.C. Jones, R.S. Frasher, & M.H. Weinburgh (Eds.),

4. *Culturally responsive teaching: Lesson planning for elementary and middle grades* (pp. 3-17). Boston: McGraw Hill.

5. Ladson-Billings, G. (1995). Toward a theory of culturally relevant pedagogy. *American Educational Research Journal, 32*(3): 465-491.

6. Marks, H.M., Newmann, F.M., & Gamoran, A. (1996). Does authentic pedagogy increase student achievement? In F.M. Newmann & Associates (Ed.), *Authentic assessment: Restructuring schools for intellectual quality* (pp. 49-73). San Francisco: Jossey-Bass.

7. McEwan, B. (2000). The art of classroom management: Effective practices for building equitable learning communities. Upper Saddle River, NJ: Merrill.

3

New Context for Learning

Creativity and innovation are becoming increasingly important for the development of the 21st century knowledge society. They contribute to economic prosperity as well as to social and individual wellbeing and are essential factors for a more competitive and dynamic society. So we should to design learning environment for creative society.

Let's step back a moment and look at the context we all find ourselves in and the challenges we face. First, every one of us recognizes that today's kids, our students, are having a new vernacular - a digital vernacular. Second, we need to find ways to tap the naturally occurring curiosities of our students so that we can turn them to do more learning on their own. Third, they have to pick up new skills outside of today's traditional educational institution. Fourth and finally, the students need to feel comfortable working in cross disciplinary teams that encompass multiple ways of knowing.

Studio based learning environment

Lave's theory (1991) focuses on learning as enculturation into a practice, often through the process of Legitimate Peripheral

Participation (LPP) in a laboratory, a studio, or a workplace setting. The spirit of LPP is that students are legitimately engaged in real work, fully participating in the technical and social interchanges and almost through osmosis are picking up not only the practice, but also the set of sensibilities, beliefs and idiosyncrasies of this particular community (of practice).

In studio-based learning environments emphasize making all work-in-progress public. As a result, every student can see what every other student is doing. Moreover, every student witnesses the thinking processes that other students are using to develop their designs. And then there is the public "crit." As a result, the brief crit holds substantial significance and presents learning opportunities for all the students – not just the one whose project is being critiqued.

Digital Learning

Dewey defines productive inquiry as that aspect of any activity where we are deliberately seeking what we need in order to do what we want to do. (Dewey, 1922 and Cook and Brown, 1999). In the net age we now have at our disposal tools and resources for engaging in productive inquiry – and learning – that we never had before. Laptops are viewed more as a kind of dinosauric technology. It's the modern, intelligent, multimedia mobile internet device that defines being digital. Now every student has a laptop with the potential of surfing the web, and Googling to get more information and gain enhanced knowledge. Of course, this is all happening while the professor is teaching.

Blogs

The net has enabled another kind of social learning platform, namely blogging (For eg. Twitter, orkut, Linken etc.,). Bringing blogs into a classroom would change everything – i.e it is not for fun and informal but it may turns out to be in a good way. When handled appropriately, classroom blogs can honor multiple ways of knowing and contributing to a class. For those who are too shy to speak out, find speaking in English challenging, or who are more contemplative, the classroom blog can serve as a way to participate in a class discussion. The classroom itself creates a kind of container for a blog – not just a free-for -all blog, but one focused on activities in the class and one tied together by the sociality of all members being in the class. It complements, but doesn't replace, the class and as a container it also allows students to contribute not just their own ideas but also adjacent material they find relevant to the topic of the class. It is also worth noting that students' entries in a classroom blog are written to be read by their peers, not just by their teacher.

Pro-Amateurs

The net is also facilitating the rise of pro-amateurs, which in turn is providing a new kind of learning platform ideally suited for the task of leaning- to-be. The term "amateur" in today's culture tends to be heard negatively. But the etymology of amateur comes from the Latin word 'amator' suggesting something you do for the love of it. Professionals do something for pay; amateurs do something out of their passion or love for it. The net is giving new impetus to the rise of the pro-amateur class today.

i. First, the letter writing practice that was so crucial to the bootstrapping efforts of the original scientific amateurs now is fostered by blogging practices.

ii. Second, social software such as Yahoo Groups and Bulletin Board Systems (BBSs) are reifying these niche communities of interest and helping others find and join them – no matter how specialized they are.

iii. Another space of activities on the net where the interaction between amateurs and professional provides a limited form of cognitive apprenticeship is Wikipedia. Many of the entries on Wikipedia first get sketched out by dedicated amateurs – pro-ams – in a field. Eventually the entries thus created catch the attention of professionals, who often start to rewrite parts of the entry. These changes, of course, are also subject to replacement by other professionals or amateurs. The entire process of additions and rollbacks is subject to public scrutiny and thus provides a glimpse into the thinking processes and scholarly practices of the field. The interested 'student' can thus become a peripheral participant in this scholarly endeavor.

A Grand Transition

The above examples are evincing the grand transition in the learning environment. To be more clear, in the 20th century, the approach to education was to focus on 'learning -about' and to build stocks of knowledge and some cognitive skills in the student to be deployed later in appropriate situations, which is appropriate for more stable environment. But the 21st century is quite different. The world is continuously changing at an increasing pace. Skills learned today are apt to be out-of -date all too soon. The concept of life-long learning is much a suitable one which warrants 'learning –to be' environment.

This apart the current approach is characterized by a *'demand-pull'* rather than the traditional 'supply-push' mode. The shift from a supply-push to more of a demand- pull basis of learning is a grand transition. The focus shifts from building up stocks of knowledge (learning-about) to enabling participation in flows of action, where the focus is on both learning-to-be through enculturation into a practice, and on collateral learning as well.

This mode of learning is closely aligned with Dewey's constructivism, but it is also somewhat different for two reasons: First, the demand-pull approach is a combination of the cognitivist and the social construction of understanding. Perhaps more importantly, it presents an approach to life-long learning that is now dramatically enabled by the net. The demand-pull approach embeds students in a rich (sometimes virtual) learning community built around a practice. It is passion-based learning.

Conclusion

The above points are going in line with Bloom's Digital Taxonomy which proves the transition of cognitive development as detailed below:

Improving these digital environments will develop millions of more technically educated people in India than other countries. So the new context of learning is necessary to access in the educational field.

Bibliography

1. Arulsamy S, Siva Kumar P,(2009), 'Application of ICT in Education', NeelKamal publications pvt ltd.,
2. Churches A, (2007), Edorigamy, Blooms Taxonomy and Approaches, http://edorigamy.wikispaces.com
3. John Seely Brown (2005) – New Learning environments for 21st century, Forum for the feature higher education
4. Siva Kumar, R, Online classroom equipped with ICT, EDUTRACK, journal of education (Oct,2008).

4

Access to Teaching Learning Materials (TLM) Among the General and Special Education Teachers in the School System

Introduction

Teaching Learning Materials (TLM) are the supportive sources for the learners to learn the contents. Some of the TLMs are customized where as others are readily available in the markets. Teachers are innovating and developing TLM according to the needs of the learners. The intension of this study is to find out the availability and accessibility of TLM with general and special education teachers in the school system. This study reveals that the customized materials are access to both general and special education teachers. The specific TLM or supportive materials are access to Special education teachers. The use of high technology like computer and laptops are access to the general education teachers.

Teaching Learning Materials (TLM) are the supportive sources for the learners to learn the contents. Some of the TLMs are customized where as others are readily available in the markets.

Teachers are innovating and developing TLM according to the needs of the learners.

Learners should be the center of instruction and learning. The role of teachers is to help learners to learn. Teachers have to follow the curriculum and provide, make, or choose materials. They may adapt, supplement, and elaborate on those materials and also monitor the progress and needs of the students.

Materials include textbooks, video and audio tapes, computer software, and visual aids. They influence the content and the procedures of learning. The choice of deductive vs. inductive learning, the role of memorization, the use of creativity and problem solving, production vs. reception, and the order in which materials are presented are all influenced by the materials.

Teaching materials is a generic term used to describe the resources teachers use to deliver instruction. Teaching materials can support student learning and increase student success. Ideally the teaching materials will be tailored to the content in which they are being used to the students and the teacher in the class. Teaching materials come in many shapes and sizes, but they all have in common the ability to support student learning.

Teaching materials here refers to teaching aids used when teachers carryout their activities in class room such as chalk, writing board, charts, apparatus , specimens , concrete materials, photographs, pictures , maps ,globes , cassettes , video recording, transparencies , projectors and computers.

Materials in the typical general Education Classroom tend to be limited. Text books, work books and work sheets are the materials commonly available in the class room. Globe, Videos, soft ware and internet resources are rarely available with many of the class rooms. Braille texts, large print texts, CDs with Audio output, sign and symbols are the materials required for children having certain limitations to learn the subjects. Universally Design Learning Materials gives students the multiple means of representation of concepts and multiple means of expression for the students to demonstrate what they have learned. Instruction is flexible and provides accessibility for all students. Every learning material we develop will be an asset for us. An investment of time or money in good teaching materials is an investment in good teaching. This study will focus on magnitude of availability and accessibility of teaching learning materials with the teachers who are interacting with the students including children with special needs.

Review of Literature

Halil Eksi (2008) conducted a case study on the use of materials by classroom teachers at primary education level. They stated that they carryout various activities for an efficient and effective education and teaching, the teachers use different materials in lesson in order to create a multi learning setting for students. They face many problems while using the materials. They also reported that the newly adapted education programme requires more material use. They also reported that the insufficient materials will create problem in future.

Nelson(2006) reported that every student needs and has the right to access the curriculum regardless of disabilities or differentiated learning styles.

Pisha and Coyne (2001) identified an approach called "Smart from the start" that is Universally Designed Learning Materials (UDL) should be part of the Curriculum Learning Environments and assessments.

Prema P (2009) Conducted an impact study on instructional and nurturing effect of Activity Based Learning on selected districts in Tamil Nadu and reported that the ABL method of learning influences the children's overall academic performance, improvement in reading, writing and numerical skills.

Rose Meyer &Hitchcock, (2006) reported that the Alternative formats of basic materials can also be provided for students with disabilities. Such as Braille text for students with Visual Impairments, large print text for students with low vision , and CD s with audio output for students with dyslexia.

Santhanam. P (2005) conducted a study on remedial programmers for children with learning difficulties in Chennai, Thiruvallur and Kancheepuram District of Tamil Nadu and reported that the intellectual capacity of the children with learning ability is significantly higher than those with learning disability. The children with learning disability show better academic performance after remedial programme. Awareness on remedial programme about learning disabilities to be conducted through print and electronic media

Aim and Objective

The main aim is to find out the accessibility of teaching learning materials to the general and special education teachers

1. To find out the availability of teaching and learning materials in the class room for general and special education teachers
2. To find out the accessibility of teaching learning materials in the class room to teach the children.
3. To find out the incidence of using the teaching learning materials in the class room by general and special education teachers

Method

Survey method.

Samples

Purposive sampling 149 teachers consisting of 82 General Education Teachers from 5 different schools and 67 Special Education Teachers working in SSA Projects up to secondary level were selected for this study.

Tool

A questionnaire consisting of 28 teaching learning materials widely used in general education and special education programme is constructed and administered with the guidelines of scoring each items on Available and used frequently (2) Available but used rarely (1) Not available (0) Refer - Appendix (A)

Procedure

The tool was constructed and administered on the general and special education teachers working in public school by indicating their choice on each items of Teaching Learning Material in the following manner Available and used frequently (2) Available but used rarely (1) Not available (0). The confidentiality on their response is promised by the author.

Result and discussion

After collecting information from the teachers the scores were tabulated and interpreted for the study. Refer Table I

From the table it is learnt that the materials of Chalk and board, Chart &flash cards models, work book, poster and text are commonly available and frequently used by both general and special education teachers.

Computer, laptop is available and frequently used by the general education teachers where as ABL materials, mobility aids and sign languages are frequently used by the special education teachers.

Pictures/Icons, graphics are rarely used materials by the general education teachers where as video, TV, tape, laptop, signature guide; adapted pencils are used rarely by the special education teachers.

Braille, Abacus, mobility cane, sign language and ABL materials are not used by general education teachers. Whereas Computers, laptop, animation, graphics, film and slides are not used by the special education teachers.

Films and graphics are not used by general and special education teachers respectively.

The study shows that there is no significant difference in Accessing the TLM among the general and special education teachers except the use of signature guide.

Conclusion

Majority of the TLM which is used in the public schools are traditionally prepared in nature which are used regularly

The innovated materials which are available in the public school to teach the students with diversified needs are minimal and used rarely.

Use of computer for teaching and learning is more common with the general education teachers than the special education teachers.

Table I : Access to TLM among the general and special education teacher's Frequency distribution

Sl. No	variable	Access to TLMs by the Educators			Access to TLMs by Special Educators			Total
		Not used	Rarely used	Fre- quently	Not used	Rarely used	Fre- quently	
1	Chalk board	0	3	79 96%		2	65 97%	149
2	Chart and flash card	6	0	76 92%	1	7	59 88%	149
3	Models	6	11	65 79%	9	19	39 58%	149
4	Video	71	5	6 7%	16	42	9 13%	149
5	Television	73	5	4 4%	16	32	19 28%	149
6	Film	77	5	0	39	22	6 8%	149
7	audio	58	10	14 17%	20	29	18 26%	149
8	Slide	67	4	11 13%	35	26	6 8%	149
9	Tape	51	15	16 19%	19	29	19 28%	149
10	Work Book	12	7	63 76%	9	18	40 59%	149
11	Poster	19	12	51 62%	29	22	16 23%	149
12	Text	10	01	71 86%	16	15	36 53%	149
13	Braille	57	04	21 25%	29	30	08 11%	149
14	Abacus	63	03	16 19%	27	24	16 23%	149
15	Mobility Can	75	02	05 6%	25	29	13 19%	149
16	Sign language	64	03	15 18%	12	23	32 47%	149
17	ABL	46	08	28 34%	09	08	50 74%	149
18	Mobility Aid	60	06	16 19%	23	18	26 38%	149
19	Book rest	47	08	27 32%	25	28	14 20%	149
20	Signature guide	19	28	35 42%	29	23	15 22%	149
21	stencils	40	22	20 24%	27	23	17 25%	149
22	Tripod pencil or pen	20	16	46 56%	23	23	20 29%	149
23	Computer	14	16	52 63%	25	23	19 28%	149
24	Adapted key board mouse	27	17	38 44%	35	19	13 19%	149
25	laptop	31	25	26 31%	28	28	11 16%	149
26	animation	36	30	16 19%	36	25	06 8%	149
27	Pictures/ Icon	20	41	21 25%	28	21	18 26%	149
28	Graphics	29	38	15 18%	60	7	0	149

Recommendation

Teachers working in the public school system need to understand the shift from using traditional materials to the innovated materials according to the needs of children with diversified in nature.

The materials need to be explored by the teachers and the students as well to optimize the learning.

Use of computer should be practiced by the special education teachers for successful mainstreaming.

The management may give the liberty to explore and innovate the materials according to the needs of the diversified group of learning.

In-service training may be organized to innovate and develop TLM to cater the diversified group of learners.

There is a need to conduct more study in this area to innovate and develop appropriate TLM which is access to all categories of learners and the teachers.

References

1. Allwright, R. L. (1990). What do we want teaching materials for? In R. Rossner and R. Bolitho, (Eds.), Currents in language teaching. Oxford University Press
2. Halil Eksi (2008) A case study on the use of materials by classroom teachers, Kasim Yildirim
3. Educational Sciences Theory and Practice 8(1) January 2008 ,305-322
4. Pisha and Coyne (2001) Incorporating Universal Design for learning principles in to the class room design.
5. Prema P (2009) Instructional and nurturant effect of Activity Based Learning An impact study in selected districts of Tamil Nadu. SSA TN Report
6. Santhanam.P (2005). Remedial programmers for children with learning difficulties. SSA TN Report.
7. The Internet TESL Journal, Vol. IV, No. 4, April 1997

   http://iteslj.org/http://iteslj.org/Articles/Kitao-Materials.html

5

Innovative Learning Environments

Introduction

In the race to achieve Education for All (EFA) goals by 2015, the importance of creating optimal conditions to enable and sustain learning has sometimes been overlooked as a 'peripheral' factor in the provision of quality education. However, a rapidly expanding body of research on the conditions of learning suggests that physical, social and organizational environments in which teaching and learning processes take place have a more central role than previously acknowledged. As the evidence gathered for this report asserts, the design and management of learning spaces is fundamental to the achievement of positive learning outcomes as well as to the health and well-being of learners.

Simply put, good learning environments foster quality learning, and bad learning environments do not. This exhaustive review of the literature on learning environments aims to provide all those who wish to fulfill the promise of EFA with evidence-based suggestions for creating and sustaining 'good' learning environments. Whether applied to formal schooling, alternative learning, or non-formal education contexts, the reflections and findings contained herein offer a rich and varied knowledge base for policy makers, educators and communities to develop strengthened policies and actions that meet local needs in the creation and maintenance of enabling places to learn.

In today's world, education systems must constantly evolve in order to effectively respond to the rapidly changing demands of the societies they serve. Innovations in curricula, methodologies, materials and technologies may require major changes in the design and organization of the environments in which they are housed. Innovations can be relatively simple and inexpensive, such as re-arranging schedules and seating patterns to allow additional time and space for guided group practice or collaborative problem solving. In a school garden environment, community members skilled in traditional methods can be invited to participate as mentors and teachers at a relatively minimal cost. In another example, teachers, school managers, parents and learners may respond to the increasing occurrence of verbal abuse and physical violence by collaborating to develop a viable policy for constructive school discipline. In yet another, university researchers can engage with teachers to design assessment tools to measure learners' perceptions of teacher and peer stereotyping based on gender, ethnicity or economic status in their classrooms and schools. To reach a common understanding of how both the physical and social dimensions of learning environments affect the quality of learning processes, an exploration of the relationship between place and process is needed. To understand this relationship, the following questions must be answered: How does one define 'a place to learn'? Why is it that children learn more effectively when there is a clear connection between the place of learning and the world in which they live? How can the different elements of learning environments be assessed in relation to local, national and international definitions of quality?

On a broader scale, educational systems undergoing reconstruction or reform may opt to undertake a radically different approach to the way schools are designed, managed and resourced in support of new visions and goals. Other systems may focus on achieving a more equitable distribution of resources in the wake of reports pinpointing clear discrepancies in the provision of basic facilities and services, such as access to drinking water and toilets. In either case, the effectiveness of an intervention or on-going change can only be sustained if it is subject to a process of assessment, reflection and incremental improvement. Thus, this review aims to raise awareness of the complete range of possible tools and methods to measure and improve places to learn. To further inspire and motivate those responsible for bringing learning environments to life, it also covers a wide range of research on innovations at various stages of planning and implementation.

This leads to consideration of how the conditions and relationships of learning impact on whether and how individuals engage with particular types of curriculum and pedagogical and assessment approaches. Learning theory now focuses on the significance of the relational and the connections between learning and positive social interactions with learners and teachers (Hattie 2003; Alton-Lee 2003, 2006), as well as the social mix of groups, classrooms and indeed schools (Thrupp 1999). Emotions and a sense of self-efficacy are now seen to have significant interrelationship with motivation and ongoing effects on learning. This means that both teachers and students have to be committed to learning together, thus limiting the extent to which curriculum and assessment policies can prescribe how they are to be enacted. Emotional management is critical to understanding and leading organisational change and informs the quality of the social interactions between teachers and learners (Hargreaves 2000b; Leithwood and Beatty 2008; Blackmore 2004, 2010).

Neighbourhood environment

A considerable body of research about schools in challenging circumstances considers context as a major factor on school effectiveness and improvement (Heppell and Chapman 2004). The neighbourhood environment is defined geographically. Key factors are whether the region is undergoing population growth or decline, and the school's location and proximity relative to other schools (public or private, primary and secondary) within education markets.

School location is mapped closely to student achievement, with studies indicating the strong association between geographical location, residential patterns, infrastructure, community health and wellbeing, levels of under-employment and unemployment with school underachievement (Teese et al 2007; Welch et al 2007; Vinson 2007). This sample of 12 case studies represents the full range of locational dis/advantage, with the rationale for ILEs arising from the desire to improve educational outcomes for students and, in some cases, provide a fair and equitable education in high poverty communities.

Policy environment

The same education, social and economic policies impact on schools differentially (Allegre and Ferrer 2010). In particular, there is significant evidence about how accountability frameworks, school improvement programs, and a range of reform policies impact significantly on an individual school's priorities and distribution of resources (Lumby 2009; Heppell and Chapman 2004; Newmann et al 1997). How a school fares on key performance indicators such as retention rates and NAPLAN tests of literacy and numeracy leads to differential treatment in terms of whether systems are more prescriptive or allow greater school autonomy in improvement plans. MacBeath (2008), in a study of 12 English schools, refers to supportive and oppressive policy environments and how they shape leadership possibilities and practices. Principal interviews indicate priorities – as to what gets foregrounded when talking about the school - professional learning or rankings. Supportive policy environments were those that challenge sloppy practices and provide ways of going forward including innovative examples in terms of pedagogy and rigorous approaches to teaching and learning. Repressive policy environments are those for which survival requires subversive activities. They tend to be overly 'prescriptive and condescending, deskilling rather than empowering teachers [and] [r]ichness and creativity are lost by formulaic prescription' while 'training is superficial' (Macbeath 2008, p.125-6). Policy environments position schools and teachers with regard to their level of autonomy and sense of agency. Recent studies on school autonomy have questioned whether greater autonomy necessarily leads to student learning improvement, and argue for the need for relative autonomy. Relative autonomy means schools do not assume all the risk and responsibility without the necessary resources, but work within a network of supports that facilitate flexiblility and encourage teachers to undertake innovative approaches by providing resources.

Built environment

A useful conceptual framework for considering these 12 case studies was developed from a literature review undertaken for DEECD (Blackmore et al 2010). This review argued there were four phases of redesign of learning spaces: designing, transitioning, consolidating, and evaluating/sustaining. The review indicated that much of the research undertaken on learning spaces and outcomes has focused on building design premised upon best practice educational and architectural principles. This research has made 'aspirational' claims about how built environments impact on learning outcomes without a significant body of empirical evidence. Little research has been done on how schools prepare for, and transition into, new learning spaces in ways that encourage innovative pedagogical practices, or that investigates which pedagogical practices get consolidated and why, or considers how to sustain exemplary practices or to evaluate the effects of new learning spaces in terms of student outcomes. Each of the 12 case studies could be identified in one or more of these phases – John Monash Science School is 6 months into their first year of establishment, others have undergone redesign over a 6-7 year time period. How one understands the relationship between the built environment and an ILE is therefore variable across the sample schools. While research has focused on virtual learning environments (Blackmore et al 2001) and built learning environments or quality of built conditions (Blackmore et al 2010), few consider the relationship between physical/virtual spaces with regard to the use of different technologies, teacher pedagogical practices and student learning outcomes.

Institutional environments

Research on both built and virtual learning spaces indicates that to fundamentally change how learners learn, teachers first have to change their mindsets and expand their pedagogical repertoires in ways that then can lead to sustained and sustainable changes in student behaviour and learning. That is, put pedagogy first. But to do so requires a culture that encourages risk taking and innovation. This, in turn, requires recognition of the powerful ways in which an institutional environment frames innovation. School cultures are informed by the student population and social mix, cultural legacies, the staff composition, leadership structures, and relationships with community (Thrupp 1999; Thrupp and Lupton 2006). Institutional environments also impact on the scope and scale of innovation and in turn how an ILE is embedded within, or marginal to, dominant school cultures. An ILE, as indicated in these case studies, can be a program at a year level, an alternative unit outside the mainstream school, or a whole school approach. Scale and focus have implications for the degree of staff involvement and therefore level of commitment to innovation: who has a sense of ownership of the innovation, and how and whether the innovation can be 'scaled up' within the school or across other schools (Datnow et al 2002).

Conclusion

Designing built environments on sound pedagogical and architectural principles that are appropriate to community needs provides new opportunities for teachers and leaders to create new partnerships and imagine new pedagogical possibilities. But the precondition to maximising these possibilities and improving student learning is changing the habits of the minds and hearts of teachers to focus on student learning. This means focusing on the purpose and rationale for change, the social practices of teaching and leading, relationships with colleagues, and organisational structures and cultures that support collaborative inquiry. At the same time, there are a range of external factors which impact on an individual school's capacity to improve student learning – the neighbourhood environment, the policy environment and the built environment. The studies indicated that it was the instability of the impact of policy and neighbourhood environments that disrupted the internal capacities to manage change in schools. Therefore there is a need to create greater internal stability and professional peer accountability

(Elmore 2007) within such schools through professional support and development.

References

1. Alexander, R. (2000). Culture and pedagogy: International comparisons in primary education London: Blackwell.
2. Allegre, A. and Ferrer, G. (2010) School regimes and education equity: some insights based on PISA 2006 British Educational Research Journal 36(3) 433-6.
3. Barron, B. (2006). Configurations of learning settings and networks: implications of a learning ecology perspective. Human Development 49: 193-224.
4. Campbell, A. & S. Groundwater-Smith (2010). Action Research in Education. London ; Los Angeles : SAGE.
5. Campbell A. McNamara, O and Gilroy, P. (2004). Practitioner Research and Professional Development in Education A thousand Oaks, CA: SAGE.
6. Campbell, A., McNamara, O., & Gilroy, P. (2004). Practitioner research and professional development in education. London: Paul Chapman.

6

Learning Without Limits: Powerful Professional Development

Introduction

Learning Without Limits is deeply committed to the power of professional development. Learning without limit leverages a variety of powerful professional development models including Professional Learning Communities (PLCs), coaching, cycles of data analysis, and input of new content. The overarching structure of professional development is the establishment of PLCs to develop collaborative learning communities that focus on equitable student outcomes.

Teaching pupils to be effective learners

Setting goals

It is important to share the goal of each lesson with pupils. This could be written on the board beside the date e.g. I know 5 words for furniture in French or I have a good understanding of present tense endings. It lets pupils know why they are there and what they are working towards. It is a good idea to remind pupils about their goal during the lesson so that they can take note of their progress. At the end of the lesson pupils should be asked to check if they have achieved this goal. Pupils could test each other then the teacher could ask for thumbs up from all the pupils who feel they have achieved something in the lesson.

Teaching pupils to be resourceful

Another part of teaching pupils to be effective learners is to teach them what resources are available to them. It is important that pupils are trained to keep their vocabulary jotters tidy with headings and an index page. They need to know where to find the meaning of a word if they are stuck; whether via the vocabulary jotter, world lists in the text book or a dictionary. Pupils should be taught early on in S1 how to use a dictionary. If a pupil says they he/she does not know the meaning of a word then the teacher should remind the pupil of the resources available.

Teaching pupils to be organised

The teachers have the date and a warm-up exercise on the board at the start of every class. This allows those pupils who are keen to learn to get started instead of waiting for the latecomers. The warm-up is always revision of the previous day's work and allows pupils the chance to review how much they have retained.

Teaching pupils learning strategies

In listening activities teachers encourage pupils to try and repeat in their head any word they can't remember the meaning of or to try and write it down to see if the written format looks familiar. As a class we practice looking at the questions while listening to the text and also reading the questions then looking away and just listening and making a few notes. Teachers should also teach the pupils Reading techniques. They learn how to recognise nouns, verbs and adjectives in a sentence so that they can divide texts up and make more sense of the words. They practice identifying cognates and making intelligent guesses at meanings of words based on the context.

Teaching pupils about pacing

Teachers encourage pupils to keep an eye on the clock while they are working and to pace themselves. I regularly let them know what time they have left and suggest what a reasonable amount of work is. Pupils also like to know how much work needs to be done. It might not always be realistic for pupils to complete a whole sheet. Teachers put a grid on the board with exercises that MUST be completed in class and GOOD indicates the exercises that the more able pupils should aim for.

Meeting the Individual Needs of Pupils Using variety to cover the different learning styles

Some of the studies show that pupils' preferences cover all four skills: listening, reading, writing and listening. Each skill received a similar number of votes. It was the same for the skill they liked the least. Almost the same number of pupils liked speaking and disliked speaking. This goes to show that pupils vary so much in their likes and dislikes. It will never be possible for a teacher to please pupils all the time. However there are strategies that the teacher can use. It is important to use variety in the lesson plans. Teachers will try to incorporate a task using each of the skills in every lesson, certainly never less than 3 of them.

Differentiation

"Children already come to us differentiated. It just makes sense that we would differentiate our instruction in response to them. (Tomlinson, 1999, p.24).

Basic Differentiation

Differentiation at its most basic level is pupils working with or without the help of their vocabulary jotter. Teachers should constantly remind pupils that if they complete the exercises without the help of the vocabulary jotter then they are working at a higher level and will learn more. By the end of the lesson all pupils should have closed their vocabulary jotter.

Catering for the different learning styles

Visual learners process information most effectively when they can see what they are learning e.g. through reading, writing and observing. Auditory learners need to hear information to help them learn e.g. via oral presentations. Kinesthetic learners learn best when they can manipulate objects e.g. by doing, touching and moving (Nordlund, 2003).

Gardner's (1993) theory of multiple intelligences suggests that pupils need to show their knowledge in different ways e.g. via pictures, talking or acting. The easiest way to do this is to take a reading exercise from the Métro book and to allow pupils to respond in different ways to the texts. Here is an example using the reading exercise. For the Benjamin speech bubble pupils could make up English questions for their partner to answer. Pupils have to show their understanding of the Sophie speech bubble by drawing a picture. For the Samuel speech bubble pupils could act out his hobbies to show understanding. The final speech bubble could be translated into English so that pupils get the chance to translate carefully e.g. time phrases.

Open and creative tasks

Pupils could be given an open and creative task which allows them to work at their own level. In Métro bleu in module 3 I give pupils the task of setting up a French school. They have to decide on a name for the school. The tasks involve making up a dream timetable, a mini school handbook (e.g. name of school, times, clubs etc) the design of a school uniform and a play outlining activities at school. I usually put pupils into ability groups and give them a week to complete the tasks.

Higher level thinking skills

Another way of differentiating work is to take a text from Metro bleu and use Blooms taxonomy to make up more challenging questions for the more able. Bloom describes six levels of thinking: knowledge, comprehension, application, analysis, evaluation and synthesis. More able pupils often need less time developing the basic facts at the knowledge and comprehension levels. Here is an example form p80. Instead of just getting pupils to list what furniture is in each room pose a more challenging question e.g. Which bedroom would you most like to have? Give reasons for your answer. Which family seems closest to your own? Which of the properties would you choose to buy?

Effects on teachers

1. Ability labelling shapes teachers' attitudes towards children and limits their expectations for some children's learning. Teachers vary their teaching and respond differently towards children viewed as 'bright', 'average' or 'less able'.
2. Fixed ability thinking reduces teachers' sense of their own power to promote learning and development through the use of their expertise and professional judgement. It therefore discourages creativity and inventiveness to overcome.
3. Fixed ability thinking encourages teachers to see differential performance as natural and inevitable, and so diverts attention from the part that school and classroom processes play in enabling or limiting learning for individuals and groups.

Effects on young people

1. Young people learn how they are perceived by teachers and respond to that perception; they tend to live up to or down to expectations.
2. Ability-labelling undermines many young people's dignity, their self-belief, their hopes and expectations for their own learning. It strips them of their sense of themselves as competent, creative human beings, leading them to adopt self-protective strategies that are inimical to learning.
3. Fixed ability thinking and ability-led practices tend to disadvantage some groups of young people. Research has repeatedly drawn attention to social class and ethnicity-based inequalities in the processes of selection, grouping and differentiation of curricula.

Effects on curriculum

1. Fixed ability thinking encourages and legitimates a narrow view of curriculum, learning and achievement.

2. By naturalising explanations of differential achievement, fixed ability thinking perpetuates the limitations and biases built into existing curricula.
3. Ability labelling and grouping by ability restrict the range of learning opportunities to which individual pupils are exposed.
4. Ability labelling and grouping encourage schools and teachers to privilege psychometric knowledge of young people over the knowledge acquired through day-to-day classroom interaction.

Conclusions

The biggest stumbling block to effective mixed ability teaching would seem to be teacher attitude. Teachers lack the knowledge of strategies to use in the classroom to cater for a wide range of ability. Setting reduces the range of ability in the class but does not remove the fact that all pupils have individual needs and learning preferences. More staff training is needed to inform teachers about catering for the different learning styles, using Bloom's taxonomy to provide challenging differentiated work and the social and academic benefits of using collaborative group work. Teachers also need to be trained to be facilitators of learning so that whole class teaching does not predominate in most lessons. Pupils need to be taught how to take responsibility for their own learning. If these strategies are followed then the four competences for a Curriculum for Excellence can be met.

References

1. Fisher, R. (2001). *Teaching Children to Learn.* Cheltenham: Nelson Thornes Ltd.
2. Gardner, H. (1993). *Frames of mind: The theory of Multiple Intelligences.* London: Fontana Press.
3. Hallam, S., & Toutounji, I. (1996). *What do we know about the Grouping of Pupils by Ability?*. London: Institute of Education.
4. Harlen, W., & Malcolm, H. (1997). *Setting & Streaming: A Research Review.* Edinburgh: SCRE.
5. Harris, V., & Snow, D. (2004). *Doing it for themselves: focus on learning strategies and vocabulary building.* London: CILT.

6. HMIE (2007). *Modern Languages: A Portrait of Current Practice in Scottish Schools*. Edinburgh: HMIE.
7. Ireson, J., & Hallam, S. (2001). *Ability Grouping in Education*. London: Paul Chapman Publishing.
8. McKeown, S. (2004). *Meeting SEN in the Curriculum: Modern Foreign Languages*. London: David Fulton Publishers.
9. Scottish Executive. (2004). *A Curriculum for excellence: The Curriculum Review Group*. Edinburgh: Scottish Executive.
10. Tomlinson, C. (1999). *The Differentiated Classroom: responding to the Needs of All Learners*. Alexandria: ASCD.
11. Nordlund, M. (2003). *Differentiated Instruction*. Oxford: Scarecrow Education.

7

Blended Learning

Introduction

This paper is about the blended learning. More than a decade ago, internet had gradually come to play a major role in the world as it was an advance technological tool provided several benefits to human being . Blended learning has gained considerable popularity in training and education in recent years. Blended learning is founded on data and measurement. Over time, the measures will get richer. Given the initial results proponents are bullish. Many of blended learning first adopters have been charter schools, simply because blended instruction requires fresh and flexible thinking. Well-developed online learning introduces possibilities of "school choice" on a course-by-course basis. Blended learning to be viewed as the combination of face-to-face and online learning, enabling learning to extend beyond the classroom and providing opportunities for reflection, interaction and future engagement with the learning material.

In recent years, with the advances of the internet and e learning technologies, a balanced mode of learning, which effectively combines the traditional face-to-face learning and e-learning has evolved yet, this blended learning mode is not widely adopted in higher and postgraduate education programs in education. One major reason in that teachers are not familiar with the practices of creating and delivering same courses in a mix of real class room and virtual environment. Another important aspect in that many teachers still do not consider the e-learning methodologies stable enough and powerful for education especially for practice activities such as laboratory and project completion. The third reason is that academic staff considers the act of teaching learning education as more than individual study and online assessment facilities provided by current e-learning solution.

For many educators and trainers, a blended learning approach provides innovative educational solutions through an effective mix of traditional classroom teaching with mobiles learning and online activities.

But what is "Blended learning" and what does it mean for students, teachers, parents and school principals? How do we harness these resources to enrich the educational experiences for our students? How do we tap in to this knowledge bank to provide relevant education and vocational training experiences for our youth? Can we use this connectivity to build online communities for isolated students and adults in rural and remote areas?

What is Blended Learning?

Blended Learning in really no more than a combination of all these approaches. For some teachers Blended learning is describing what they have been doing successfully for years. That is using a range of resource and activities to provide individualized, student-centered learning experiences for their students. The real difference today is the unparalleled access to the internet with its rich sources of information and services and more importantly, the connectivity it offers students and teachers. Particularly, the ability to create online communities and support networks. In addition, there is a growing use of mobile technologies such as flip cameras, voice recorders, mobile phones and GPS devices extending learning beyond the class room walls.

Definition of Blended Learning

1. International Association for K-12 on line learning (2008) : Ultimately, the exact definition of Blended Learning beyond some combination of online and face-to-face, may not matter.
2. Singh(2003): "The concept of blended learning is rooted in the idea that learning is not just a one-time event-learning is a continuous process. Blending provides various benefits over using any single learning delivery medium alone".
3. Dziuban, Hartman and Moskal(2004): Blended learning should be viewed as a pedagogical approach that combines the effectiveness and socialization opportunities of the class room with the technologically enhanced active learning possibilities of the online environment, rather than a ratio of delivery modalities.

Rotational Model

The common feature in the rotation model is that, within a given course, students rotate on a fixed schedule between learning online in a one-to-one, self-paced environment and sitting in a classroom with a traditional face-to-face teacher. It is the model most in between the traditional face-to-face classroom and online learning because it involves a split between the two and, in some cases, between remote and onsite. The face-to-face teacher usually oversees the online work.

Flex Model

Programs with a flex model feature an online platform that delivers most of the curricula. Teachers provide on-site support on a flexible and adaptive as-needed basis through in-person tutoring sessions and small group sessions. Many dropout-recovery and credit-recovery blended programs fit into this model.

Self- Blended

The nearly ubiquitous version of blended learning among American high schools is the self-blend model, which encompasses any time students choose to take one or more courses online to supplement their traditional school's catalog. All supplemental online schools that offer a la carte courses to individual students facilitate self-blending.

Enhanced Virtual Model

In fact the teacher increase the programmes that fit in the face-to-face driver category all retain face-to-face teachers to deliver most of their curricula. Face-to-face check-ins are sometimes optional and other times required.

Benefits of Blended Learning

1. Increase widespread adoption of effective blended learning models
2. Blended may be defined at the course program or student services level
3. Blending may be across institutions.
4. Seeking effective conceptual models and implementation practices.
5. Demonstrated efficiency(Ex: Classroom utilization)
6. Pedagogical richness; blended learning could be an effective means of enhancing learning by blending traditional classroom learning and online learning
7. Students can pace their own learning and become self-directed learners;
8. Greater flexibility offered by blended learning through the use of ICT, thus reducing the on campus face-to-face hours.
9. Opportunity to evaluate student learning using more reliable authentic assessment strategies;
10. Rich and immediate feedback which leads to significant reductions in time taken be students to achieve a desired level of performance(Anderson, Conrad and Corbett, 1989)

Barriers to the Growth of Blended Learning

If existing blended learning schools are getting good results, why hasn't the practice spread more widely? One obvious answer in that the current schools are very new. Hardly any have more than just a few years of experience. Moreover starting a new school – or radically transforming any older schools structure – in a complicated under activity that is not for the faint of heart.

Bottleneck 1 : A lack of Research:

While blended learning proponents can point to some initially good test scores, there in little solid date published in peer-reviewed journals. "Honestly, it is so early on, no one knows what works and doesn't work". Says Daine Tavenner, leader of summit public schools. "Indeed"notes scott Benson, who directs blended learning grants at the Bill and Melinda Gates Foundation. "Part of me is really nervous-that the dialogue and enthusiasm is outpacing the results.

Bottleneck 2 : The Dilbert reaction

Another bottleneck showing blended learning has to do with what it look like compared to the archetypal vision of Education, or at least education as grown-ups was nostalgic about it. "There is a lot of 'small c' conservation" among parents and educators, says Michael Horn of the Inn sight Institute. They says "This is how I went to school. Why shouldn't my kids have the same experience?"

Bottleneck 3 : Misguided policy

Education policy is often the object of tug-of-war among different interest groups scads of local, state, and federal policies create obstacles for blended learning even when that's not the explicit intention. Many of blended learning's first adopters have been charter schools rather than traditional district-run schools. Simply because blended instruction requires fresh and flexible thinking among administrators and teachers and that is more common at charters. But even within the charter-school sector there are serious legal and administrative obstacles.

Bottleneck 4 : Inertia

Perhaps the biggest barrier to the growth of blended learning in that public education by nature trends to be glacial in its rate of movement and change. The hundreds of billions of dollars spent nationally on public schools have created entrenched lobbies dedicated to protecting the status quo. More neutrally schools are the heart of many communities and they have along traditions that people naturally, protect. Sometimes educational innovation is great, but often it is just faddish, says Micheal Horn of the innosight institute. "There are a lot people jumping in and doing blended learning because it is the cool thing to do right now without giving a lot of thought to why or what problem they resolving". A bad precedent could sour the movement quickly.

Conclusion

Blended learning may contribute to creating powerful learning environment in numerous ways. Impact of blended learning approach on higher education and the provided acceptance of blended learning as a model of delivery in higher education, as blended learning does not have a pedagogy of its own. Shift in focus to the constructivist pedagogical Philosophy, its strength is drawn from theoretical perspectives of established theories and those derived from them.

References

1. 1. U.S. Department of Education, Evaluation of evidence - Based practices in online learning: A Meta – Analysis and Review of online learning studies. "September 2010, http://www2.ed.gov.rschstat/eval/tech/evidence-based-practices/final report.pdf.
2. Matt Richtel " At waldort school in silicon vally. Technology can wait" New York Times, October 22, 2011, http://www.mytimes.com/2011/10/23/technology/at-waldorf-school-in-silicon-valley-technology.com-wait.html.
3. Dziuban, C.D., Hartman, J.L., &Moskal, P.D.(2004). Blended learning, Educause center for Applied Research, Research Bulletin, 7, retrieved January 15,2008, from http://www.educause.edu/ir/library/pdf/ERB0407.pdf.
4. International Association for K-12 online learning (2008).

8

Blended Learning A Pedagogical Approach to Teach in Smart Classrooms

Introduction

Blended learning means many things to many people even within our relatively small online learning community. It is referred to as both blended and hybrid learning with little or no difference in the meaning of the terms among most educators. In general terms, blended learning combines online delivery of educational content with the best features of classroom interaction and live instruction to personalize learning allow thoughtful reflection, and differentiate instruction from student to student across a diverse group of learners. Definitions of blended learning range from some so broad that practically any learning experience that integrates some use of educational technology might quality, to others that focus a specific percentage combination of online curriculum and instruction in a face to face setting.

Blendend Learning

Blended learning consists of two features

1. It is a planned combination of online learning and face to face instruction using a variety of learning resources.

2. It is an educational format that integrates online learning techniques including online delivery of materials through web pages, discussion boards and e-mail with traditional teaching.

Ingredients of Blended Learning

1. **Self paced leaning**: recorded live events, Internet based which helps the learner to learn at his own pace.
2. **Assessment**: it is both live and online measure of learner's knowledge to determine prior knowledge as well as to measures learning transfer.
3. **Live events**: synchronous teacher led learning environment in which all learners participate at the same time. It can be in real classroom.
4. **Collaboration**: it implies a more dynamic communication and interaction among many learners that brings about knowledge sharing.

Emergence of Blended Learning

In recent years, ICT has paved the way for accelerating the paradigm shift through providing more flexible ways of learning. The demand of new technologies and 24/7 global environment cannot be satisfied with the only source of classroom instruction, with its inherent classroom limitations.

Blended learning proves to be an effective step whereby allows a faculty to bring with a course that is mostly face to face and then switch it over to the online component as soon as the student's expertise in the field increases. Broadly, blended learning models comprise of the following elements like learning through information, learning through collaboration, learning through interaction and learning through experience mixed in varied proportions according to and organisations requirements.

On the other hand the significance of face to face instruction cannot be ignored since the live human interaction in teaching or learning cannot be denied to a large extent. Keeping all these in view, a consensus has emerged among educationists working in the area that there is a need for tapping the wide applicability of online learning the with face to face instruction and then evolve blended learning.

Smart Classrooms

Smart classrooms are technology enhanced classrooms that foster opportunities for teaching and learning by integrating learning technology, such as computers, specialized software, audience response technology, networking and audio/ visual capabilities. The smart classrooms demand learning initiative that assists educators to make to make ICT integral to leaning. The challenge lies in shifting from teaching and learning about ICT to teaching and learning with and through ICT. This means rather than using technology to do old things in new ways and use technology to enable and transform teaching learning and the curriculum.

Smart Classrooms Via-A-Via Blended Learning

Smart classrooms uses following elements mixed in varied proportions according to an organization requirements of blended learning.

1. Learning through information
2. Learning through interaction
3. Learning through collaboration
4. Learning through classroom interaction
5. Virtual fieldtrips
6. Blogs

The success of a blend largely depends on the right mix of the elements. A good blend would provide optimum role of live interaction. It is essential to provide a good support and training model and should keep the cultural components in mind. A successful blend would strike the right balance between innovations and mass utility. Some of the basic factors which should be considered in identifying blend are

1. Student profile

2. Hours of learning
3. Teaching style
4. Resource availability
5. Training implementation

Conclusion

The challenges in a blended learning environment can be looked in two different perspectives learner perspective and teacher perspective. In focusing learner perspective, there is a need to consider the learning style and perceptual skills and abilities of students while designing blended learning strategy. Learner's proficiency in using ICT is also important in a blended learning environment. It is the responsibility of authorities to provide necessary leaning support in providing access to online learning so that out students become blended learners with self regulatory authentic learning experience.

References

1. Dutta, subrat (2003). Impact of information communication technology on society. Yojna. 47, no. 7. Ibid (2003) yojna. 47, no. 7.
2. Talawar, M.S. & Pradeep Kumar, T. (2009). Podcasting a new trend of web-based technology in education, University news, Vol. 47, No. 30, pp 13-15.
3. Sonkambl, C. & Pagare, p. (2010). Use of blended learning approach in teacher education. In Z, Proceedings of global learn asia pacific.
4. Valiathan, P. (2002). Blended learning models, ASTD learning circuits.

9

Cloud Computing and Access to Public Services Among the Teacher Trainees of Special Education Programme

Introduction

Network-based services, which appear to be provided by real server hardware and are in fact served up by virtual hardware simulated by software running on one or more real machines, is often called cloud computing.

Student often search the materials through internet to update their knowledge. People stated doing their business by sitting at their hose. We make all our planning with the help of computer, laptop or mobiles connected to internet. Any kind of services are available at door step by clicking a mouse.

An attempt is made to study the accessibility of public services among the teacher trainees of Special Education College through cloud computing in their academic and day to day life.

Network-based services, which appear to be provided by real server hardware and are in fact served up by virtual hardware simulated by software running on one or more real machines, is often called cloud computing.

Cloud computing is computing that involves a large number of computers connected through a communication net work such as the internet, similar to utility computing. In science cloud computing is a synonym for distributed computing over a net work, and means the ability to run a programme or application on many connected computers at a same time.

The cloud computing was available via thin clients /terminal computers known as static terminals in the beginning. Later it becomes time sharing in the industry and in 70's it become Remote job Entry process associated with IBM and Others.

The term cloud computing is mostly used to sell hosted services in the sense of application service provisioning that run client server software at a remote location. Such services are given with the acronyms of 'SaaS' (Software as a Service), 'PaaS' (Platform as a Service), 'IaaS' (Infrastructure as a Service), HaaS (Hardware as a Service), and finally, EaaS' (Everything as a Service)

End users access cloud based applications through a web browser, thin client or mobile applications, while the business software and users data are stored on servers at a remote location.

This cloud services may be offered in a public private or hybrid net work Amazon Web services, Google apple engine, Oracle Zoho and Azure are some of the venders. This allocate space for a user to deploy and manage software "in the cloud" The client devices of cloud computing are desk top computers, laptops, tablets and smart phones.

With the help of cloud computing Searching study materials, Results, E-banking, E-ticketing, E –Payment are common now and that becomes part of our life.

This study will focus on the accessibility of cloud computing for availing the public services by the student trainees undergoing teacher training programme in a special education college for their academic and other personnel use.

Review of literature

1. Jake Gardner explains that while unregulated usage is beneficial for IT and tech moguls like Amazon ,the anonymous nature of the cost of consumption of cloud usage make it difficult for business to evaluate and incorporate it in to their business plan.
2. Slovoj Zizek points out that although cloud computing enhances content accessibility this access is increasingly grounded in the virtually monopolistic privatization of the cloud which provide this access
3. Zizek criticizes the argument purported by the supporters of cloud computing that this phenomenon is part of the natural evaluation of the internet sustaining that the quasi monopolies yet prices at will but also filter the software they provide to give its universality a particular twist depending on commercial and ideological interests
4. European commission (2012) has issued an analysis of the relevance of the open research issues for commercial stabilization in which various experts from industry and academia identify in particular following major concerns 1. Open interoperation across (proprietary) cloud solutions at IaaS, PaaS and SaaS levels 2. Managing multi tenancy at large scale and in heterogeneous environments 3. Dynamic and seamless elasticity from in house clouds to public clouds for unusual (scale, complexity) and/or infrequent requirements 4. Data management in a cloud environment, taking the technical and legal constraints into consideration
5. Johnson (2013) reported that Virtualization and cloud orchestrian turned a corner here to take virtualization to its logical conclusion of allowing business users to access their desktops from any laptop ,tablet or smartphone
6. Newman(2013). Reported that the new programming of elastic computer cloud may change the carbon and electricity cost of developing cloud computing and minimize the wastages.

7. Rozenfeld.M.(2013) Stated that as we become more reliant on mobile phones and tablets, central storage of data and fast access to systems in the cloud become essential to enable ubiquitous and anytime access. To these ends, the technologies that support the cloud must become faster, more cost-effective, and more secure
8. Xu.J.S.etall (2013) developed a model to service document mechanism which will protect the security of the programme in the cloud computing.

Aim

This study will aim to understand the use of cloud computing with the teacher trainees in their academic and their personal works

Objective

1. To find out the application of cloud computing as a supportive programme for academic works of the student trainees
2. To find out the use of cloud computing in their day to day life.

Method

Survey method

Sampling

Purposive sampling

71 student trainees from a teacher training college offering special education programme is selected for this study.

Tool

A questionnaire consisting of 20 items comprising of the use of personal computer, laptop and mobile which is connected to internet for searching the educational materials, booking tickets, and availing other services at college, home and other places were developed for administering on the individuals. Refer Appendix A.

Procedure

The tool is given to individuals and requested to give their response on each item by scoring (2) for frequently used (1) for occasionally used (0) for never used against to the question Refer Appendix A

Result and Discussion

After obtaining the response from the student trainees the scores were tabulated and reported

From the table it is revealing that access to study materials using computes at college is more than that of at any other places. Accessing the study materials using laptop seems to be more at home that that of at any other places. Accessing the study material using cell phones are very minimal.

Table I: Cloud computing and access to public services among the teacher trainees of a special education college.

Sl.No		Diploma			Degree			PG			Total
		Not used	rare	fre-quent	Not used	rare	fre-quent	Not used	rare	fre-quent	
1	computer at college	22	22	02	09	11	00	03	00	02	71
2	computer at home	40	04	02	16	03	01	02	00	03	71
3	computer outside	36	09	01	12	04	04	04	01	00	71
4	laptop at college	44	02	00	18	01	01	05	00	00	71
5	laptop at home	41	04	01	16	03	01	03	00	02	71
6	laptop outside	40	04	02	11	09	00	04	01	00	71
7	cellphone at college	37	07	02	17	00	03	03	01	01	71
8	cellphone at home	36	05	05	12	04	04	04	01	00	71
9	cellphone outside	40	05	01	14	06	00	04	01	00	71
10	online shopping	46	00	00	16	04	00	04	00	01	71
11	online banking	46	00	00	16	03	01	03	01	01	71
12	online payment	45	01	00	18	02	00	03	01	01	71
13	e-money order	46	00	00	19	01	00	05	00	00	71
14	online business	45	01	00	19	01	00	04	00	01	71
15	online movie reservation	42	03	01	15	05	00	04	00	01	71
16	online journey reservation	44	02	00	12	08	00	01	02	02	71
17	online doctor appointment	46	00	00	16	04	00	05	00	00	71
18	online application submission	40	06	00	13	04	03	03	00	02	71
19	online exam	42	04	00	13	05	02	04	00	01	71
20	online result	33	12	01	01	14	05	02	01	02	71
21	online game	43	03	00	08	10	02	05	00	00	71
22	online communication	37	09	00	08	09	03	01	02	02	71

Accessing the exam result through internet is more common with the students. Ticket booking for their travel also fairly observe with the students.

Very few students are accessing internet for other purposes like banking , shopping submission of online applications and chatting with others.

Postgraduate students are accessing more public services through cloud computing followed by the degree and diploma students. Statistically there is no significant difference observed in this study

Conclusion

The personal computer is very supportive for student trainees to collect the study materials in the college. The laptop is useful for the trainees tot store and does the review at home. The mobile phone is used for commercial business. The government is providing laptop to the student further it needs to be connected with clouding system so that the public service will be accessed easily.

This study is limited and there is a need of conducting more study on identifying the needs of student to access the public services.

Recommendations

Every college needs to provide the wi-fi facilities to access the public services to the students

Government can bring out a scheme of access to internet facilities to laptop issued at school so that the public services can be availed at any movement.

Reference

1. "The NIST Definition of Cloud Computing " (2011) National Institute of Standards and Technology Retrieved 24 July 2011.
2. What is cloud computing Amazon Web Services 2013-03-19 Retrieved 2013-03-20.
3. Baburajan ., Rajani (2011). The raising cloud storage market opportunity strengthens Vendors info tech it.tmc.net.com 2011 -07-24 retrieved 2011 -12-02

4. Dan Sullivan (2014) Cost of the cloud a developers guide to reducing your Bill Retrieved 2014 -11-27

5. Sinmon Garfrinkel 2011) The cloud imperative technology review (MIT) Retrieved 31 May 2013.

6. Danielson, Krissi (2008-03-26). "Distinguishing Cloud Computing from Utility Computing". Ebizq.net. Retrieved 2010-08-22

7. Johnson.C.R.(2013) Cloud based virtualization goes mobile 5/24/2013 Los Angel

8. Newman.L.H.(2013). New algorithms reduce the carbon cost of cloud computing

9. Rozenfeld .M.(2013) Bridging the gap in the cloud paper presented in the conference on how silicon system can lead to a more mobile and connected world. In San Francisco

10. Xu.J.S.etall (2013) Secure document service for cloud computing University of Post and Telecommunication China

10

Designing Learning Environment of Tomorrow with An Indian Perspective

Introduction

How to design a powerful learning environment so that learners can thrive in the 21st century? Designing Learning Environment of Tomorrow is an ambitious topic which necessitates an international study that responds to this challenging question. This paper is based on in-depth analysis of powerful 21st century learning environments that have taken the innovation journey. Designing Innovative Learning Environments presents a wealth of international material and features a new framework for understanding the learning environments. It aspires to become an effort through strong design strategies with corresponding learning leadership, evaluation and feedback.Open up to partnerships to grow social and professional expertise, and to sustain renewal and dynamic growth. It aims to promote 21st century learning environment through the application of various learning principles. In conclusion it offers pointers to how this can be achieved, including the role of technology, networking, and changing organizational cultures. This paper will prove to be an invaluable resource for all those interested in learning and teaching. It will be of particular interest to teachers, education leaders, parents, teacher educators, advisors and decision-makers and the research community

Education is a fundamental human right. It provides children, youth and adults with the power to reflect, make choices and enjoy a better life. It breaks the cycle of poverty and is a key ingredient in economic and social development. *UNESCO 2005*

What constitutes learning in the 21st century? Should reading, watching, writing, memorizing facts, and then taking exams be the only way to learn? Or could technology make learning more interactive, collaborative, and constructive? Could learning be more engaging and fun? We need to construct, access, visualize, and share information and knowledge in very different ways than we did decades ago. The amount and types of information created, shared, and critiqued every day is growing exponentially, and many skills required in today's working environment are not taught in formal school systems. In this more complex and highly-connected world, we need new training and competency development—we need to design a new learning environment.

The aim of this paper is to promote systematic design thinking that will cause a paradigm shift in the learning environments of today and tomorrow. All of us have been involved in the teaching learning process at some point in our lives; in this paper I invite educators, school leaders, researchers, students, parents, entrepreneurs, computer programmers, illustrators, interface designers, and all those who are interested in working together, to create a new learning environment for the future generation.

I also intend to identify advantages, disadvantages, limitations, and potentials of some unique ways of teaching learning process which will pave way to a paradigm shift from the usual conventional, stereotyped thinking about the process of learning in future. I would like to describe how online communication, collaboration, and visualization technology play a role in the behavioral, cognitive, constructivist, and social dimensions of learning in future. I would describe the major components and processes involved in development of interactive education systems for future learning environment. To communicate rationales of learning technology design approaches through team-oriented collaborations and to evaluate the value of ideas, principles, and techniques used in educational media or systems.

As the development of modern technology leads us to Team Project based learning, the teachers of tomorrow have to design a new learning model catering to 21st century environments and learners. Each country will design and develop an application or system that combines team interaction activities and learning support features in ways that are effective and appropriate for today's computing and communication devices. Students must consider potential uses with various learning devices (e.g., tablet, phone, PC), infrastructure requirements (e.g., cellular network, wi-fi, Bluetooth), and any special circumstances that irrelevant. In addition, each teacher must create and defend a learning model for the progress of future society.

Designing Today's Schools For Tomorrow's World

Many existing schools are still based on the 18th and 19th century model of infrastructure. These schools embody the concepts of conformity, formal teacher-centred teaching and a hierarchy of subjects. From a physical perspective, the traditional classroom was arranged like an egg crate. This historical model has been associated with an emphasis on control of students and on teacher-centred, lecture-format learning. Today, we look beyond this traditional template of learning to a more interactive, collaborative and inquisitive student-centred approach to learning. However, while pedagogical changes are taking place within the classroom, the design of new learning spaces is only now beginning to catch up.

During the past decades, the academic community has seen a strong emphasis on learning rather than teaching, and new learning spaces must allow for interactive, formal and informal, and peer-to-peer learning experiences.

The traditional 'lesson' has not been done away with, but is only one of the numerous ways that students will engage in learning. The new learning paradigm necessitates that the entire school be a learning environment rather than a set of rectangular structure with a specified number of seats for focused and approved activities.

Many education departments of different states in India and school policy makers of the world are now promoting new pedagogical practices and require facilities that will enable the new collaborative and experience-based learning approaches to happen.

Building the Education Revolution

The Central and State Governments in India funding focused on the provision of teachers, permanent buildings, infrastructure and bare necessities of school. However, many schools are lacking the basic amenities that are essential for an institution.

There is a vast array of vintages and models of dilapidated classrooms currently in use. Older models are gradually being phased out, but this will take time to complete. One issue this raises is that different models and vintages cannot be easily co-located to create multi-unit learning centers or phase setting institutions.

There are many variables around the provision of restructured classrooms across India. These include: climate-related issues; site conditions; locations in suburban, rural and remote communities; transportation; and the availability of skilled and affordablelabour.

Fundamental Needs

Children are ready to learn only when basic needs such as food, water, warmth, toilets and security are met. In addition to these basic needs, other qualities are important in an ideal learning environment. These include natural light, comfortable furniture, indoor air quality and non-toxic materials in and around schools .

A major consideration and concern for both educators and students is hygienic conditions. Many children, notably marginalized, indigenous tribal children, have both temporary and chronic health issues. A child who cannot hear or speak clearly in class will lose interest very quickly.

Good teaching, learning facilities will reduce student and teacher absenteeism due to lack of infrastructure and repeat instruction, improving attention spans and educational outcomes in children.

Creativity and the New Learning Models

Twenty first century learning spaces must be agile, able to be easily reconfigured to engage different kinds of learners and teachers, and able to accommodate individual, small group and large group activities.

Current and future economies of the world depend on innovation and creativity, skills that need to be encouraged. For true innovation and creativity to occur, learning spaces should facilitate people working collaboratively across disciplines. Spaces should allow teachers and students to group and regroup and classes to be easily reconfigured (Robinson 2009).

Gardner's theoretical work in the 1980s was important in that it broadened teachers' concepts of students' cognitive abilities to include spatial, linguistic, logical-mathematical, bodily-kinesthetic, musical, interpersonal, intrapersonal and naturalistic skills. His 'frames of mind' or 'multiple intelligences' helped educators understand that people have preferred ways of learning, and a variety of skills and talents. Traditionally, schools had mainly focused on fostering mathematical and literary skills.

In 2007 Gardner outlined five cognitive abilities he believed would need to be cultivated, lead to useable knowledge and be sought by leaders in the future. They are useful guidelines for thinking about education in the 21st century: The Disciplinary Mind: the mastery of major schools of thought, including science, mathematics, and history, and at least one professional craft. The Synthesizing Mind: the ability to integrate ideas from different disciplines or spheres into a coherent whole and to communicate that integration to others The Creating Mind: the capacity to uncover and clarify new problems, questions and phenomena. The Respectful Mind: awareness of and appreciation for differences among human beings and human groups. The Ethical Mind: fulfillment of one's responsibilities as a worker and as a citizen.

Changes in society and the unknown future challenges and technologies facing learners have led to the need for what can be described as anywhere, anytime, ubiquitous learning (Cope

&Kalantzis, 1999) and problem solving approaches. Twenty-first century learning theories emphasise the importance of authentic learning and providing students with opportunities and spaces to develop their creative and critical thinking skills (Newton & Fisher, 2009; McGuinness, 1999 & 2010). Indian learners will need to develop skills to analyse and respond to authentic situations through inquiry, imagination and innovation. New pedagogies, including problem and inquiry-based learning approaches, require students to plan and organize their learning activities with their peers, to tackle big ideas, become technologically literate and develop cultural awareness.

A learning environment aided by learning technologies and rich in evocative images and objects, triggers active learning by allowing students to engage with what appeals to them. The community, the landscape and faraway places can be brought to the classroom enabling a rich cultural diversity to be explored. The acknowledgement and visual stimulus provided by the display of student work in this digital era is important, and display space is a high priority with educators, particularly those working in primary and secondary schools. The digital divide between the urban and rural schools in Private and Government schools is vast and this gap should be filled with appropriate funding from both Central and State Governments.

Conclusion

The basic structure of teaching spaces does not seem to have evolved much over the past century. This fact inspired the researcher to investigate the reason why, despite the recent changes in pedagogy and the widespread use of information technology inside classrooms and school spaces, the physical learning environment has not yet changed in keeping with this evolution. In order to plan and construct effective physical learning environments, not only technical specifications need to be elaborated; qualitative aspects also need to be considered (Nuikkinen 2009, p. 64).In terms of teaching methods, Indian schools must recognize that what engages this generation of learners is very different from what may have engaged previous generations. Students today have grown up in a world where laptops, computers, cell phones with browsers, and other personal digital devices are common tools, and instant messaging, blogs, and wikis are common modes of self-expression.

The knowledge explosion of twentieth and the present century makes it mandatory for a harmonious growth of the people living in all parts of the world with equal opportunities in education and employment avenues. The role of technology, networking, and changing organizational cultures prove to be an invaluable resource for all those interested in learning and teaching. Designing learning environment of tomorrow is of paramount importance for the society across the continents and of particular interest to teachers, education policy makers, parents, teacher educators, advisors and decision-makers nationally and internationally. We need to create a long-term shared vision. Sometimes the policy development process starts with someone—often the Prime Minister or President, —who articulates a high-level vision of what education should be like to ensure the Nation's future wellbeing. Private-public partnerships can also play an important role. In addition to contractual arrangements with the private sector, some companies may be able to contribute resources or programs that would help designing learning environment of tomorrow.

References

1. Future Proofing of Schools – designing today's schools & tomorrows world –e-content
2. The future of the Physical learning environment- school facilities that support the user by Marco Kuuskorpi, Kaarina, Finland NuriacabellosGonzaliz Spain
3. Apple classroom of Tomorrow Today Learning in the 21st century
4. Intel teach to the future initiative – a world programme
5. Policy for Educational Transformation: An Educational Policy brief Robert B. Kozma, Ph.D.Kozmalone Consulting

11

Effectiveness of Educational Software on Achievement in Chemistry Among Students of Standard XI

Introduction

The instruction through Educational Software has been making wonders in the class room activities. 'Eureka Educational Software' has developed Educational Software in the name of "Designmate" for different subjects such as Mathematics, Physics, Chemistry and Biology for the Standards from VI to XII. More animations and interactions are incorporated in this Software. The Investigator wanted to know, the effectiveness of the Eureka Educational Software on the Achievement in Chemistry. Hence the Investigators were aimed to study the Effectiveness of Educational Software on Achievement in Chemistry among the Students of Standard XI. The study belongs to an Experimental Research. The sample of the study based on the half – yearly performance of the students, they are divided into two groups. The total number of students 79, of which 37 belonged to Control Group and 42 belonged to Experimental Group. The Eureka Educational Software "Designmate" was the Dependent Variable and the Achievement in Chemistry was the Independent Variable. The developed Achievement Test in Chemistry by the Investigator was conducted before and after the treatment for both Control and Experiment Groups. Then the Investigator taught Chemistry through Educational Software to the Experimental Group. Similar topics in Chemistry were taught through Lecture Method to the Control Group. The collected data was analysed by using different statistical techniques such as Mean, Standard Deviation and 't' test. The study found that the Achievement made through Educational Software by Experimental Group was significantly higher than the Control Group.

Computer Assisted Instruction (CAI) has emerged as an effective and efficient media of instruction in the advanced countries of the world. CAI is being used in the formal and non – formal educations at all levels. In India too computer has been introduced in most of the areas such as data processing, decision making, etc., It has impact on the working methods of research and development in the field of Science and Technology. First CAI attempt was made around 1961 when University of Illinosis produced Programmed Logic for Automatic Teaching Operation (PLATO). Hence, the use of computer in general education started from early sixties. The Computer Assisted or Aided Instruction may be defined as the use of computer as an integral part of an instructional system, the learner generally engaging in two – way interaction with the computer via terminal.

"Designmate', is a Educational Software developed by Eureka Educational Software which is a 17 years old Multimedia Production House, involved into various activities like making of interactive presentation, animated films, music videos, special effects. They are the first people in India to do a full four minute animated music video where a live character interacts and dance with a computer generated character Anaida's "Hoo Halla Hoo". They received an award for Best Animation from Autodesk. Eureka Educational Software developed 'Designmate', which were converting the entire textbooks into colourful 3D animated movies with interactive games and puzzles. Bringing a visually beautiful and interesting learning experience, enhancing the student's learning and retention capabilities. This Education Software was distributed to Schools via

Server and LAN. This Education Software covers Science and Mathematics subjects from class VI to XII.

Objectives of the Study

The objectives of the study are

(i) To find out the significant difference between the Pre – Test Scores of the Control and Experimental group.

(ii) To find out the significant difference between the Post – Test Scores of the Control and Experimental group.

(iii) To find out the significant difference between Control and Experimental group at the Pre – Test and Post – Test Scores.

(iv) To find out the effect of Educational Software on Achievement in Chemistry with respect to different variables such as of Gender, Caste and Science Marks secured in Standard X.

Hypotheses

The following hypotheses were formulated to realize the above objectives.

(i) There is no significant difference between the Pre- Test and Post – Test Scores of the Control group and Experimental group.

(ii) There is no significant difference between the Control group and Experimental group at the Pre – Test and Post – Test Scores.

(iii) There is no influence of Gender, Caste and Science Marks secured in Standard X (SMSX) over the effect of Educational Software on Achievement in Chemistry.

Nature of the Research

The present investigation is Experimental in nature, because the investigators aimed to compare the Effectiveness of Teaching Chemistry to the XI Standard Students through Teaching and through Eureka Educational Software.

Sample Selection

The investigators selected XI Standard Students of Periyar Centenary Memorial Matriculation Higher Secondary School, K.K. Nagar Trichy to carry out the Experiment because the School have been posed with well equipped computer facilities. Based on the half – yearly performance of the Students, they are divided into two groups. The total number of students 79, of which 37 belonged to Control Group and 42 belonged to Experimental Group.

Development of Tool

The Eureka Educational Software, 'Designmate' was the Dependent Variable and the Achievement in Chemistry was the Independent Variable. The Eureka Educational Software was given to the Post Graduate Teachers who are handling Chemistry in the nearby schools for content validity. The opinion of them was highly satisfactory.

The developed Achievement test questionnaires were framed by the investigators with the guidance of the subject experts covering the following items such as Knowledge, Understanding, Application and Skill. These questionnaires were validated by Test – Retest method among the Student of XI Standard. The obtained 'r' value 0.74 shows that the tool is highly valuable. Thus the Validity and Reliability of the tool were established. The developed Achievement Test in Chemistry was conducted before and after the treatment for both Control and Experiment Groups. Then the Investigators taught Chemistry through Educational Software to the Experimental Group. Similar topics in Chemistry were taught through Lecture Method to the Control Group.

After the finalization of the tool, the investigators had given 40 items to the Students. Each item was in the form of multiple choices with an incomplete statement. For each item four alternative answers were given. Only one was the correct answer. The Students were requested to write the response in the form of correct alpha bate a, b, c and d. Each × responses carry 1 mark.

Data Analysis

Thus the data collected in this manner undertake analysis by using different statistical technique. Mean and SD were calculated for each Variables to calculate 't' values which is the test of significance of the difference between two means. The following tables contained the data regarding the Control group and Experimental group with the following variables such as Gender, Caste and SMSX.

Table 1.1 : Mean and SD of the Student towards Achievement Score for different Category of Control Group

Sl.No	Variable	Category	Sample Size	Mean		SD	
				Pre-Test	Post-Test	Pre-Test	Post-Test
01.	**Gender**	Boys	18	20.83	65.97	9.09	13.31
		Girls	19	15.53	62.5	12.05	17.37
02.	**Caste**	OC/BC	23	22.07	65.43	11.48	16.57
		MBC/SC/ST	14	11.61	62.14	6.09	13.69
03.	**SMSX**	Above 70%	21	21.55	68.21	10.73	11.34
		Below 70%	16	13.59	62.66	9.72	16.31
04.	**Total**		37	18.11	64.19	11.03	15.63

From the above table 1.1 it is revealed that the average Mean Score of the Student towards Achievement Score for different category is 18.11 at Pre – Test level and 64.19 at Post – Test level which show the effectiveness of Lecture Method. Moreover at the Pre – Test level the minimum score at the is 11.61 and the maximum score is 22.07. At the Post – Test level 62.14 is the minimum score and 68.21 is the maximum score.

Table 1.2 : Mean and SD of the Student towards Achievement Score for different Category of Experimental Group

Sl.No	Variable	Category	Sample Size	Mean		SD	
				Pre-Test	Post-Test	Pre-Test	Post-Test
01.	**Gender**	Boys	21	25.6	81.67	9.66	10.24
		Girls	21	13.81	70.12	7.82	10.62
02.	**Caste**	OC/BC	26	21.63	76.44	10.56	11.99
		MBC/SC/ST	16	16.56	74.68	9.84	12.58
03.	**SMSX**	Above 70%	18	18.89	78.89	10.28	9.33
		Below70%	24	19.9	73.65	11.24	13.11
04.	**Total**		42	19.70	75.89	15.63	11.93

Above table shows that the average Mean Score of the Student towards Achievement Score for different category is 19.70 at Pre –

Test level and 75.89 at Post – Test level which show the Eureka Educational Software has considerable effect in Teaching Chemistry. Moreover at the Pre – Test level the minimum score is 13.81 and the maximum score is 25.6. At the Post – Test level 70.12 is the minimum score and 81.67 is the maximum score.

Table 1.3 : Significant Difference between the Mean scores of Control Group and Experimental Group at Pre – Test level

Group	N	Mean	SD	t value	Remarks
Control	37	18.11	11.03	0.661	NS
Experimental	42	19.70	10.58		

NS: Not significant

The above table 1.2 reveals that the obtained mean Student Achievement Scores in Chemistry of the Control group and Experimental group are more or less same. The calculated 't' value also indicates there is no significant difference at 5% level between Control group and Experimental group at Pre- Test level. Hence the stated Null Hypothesis is that, there is no significant difference between the mean Student Achievement Scores in Chemistry of the Control group and Experimental group at the Pre – Test level is accepted.

Table 1.4 : Significant Difference between the Mean scores of Control Group and Experimental Group at Post – Test level

Group	N	Mean	SD	t value	Remarks
Control	37	64.19	15.63	**4.01**	S
Experimental	42	75.89	11.93		

S: Significant

It is evident from the table 1.3 that the obtained mean value of Experimental group is greater than the control group. The calculated 't' value shows that there is significant difference between the Control group and Experimental group. Hence the stated Null hypothesis that there is no significant difference between Student Achievement Scores in Chemistry of Control group and Experimental group at Post – Test level is rejected.

Table 1.5 : Influence of various Category over the performance of the Control Group and Experimental Group at Pre – Test level

Category	Group	N	Mean	SD	t value	Remarks
Boys	Control	18	20.83	9.09	1.59	NS
	Experimental	21	25.6	9.66		
Girls	Control	19	15.53	12.05	0.54	NS
	Experimental	21	13.81	7.82		
OC/BC	Control	23	22.07	11.48	0.14	NS
	Experimental	26	21.63	10.56		
MBC/SC/ST	Control	14	11.61	6.09	1.68	NS
	Experimental	16	16.56	9.84		
Above 70%	Control	21	21.55	10.73	0.78	NS
	Experimental	18	18.89	10.28		
Below 70%	Control	16	13.59	9.72	1.88	NS
	Experimental	24	19.9	11.24		

The above table 1.4 shows that the calculated 't' values of Control group and Experimental group at the Pre – Test level at various Categories has no significant difference at 5 % level. Hence it is concluded that Gender, Caste, SMSX has no influence over the performance of Control group and Experimental group at the Pre – Test level. Therefore the stated Null hypothesis is that, there is no influence of Gender, Caste, SMSX over the performance of Student Achievement Scores in Chemistry of the Control group and Experimental group at the Pre – Test is accepted.

Table 1.6 : Significant Difference between the Mean scores of Pre – Test and Post – Test for Control Group

Test	N	Mean	SD	t value	Remarks
Pre	37	18.11	11.03	**14.62**	**S**
Post	37	64.19	15.63		

It is evident from the table 1.5 that the obtained mean value of Post – Test is greater than the Pre - Test. The calculated't' value shows that there is significant difference between the Pre – Test and Post – Test conducted for the Control group. Hence the stated Null hypothesis that there is no significant difference between Student

Achievement Scores in Chemistry for the Pre – Test and Post – Test of Control group is rejected.

Table 1.7 : Significant Difference between the Mean scores of Pre – Test and Post – Test for Experimental Group

Test	N	Mean	SD	t value	Remarks
Pre	42	19.70	10.58	**22.61**	**S**
Post	42	75.89	11.93		

The above table 1.6 reveals that the obtained mean Student Achievement Scores in Chemistry of the Post – Test is greater than Pre – Test of Experimental group. The calculated 't' value also indicates there is significant difference at 5% level between Pre – Test and Post – Test of Experimental group. Hence the stated Null Hypothesis is that, there is no significant difference between the mean Student Achievement Scores in Chemistry for the Pre – Test and Post – Test of Experimental group is rejected.

Table 1.8 : Influence of Gender over the performance of the Control Group and Experimental Group at Post – Test level

Gender	Group	N	Mean	SD	t value	Remarks
Boys	Control	18	65.97	13.31	**4.02**	S
	Experimental	21	81.67	10.24		
Girls	Control	19	62.5	17.37	1.52	NS
	Experimental	21	70.12	10.62		

The above table 1.8 shows that the calculated 't' values of Control group and Experimental group at the Post – Test level of the Boys has significant difference between the mean scores at 5 % level. The above table also reveals that the calculated 't' values of Control group and Experimental group at the Post – Test level of the Girls has no significant difference between the mean scores at 5 % level. Therefore the stated Null hypothesis is that, except Boys the Girls has no influence over the performance of Student Achievement Scores in Chemistry of the Control group and Experimental group at the Post – Test is accepted.

Table 1.9 : Influence of Caste over the performance of the Control Group and Experimental Group at Post – Test level

Caste	Group	N	Mean	SD	t value	Remarks
OC/BC	Control	23	65.43	16.57	**2.63**	S
	Experimental	26	76.44	11.99		
MBC/SC/ST	Control	14	62.14	13.69	**2.62**	S
	Experimental	16	74.68	12.58		

The calculated 't' values from the above table reveals that Control group and Experimental group at the Post – Test level of the Caste has significant difference between the mean scores at 5 % level. The mean values of the above table shows that there is influence of caste over the performance of Control group and Experimental group at the Post – Test level. Hence the stated Null Hypothesis is that, there is influence of caste over the performance of Student Achievement Scores in Chemistry of the Control group and Experimental group at the Post – Test is rejected.

Table 1.10 : Influence of Students secured Science Marks in Standard X over the performance of the Control Group and Experimental Group at Post – Test level

SMSX	Group	N	Mean	SD	t value	Remarks
Above 70%	Control	21	68.21	11.34	**3.43**	S
	Experimental	18	78.89	9.33		
Below 70%	Control	16	62.66	16.31	**2.45**	S
	Experimental	24	73.65	13.11		

It is evident from the table 1.10 that the obtained mean value of Experimental group is greater than the Control group. The calculated 't' value shows that there is significant difference between the Control group and Experimental group at the Post – Test level with respect to SMSX at 5 % level. The mean values of the above table shows that there is influence of SMSX over the performance of Control group and Experimental group at the Post – Test level. Hence the stated Null Hypothesis is that, there is influence of SMSX over the performance of Student Achievement Scores in Chemistry of the Control group and Experimental group at the Post – Test is rejected.

Findings & Discussion

The salient findings of the study are i) the Eureka Educational Software has considerable effect in Teaching Chemistry, ii) there is a significant difference between the mean scores of Pre – Test and Post – Test level for both Control Group and Experimental Group, iii) Gender, Caste and SMSX has no influence over the performance of Student Achievement Scores in Chemistry of the Control group and Experimental group at the Pre – Test level, iii) Caste and SMSX has influence over the performance of Student Achievement Scores in Chemistry of the Control group and Experimental group at the Post – Test level and v) Experimental group Boys show significant higher mean scores in the Achievement Scores than the Control group, but Girls has no influence over the performance of Student Achievement Scores in Chemistry of the Control group and Experimental group.

While conducting the Pre – Test it was observed that both Control and Experimental group's posse's similar level of pervious knowledge on the selected contents in Chemistry. The same trend was observed with respect to different variables such as Gender, Caste and SMSX. When the analysis was made between Pre – Test and Post – Test Scores of the Control and Experimental groups it was observed that both methods of teaching such as traditional Lecture Method and Educational Software method, Educational Software method is found to be effective method. While comparing the Mean Achievement Scores between Control and Experimental group it was observed that students who learnt through Eureka Educational Software score significant higher than the Control group Students. The significant difference of the Experimental group may be due to the reason that the Eureka Educational Software has incorporated with interactive presentation, animated movies, special effects and puzzles, these special features might have attracted the Experimental Students to score more marks.

It is interesting to note when comparing the Achievements of Girls Students between Control and Experiment groups the effectiveness was not significant as the Girls Students might not show interest towards Computer Assisted Instruction at XI Standard level.

Education Implications

This Experimental Study established the positive result on Achievement, so the Educational Institutions may be encouraged to use the Computer Assisted Instruction for the Teaching Learning process. Subject experts may concentrate on preparing Software packages in all the units of the all the subjects and distribute them to Schools. This may make the Students more interest towards Educations and it also make the Teachers to save their time.

Conclusions

Eureka Educational Software is more suitable method for teaching Chemistry at XI Standard level. Eureka Educational Software is the one of the best method in the Teaching Learning process of Chemistry for XI Standard Students without considering the individual variables such as Gender, Caste and SMSX this is due to the subject contents are taught through more animations and interactions. Due to this Educational Software Students concentrations increased and they easily understood the subject contents. At the Post – Test level the Girls shows no significant difference in the Achievement Scores in Chemistry of the Control group and Experimental group.

Reference

1. Ramesh Chandra (2004). Impact of Media and Technology in Education, Kalpaz Publications, New Delhi.
2. Rao, V.K.(2005). Instructional Technology, APH Publishing Corporation, New Delhi.
3. Rawat, S.C. (2004). Essentials of Educational Technology, R.Lall Book Depot, Meerut.
4. Zaidi, S.M.(2004). Educational Technology, Anmol Publisher Pvt. Ltd New Delhi.
5. www.knewton.com/flipped-classroom
6. en.wikipedia.org/wiki/Flip_teaching
7. *www.core-learning.com/pt_software_school.asp*

12

E-learning: An Innovative Techno-pedagogy in the Digital Era

Education is the provision of a series of learning experiences to students in order to impart knowledge, values, attitudes, and skills with the ultimate aim of making them a productive member of the society. Changes in the economic and social fundamentals in the society call for the transformation in the skills, capabilities and attitudes of the masses. This requires a shift in the delivery and methodology used in the current education system. E - Learning is a technology which supports teaching and learning via a computer web technology. E-learning provides lot of opportunities for the students when comparing to other media of learning. This paper mainly focuses on the impact of E-learning on teaching and learning process both from teacher's view point and student's effectiveness in learning.

The root meaning of education is given as bringing up or leading out or making manifest the inherent potentialities in a pupil. Education in broad term means, *"the life- long process of acquiring new knowledge and skills through both formal and informal exposure to information, ideas and experiences"*. A shift from teacher -centered instruction is needed to enable student to acquire the new dimensions of knowledge and skills. This new environment also involves a change in the role of both teachers and students. In the modern era, we have seen phenomenal developments in the application of media and technology in education in the recent past. E-Learning specifically, is becoming a prominent learning environment aimed at providing student - centric, self-paced instruction using the electronic medium of World Wide Web. E-Learning environment can be perceived as a flexible learning environment in which the body of knowledge is logically and sequentially arranged with considering the possible all types of learning styles. Therefore, it becomes a learning resource that suits all types of learners. In this paper, it has been stressed the need of electronically enabled learning environment by developing e-learning materials to make teaching learning experiences joyful and successful.

E-learning and E-teaching:

E-Learning is a technology which supports teaching and learning via a computer web technology. E-Learning is internet-enabled learning. E-learning provides faster learning at reduced cost, increased access to learning and clear accountability for all participants in the learning process. (Rosenberg. 2001)

E-Teaching is the facilitation of live teaching with streaming lectures, white boards, downloadable slide sets and discussion forums (Mishra, 2005). E-Learning is about the automation of an existing teacher-centered educational approach, while e-learning means innovative students-centered approach that is more consistent with adult learning theory. Thus E-teaching and E-learning enables the students for continuous updating of knowledge, enhances their IT skills and paves way for time management in the teaching learning process.

ICT – A Necessity Tool in the Digital Era

"India can become one of the developed countries in the world by year 2020, if we adopt technology as our tool. For this, the teaching community should change its mind set and enthuse the students by means of technology" (Abdul Kalam, 2004).

ICTs are powerful tools having potential to transform the educational systems and opportunities for all students including those who are normally excluded by virtue of their special circumstances and special educational needs. Use of ICTs can break down some of the barriers that lead to under achievement, student disaffection and educational exclusion (Swarts, 2006) E-learning is fast becoming a major form of learning. Multimedia offers ideal opportunities for creating and presenting visually enriched learning environments. Management institutes and educators have attempt an increased incorporation of collaborative group work, problem, solving and decision making through technology as an integral component of pedagogy (Sharma, 2007) ICT powers our access to information, enables new form of communication, and serves many online service in the spheres of commerce, culture, entertainment and education.

E-Learning Efficiency in Teaching Learning Process:

Improving the quality of education and training is the critical issue in the educational sector. E-learning can enhance the quality of education by increasing learner motivation and engagement, by facilitating the acquisition of basic skills and by enhancing teacher training. Multimedia computer software that combines text, sound and colorful moving images can be used to provide challenging and authentic content that will engage the student in the learning process. E-learning can increase learner motivation as it combines the media richness and interactivity with the opportunity to connect with real people and to participate in real world events. The transmission of basic skills and concepts that are the foundation of higher order thinking skills and creativity can be facilitated by e-learning through drill and practice. E-learning can support and scaffold the students for their own learning. And it also helps the students to clarify their doubts in any time. From this, students get wide knowledge and learning experience. (Sivarajan, 2010). ICT supports the students for independent learning and helps the learner for self construction of knowledge.

E-Learning promotes collaborate learning, depends understanding, provide flexible and rich medium for students to access learning materials. It also provides a single experience that accommodates the distinct learning styles of auditory learners, visual learners and kinesthetic learners. In short, computer based networking system has provided the present day teacher to deliver the effective instruction in the class room.

Role of a e-teacher

E-teacher has to adapt continuous professional development in the educational use of technology. In this sense, teachers have to be ready to make use of the possibilities that ICT offer, such as different learning contexts, focused on the students, presenting them with several types of interaction, offering different degrees of control of their own learning and promote collaborative tasks. Hence the e-teacher need to (i) Look at the subject content in a new way and re-think and adapt innovative course delivery (ii) Gain computational proficiency so that there is understanding of both its strength and its weaknesses (iii) Develop positive attitude towards e-learning (iv) Encourage students to set their own objectives and agendas (v) understanding of different learning styles of students.

Conclusion

Integration of ICT in education is inevitable in the digital era. Success of ICT based education depends upon the teacher's ability to keep pace with the developments of modern society. E-learning is a learning process created by interaction with digitally delivered content, network, based services and tutoring support. Thus, E-learning enables the students for continuous updating of knowledge, enhances their skills and paves way for time management in the teaching learning process.

Reference

1. Sharma. K. (2007). *India in the knowledge economy an electronic Paradigm,* International Journal of Educational Management Vol. 21, No.6, PP. 543 – 568
2. Sivarajan, K. (2010). *Information and communication Technology and Communication Skills,* Calicut university central co-operative store.

3. Rosenberg, M.J. (2001). *E-learning strategies for delivering knowledge in the digital age.* Newyork MC Graw Hill.
4. Mishra, S. (2005) *Development of e-learning in India,* University News, 43(11), pp. 14-20
5. Swarts (2006). *Web based technology in education,* APH publishing corporation, New Delhi.

13

Engineering Chemistry Teaching Through VAI

Introduction

Video assisted instruction can provide a consistent form of teaching and can communicate certain concepts in a visual and realistic manner. Refers to recording, manipulating, and displaying moving images, especially in a format that can be presented on a television. VAI may also be helpful to look through lesson plans from other institutions for ideas on how video has been used effectively to illustrate specific topics. The investigators followed experimental research for their study. The aim of experimental research is to establish cause and effect relationship between variables and conditions. Establishing cause and effect relationship between the Phenomenon is the fundamental concern of experimental research. In this present study, 120 samples were selected from three Engineering colleges located in Cuddalore district based on the mark scored in pre-test which was constructed and administered by the Investigator before giving the treatment. If a video has been chosen to demonstrate a specific topic, does it do so succinctly and effectively. Pre-viewing: Before viewing it is important to prepare students for what they are about to see and to introduce the broad topic. Any parts of the video that you believe will challenge students can be outlined at this time. Pre-viewing exercises such as brainstorms may help to focus attention. Viewing: Continuous interruptions during viewing risk breaking concentration and should be avoided. However, students can be given simple tasks to carry out while watching a video which will help them to engage with the video's content. A balance has to be found which doesn't ask too much of students, but does help to keep them active. Predefined pause points may also act to engage students by eliciting opinions during the viewing process. Post-viewing: Many different types of activity might follow on from watching a video. Content might be used to begin a discussion, individual reports might be written from different perspectives students could role-play further scenarios. Sourcing video: When searching for video clips, consider television broadcasters online resources, such as the BBC or ITN. Websites such as YouTube, BUFVC, Teacher Tube can also be very useful. The technology requirements and the sources for selecting appropriate videos were described. If one will be teaching in one of the content areas in which there are clips and guidelines ready to use and many of those clips are on the survey top 40, one will be in great shape. Every one we have to decide how a person want to use the clips and where and when to embed them. If one teaching in other disciplines, start with the top 40 and begin extracting the clips one wants. Gradually, everyone will accumulate their own pool for use semester after year. Draw on every one creativity, imagination, and artistic gifts in applying these clips and those of our own choosing to our teaching. That will inevitably make the greatest difference in our classroom. In the years to come, students will request DVDs of your classes to download onto their iPhones and PCs. Then they can play and relive those magical teaching moments. Chemistry needs the support of VAI but it is very essential if science like chemistry is taught without VAI, that will be useless at all levels. Changing method according to the need is most important, so blended teaching in chemistry also inevitable.

The use of educational video offers many favorable characteristics in the variety field of science area. Video instruction can provide a consistent form of teaching and can communicate certain concepts in a visual and realistic manner. Furthermore, video education has been shown to be superior to traditional method and improve knowledge. The purpose of this study was to evaluate how the implementation of an educational video on the teaching would influence the understanding of educational process and satisfaction in a group of students.

What is Video

1. Refers to recording, manipulating, and displaying moving images, especially in a format that can be presented on a television.
2. Refers to displaying images and text on a computer monitor. The video adapter, for example, is responsible for sending signals to the display device.

Why video?

There are an endless number of ways to exploit video in order to create motivating, memorable and inclusive learning experiences. However, watching a video can also be a passive experience and so teaching methods must be used which instead turn it into a springboard for student action and interaction. Before deciding to use video for teaching purposes, it is vital to watch all the material to be shown to students beforehand, just in case there is any unnecessary or unsuitable content. It VAI may also be helpful to look through lesson plans from other institutions for ideas on how video has been used effectively to illustrate specific topics. If a video has been chosen to demonstrate a specific topic, does it do so succinctly and effectively?

Video and lesson structuring

A lesson plan that involves video material might be thought of in terms of three distinct phases:

Pre-viewing

Before viewing it is important to prepare students for what they are about to see and to introduce the broad topic. Any parts of the video that you believe will challenge students can be outlined at this time. Pre-viewing exercises such as brainstorms may help to focus attention.

Viewing

Continuous interruptions during viewing risk breaking concentration and should be avoided. However, students can be given simple tasks to carry out while watching a video which will help them to engage with the video's content. A balance has to be found which doesn't ask too much of students, but does help to keep them active. Predefined pause points may also act to engage students by eliciting opinions during the viewing process.

Post-viewing

Many different types of activity might follow on from watching a video. Content might be used to begin a discussion, individual reports might be written from different perspectives or students could role-play further scenarios.

Sourcing video

When searching for video clips, consider television broadcasters online resources, such as the BBC or ITN. Websites such as YouTube, BUFVC, Teacher Tube can also be very useful, but remember to check for potential rights issues. Remember, not everything on the web is legally posted. If in doubt, don't use it! It is also important to check for any policies your host institution might have for using video. Academic libraries often hold an ERA license, which allows recorded off-air materials to be used for teaching purposes.

Creating video

Video documents can make effective reference material but creating your video content is also a rewarding experience, which can be carried out simply and with inexpensive equipment. Via role-play, students or groups of students can become engaged with extremely difficult topics. Simple editing can illustrate how information can be shaped to deliver a message. Students can be given the opportunity to produce assessed audiovisual materials or 'video essays'. Web sites such as Flickr now host video clips and offer a powerful broadcasting platform for student output. Creating simple video recordings of lectures allows information to be presented at the student's own pace with instant playback, rewind and pause. This may be particularly useful for students who are less suited to the familiar lesson scenario.

Computer Assisted Teaching and Video Assisted Teaching

The term CALI (computer-assisted language instruction) was in use before CALL, reflecting its origins as a subset of the general term CAI (computer-assisted instruction). CALI fell out of favour among language teachers, however, as it appeared to imply a teacher-centred approach (instructional), whereas language teachers are more inclined to prefer a student-centred approach, focusing on learning rather than instruction. CALL began to replace CALI in the early 1980s (Davies & Higgins 1982: p. 3) and it is now incorporated into the names of the growing number of professional associations worldwide. A combination of face-to-face teaching and CALL is usually referred to as blended learning. Blended learning is designed to increase learning potential and is more commonly found than pure CALL. Engineering college the objective of the study was to determine the effects of video-assisted Instruction on the academic achievement of pupils in teaching Chemistry. The true experimental method under the category of posttest-only, equivalent-groups design was used in this study to gather and interpret its data. Validated achievement test, adopted documents (lesson plans), videotapes will be used to gather data from the respondents. T-test was the statistics used to treat the data. The learning of chemistry poses two great difficulties from the very beginning. The first is the usable nature of the fundament particles on which the whole science depends. Students are expected to become familiar with electrons and nuclei, atom, ions and molecules that may remain forever invisible. The second difficulty is the inherent complexity of over the seemingly simplest phenomena, which has caused far two wide a gap between inter portative and descriptive chemistry. Indeed explanations of many common chemical phenomena have not even been available. For these reason students have been expected to memorize for too much without understanding.

Teaching of Chemistry

The science of the composition, structure, properties, and reactions of matter, especially of atomic and molecular systems. This definition further evolved until, in 1947, it came to mean the science of substances: their structure, their properties, and the reactions that change them into other substances - a characterization accepted by Linus Pauling. The learning of chemistry poses two great difficulties from the very beginning. The first is the usable nature of the fundament particles on which the whole science depends. Students are expected to become familiar with electrons and nuclei, atoms, ions and molecules that may remain forever invisible. Chemical engineering is applied chemistry. It is the branch of engineering concerned with the design, construction, and operation of machines and plants that perform chemical reactions to solve practical problems or make useful products.

Methodology

The investigators followed experimental research for their study. The aim of experimental research is to establish cause and effect relationship between variables and conditions. Establishing cause and effect relationship between the Phenomenon is the fundamental concern of experimental research.

Experimental research deals with three types of variables the dependant, independent and controlled. The setting in which experimental research is conducted is usually standardized and well defined. The experimental research is conducted in highly controlled situation. The experiment is generally regarded as the most sophisticated research method for testing hypothesis.

In this present study, there are 120 samples selected from three Engineering colleges located in Cuddalore district based on the mark scored in pre-test which was constructed and administered by the Investigator before giving the treatment. Three groups were equated numerically based on their achievement in pre-test out of divided three groups, First group second group was treated with developed VAI software, called Experiment. Group II and Third group were treated with conventional method, called controlled group.

Merits of VAI

Video assisted training is not just sitting down and watching television. A video assisted curriculum has three distinct parts. First, there is a facilitator who guides the discussion; second, the video cassette that contains consistent current information; third, handouts for the participants so they can be actively involved in the process. All programs come with a facilitator's manual giving all the information a local person would need to conduct the sessions. An agency that invests in this type of training receives three major advantages. The biggest advantage is a onetime investment which will allow the agency to train as many people as they want over a long time. This means the cost per person drops every time the video curriculum is used to make it very cost effective investment. Some other strong points of the programs are flexibility because you can present the curriculum at one time or divide it. Consistencies, the video cassettes contain the correct information, and you will not have people getting different messages from different people especially information is regulations.

5. The Role of Media in Education

The role of media and technology in education is quite obvious in today's educational settings. Schools are loaded with computers and even here at Northern Michigan University students receive a laptop to help them with academic studies. This is part of NMU's Laptop Initiative plan that believes providing every student with a laptop will help improve their academic performance. However media comes in many different forms, such as; internet, TV, radio, and books, all of these media have affected the way students learn. Around the world students are being globally connected with one another via internet. These mass media tools have made the world a smaller place in a way, also called (globalization). The way media affects education are great and varied when you think about it. Back when Columbus sailed the ocean blue the world had the misconception that the earth was flat, and why did they have this theory? Because that is what was printed on every map that was distributed back then making media at fault. Media is such a massive part of our lives and it is everywhere we turn. How could it not affect our lives in terms of education? Before we can dive into all the benefits of media to education it is important that the educators of students and students themselves become what is called “media literate”. This is the ability to decipher the hidden messages in mass media. Teacher education needs media literacy as an essential tool and topic in the new millennium. Let’s face it, media has changed the world. Media such as internet, is constantly growing and changing, thus educators must stay with the times and keep up by using these tools for their students. With the help of new media power teachers would be more able to offer students information from around the world at an even faster and easier rate.

Science through Video

Inquiry-based teaching, central to the National Science Education Standards and the Benchmarks for Science Literacy, should not be an isolated occurrence, but a comprehensive and ongoing approach. However, many teachers hesitate to teach science through inquiry because they did not learn this way themselves, when they were students or during their preparation to become teachers. This workshop shows inquiry teaching and learning in action, with real teachers and students in real classrooms. Whether you have already experimented with inquiry teaching and want to enhance your practice, or are new to the approach and want to know how to make it work, this workshop will help you understand the process and how it benefits students, and give you strategies to use in your classroom. Science teachers frequently scour the Web for short videos, knowing they can be powerful tools for demonstrating hard-to-explain concepts and piquing students’ interest in their subject. The new Science take series in the times is full of such videos, taking advantage of time-lapse photography and high-speed video to reveal the natural world’s secrets. Additionally, the Creature Cast series uses short animated films to explain scientific ideas and show the beauty in nature. Below several ways one can use these short science videos found in research work.

Educational Video and the Classroom

There is substantial research promoting the use of video in the classroom as a dynamic resource for supporting curricula. According to a recent teacher survey, 94% of classroom teachers have effectively used video during the course of the last academic year. And most teachers were using it frequently - on average, once per week. But why?. As educators, our aim is to get students energized and engaged in the hands-on learning process, and video is clearly an instructional medium that is compelling and generates a much greater amount of interest and enjoyment than the more traditional printed material. Using sight and sound, video is the perfect medium for students who are auditory or visual learners. With the added use of subtitles each child then has the choice to watch, listen to, or read each presentation. Video stimulates and engages students creating interest and maintaining that interest for longer periods of time, and it provides an innovative and effective means for educators to address and deliver the required curriculum content.

Video and its Experience

Consider teaching with the voices from the past by introducing students to great historians, political figures and famous people who lived centuries ago. Envision the classroom in which children hear the cry of a nearly extinct species and see the colors and hear the sounds of animals that thrive only in a remote wilderness half way around the world. And what about investigating the laws of motion, sound and energy transfer by viewing the launch of the space shuttle on its voyage into space? Think about how much easier it would be to understand the diverse cultures of people who live in other areas of the world if you could encounter them in their own environments - hearing their songs, observing their rituals or listening to their silence.

The benefits of using video in education includes providing a sensory experience that allows concepts and ideas to actually become an experience and come to life as students are guided through each adventure.

Video as a Flexible Teaching Component

The more interested and engaged students are, and the more interactive each learning session is, the more students will enjoy, learn from and retain information from the lesson.

Video provides a means of interactive instruction and is a very flexible medium. Having the ability to stop, start and rewind is absolutely invaluable. It provides the option to stop each video and challenge students to predict the outcome of a demonstration, and elaborate on, or debate a point of historical reference. You also have the option to rewind a section of the video to review a segment to ensure that children understand a key concept. You can ensure to add further interactivity by copying activities, conducting discussions or repeating demonstrations and experiments in the your classroom.

Effectively Utility of Video in The Classroom

Research has demonstrated that the most effective way to use video is as an enhancement to a lesson, or unit of study. Video should be used as a facet of instruction along with other resource material available to you for teaching a particular topic. Teachers should prepare for the use of a video in the classroom in the same way they do with other teaching aids or resources. Specific learning objectives should be determined in advanced, instructional sequences should be developed and reinforcement activities planned.

Video Support Tools

If students and teachers are to receive the maximum benefits from the use of video in education, the video should be supported by a selection of other tools and resources that enable each topic to be fully investigated and explored. The use of online video should be supported by the use of an interactive word glossary, dictionary, thesaurus and an online encyclopedia. Access to lesson plans specially written to be used in conjunction with the video help not only to minimize lesson preparation time, but also help provide valuable additional learning activities and projects that further enhance the use of the video as an educational aid. Increases student motivation, enhances learning experience, higher marks of development potential for deeper learning of the subject, development of learner autonomy, enhances team working and communication skills, a source of evidence relating to skills for interviews, learning resources for future cohorts to use.

Conclusion

The technology requirements and the sources for selecting appropriate videos were described. If one will be teaching in one of the content areas in which there are clips and guidelines ready to use and many of those clips are on the survey top 40, one will be in great shape. Every one we have to decide how a person want to use the clips and where and when to embed them. If one teaching in other disciplines, start with the top 40 and begin extracting the clips one wants. Gradually, everyone will accumulate their own pool for use semester after year. Draw on every one creativity, imagination, and artistic gifts in applying these clips and those of our own choosing to our teaching. That will inevitably make the greatest difference in our classroom. In the years to come, students will request DVDs of your classes to download onto their iPhones and PCs. Then they can play and relive those magical teaching moments. Chemistry needs the support of VAI but it is very essential if science like chemistry is taught without VAI, that will be useless at all levels. Changing method according to the need is most important, so blended teaching in chemistry also inevitable.

Reference

1. Agarwal, D.D (1998). Modern Method of teaching Chemistry. New Delhi, Sarup Cep Sons.
2. Abrams Arnold, H. Effectiveness of Interactive Video in Teaching Basic Photography Skills DAI., 4(11): 3326-A, 1986
3. Sundararaja Rao, T.R and Rajaguru, S. Effectiveness of Video Assisted Instruction of the Achievement of Slow learners. Journal of Educational Research and Extension. Vol.32 No.2. Oct 1995.
4. K. J. Howard-Quijano, Y. M. Huang, R. Matevosian, M. B. Kaplan and R. H. Steadman, (2008). "Video-assisted instruction improves the success rate for tracheal intubation by novices". *Oxford Journals*, Vol.101(4), pp.568-572.
5. Wolfra Lasser, Production and Design of Instructional Video and T.V and distance Education.\Journal of Research in Educational Media. Vol.1(4), July-1994.

14

Fillipped Classroom Pedagoggy-beyond Digital Age Learners

Introduction

Pioneered by Jonathan Bergman and Aaron Sams, chemistry teachers at Woodland Park High in Colorado, "flipped" classrooms invert traditional teaching methods by delivering lectures online as "homework" and shifting engagement activities into the classroom. By making this "flip" teachers are able to spend class time working directly with students to provide hands-on instruction and support. The flipped classroom is a teaching strategy that allows instructors to more actively engage with students in the classroom. In the flipped classroom, instructors typically assign recorded video lectures as homework, and use class time for active learning exercises and direct engagement with students. As Mung Chiang from Princeton said, "class time is for two-way interactions." Flipped classrooms help to make these two-way interactions possible.

Flipped Classrom

The flipped classroom describes a reversal of traditional teaching where students gain first exposure to new material outside of class, usually via reading or lecture videos, and then class time is used to do the harder work of assimilating that knowledge through strategies such as problem-solving, discussion or debates. The purpose of flipping the classroom is to shift from passive to active learning to focus on the higher order thinking skills such as analysis, synthesis and evaluation (Bloom). In flipped classrooms, students watch online lectures outside class and participate in engaged learning activities inside class. This approach allows instructors to more deeply engage their students with evidence-based learning practices that can significantly improve student outcomes.

Flipped Learning

Flipped learning is a pedagogical approach in which direct instruction moves from the group learning space to the individual learning space, and the resulting group space is transformed into a dynamic, interactive learning environment where the educator guides students as they apply concepts and engage creatively in the subject matter.

Key Elements of the Flipped Classroom

1. Provide an opportunity for students to gain first exposure prior to class.
2. Provide an incentive for students to prepare for class.
3. Provide a mechanism to assess student understanding.
4. Provide in-class activities that focus on higher level cognitive activities

Flipped Classrooms Characteristics

1. The in-class learning environments are *highly* structured (often planned down to the minute).
2. The in-class activities involve a significant amount of quizzing, problem solving and other active learning activities, forcing students to retrieve, apply, and/or extend the material learned outside of class. These activities are often slightly easier than those tackled outside of class, and are directly relevant to the out-of-class work.

3. Students are heavily incentivized through grading, in-class activities, and instructor expectations to complete out-of-class work and attend in-person meetings.

Teachers and Students Role and Expectations in the Flipped Classroom

Students take more responsibility for their own learning and study core content either individually or in groups before class and then apply knowledge and skills to a range of activities using higher order thinking,

Teaching 'one-to-many' focuses more on facilitation and moderation than lecturing, though lecturing is still important. Significant learning opportunities can be gained through facilitating active learning, engaging students, guiding learning, correcting misunderstandings and providing timely feedback using a variety of pedagogical strategies.

There is a greater focus on concept exploration, meaning making and demonstration or application of knowledge in the face-to-face setting.

Flipped Classroom Practices

1. Need to Know

If the flipped classroom is truly to become innovative, then it must be paired with transparent or embedded reason to know the content.

2. Engaging Models

One of the best ways to create the "need to know" is to use a pedagogical model that demands this. Whether project-based learning (PBL), game-based learning (GBL), Understanding by Design (UbD), or authentic literacy, find an effective model to institute in your classroom.

3. Technology

Since the flipped classroom is about recorded video, then obviously students would need the technology to do this. There are many things to consider here, video recording, pod casting, online notes, Audio tapes, etc.,

4. Reflection

5. Time and Place

If you have a blended learning environment, that of course provides a natural time and place to watch the videos, but it will be difficult to ensure all students watch a video as homework.

Web Tools for Flipped Classrooms

Below is a simple list designed to help get any educator, administrator, student, or parent a bit more familiar with some of the most popular web tools for flipped classrooms.

Comparison between Normal and Flipped Classroom

	Non Flipped Classroom Environment	**Flipped Classroom Environment**
Before Class	Students assigned something to read.	Students guided through learning module that asks and collects questions.
	Instructor prepares lecture.	Instructor prepares learning opportunities.
Beginning of Class	Students have limited information about what to expect.	Students have specific questions in mind to guide their learning.
	Instructor makes general assumption about what is helpful.	Instructor can anticipate where students need the most help.
During Class	Students try to follow along.	Students practice, performing the skills they are expected to learn.
	An instructor tries to get through all the materials.	Instructor guides the process with feedback and mini-lectures.
After Class	Students attempt the homework, usually with delayed feedback.	Students continue applying their knowledge skills after clarification and feedback.
	Instructor grades past work.	Instructor posts any additional explanations and resources as necessary and grades higher quality work.
Office Hours	Students want confirmation about what to study.	Students are equipped to seek help where they know they need it.
	Instructor often repeats what was in lecture.	Instructor continues guiding students toward deeper understanding.

Improved educational outcomes:

Studies have shown that flipped classrooms and blended learning environments can significantly improve educational outcomes when compared to traditional classrooms.

Efficiency

Lecturing and assignment grading are time-intensive activities. The long-run time savings from automating some of the repetitive lecture and grading activities allow faculty members to spend more time on active learning activities, teaching problem solving, and giving students personal attention and individual help. Similarly, auto graded assignments allow instructors to quickly and efficiently evaluate each student's understanding of learned concepts.

Interactive lectures

Instructors are able to intersperse in-video quizzes throughout their lectures, making the student lecture experience more interactive, dynamic, and personalized than traditional lectures.

Instructors are also able to implement elements that would be difficult to incorporate into traditional lectures, such as animations, simulations, interviews with distinguished individuals in the field, etc.

Data and analytics

In blended learning environments, educators are able to collect such data on student performance, giving opportunities to target their lessons and address gaps in student comprehension while refining their teaching strategies for subsequent offerings of the course. This is particularly useful for those employing

Student-driven lectures

Despite the great variance of student learning styles and ability that exist in classrooms, traditional lectures are often one-size fits all. Video lectures, on the other hand, put students in the driver's seat, and allow them to engage with the material at their own pace, review confusing concepts, or break the lectures into easily-digestible chunks. More generally, flipped classrooms allow instructors to more easily implement a variety of differentiated instruction techniques.

Mastery learning

In mastery learning, students are encouraged to master each concept before proceeding to the next.

Some other Benefits

1. More time for interaction between teachers and students.
2. Students can review content at their own pace and as frequently as they need.
3. Active classroom leads to more engaged students.
4. More flexibility to accommodate learning differences.

Basic Components of a Flipped Classroom

1. A blending learning of direct instruction (where the teacher supplies the knowledge base) with constructivist learning (where the students are ultimately responsible to construct their own knowledge). An increased interaction between students and teacher.
2. An increased interaction between students and teachers.
3. An environment where students take responsibility for their own learning.
4. A classroom where the teacher is not the center of attention, but instead, serves as a guide or facilitator of learning.
5. A blending of direct instruction (where the teacher supplies the knowledge base) with constructivist learning (where the students are ultimately responsible to construct their own knowledge).
6. A classroom where students who are absent due to illness or extra-curricular activities such as athletics or field-trips, don't get left behind.
7. A class where the curriculum and lessons are always available for review or remediation.
8. A class where all students are engaged in their learning.
9. A place where all students can get a personalized education.

Advantages of Flipped Classroom

1. Active vs. Passive Learning

Moving lectures out of the classroom, students are able to become active participants in the learning process through learning activities delivered during the class period.

2. Self-paced Instruction

Lectures are available on online 24/7, students are able to learn at the pace that best suits them. They can stop and rewind explanations of concepts they find difficult and refer back to past lectures to review older content.

3. Multiple learning styles

Different students learn in different ways, so by delivering instruction in multiple forms, the likelihood for engagement and retention are improved.

4. Varied instruction

It offering instruction in multiple forms, students are likely to remain motivated throughout the learning process.

5. Social interaction

It added class time for collaborated activities, social interaction promoted amongst the students and student and teacher.

6. 21st century preparation

Using technology for educational purposes at an early age develops technical skill and provides student with the working knowledge at 21st century tools and resources.

Disadvantages of Flipped Classroom

7. Non-Universal accessibility

All students are capable of accessing online instructions cannot possible at home this can set them back in the learning process and limit their progress.

8. Additional time and effort

It creating online lessons and coming up with encaging learning activity for on entire requires a significant amount of additional time and effort that some or not willing are able to commit.

References

1. Bergmen, J. and Smith, A. (2012) Flip Your Classroom: Reach Every Student in Every Classroom, Every Day. International Society for Technology Education.
2. Green, G. (2012). My View: Flipped classrooms give every student a chance to succeed Retrieved from.
3. Michaelsen, L.K., Knight, A.B., & Fink, L.D. (2004). *Team-Based Learning: A transformative use of small groups in college teaching.* Sterling, VA: Sylus Publishing.

15

Cloud Computing in Education and Student's Needs

Introduction

Cloud computing is not just a buzz-word, it represents a strong direction of IT industry development. Speaking of cloud computing we should distinguish three different service models: Infrastructure as a Service (IaaS), Platform as a Service (PaaS) and Software as a Service (SaaS). The scope of this work is a model of Software as a Service. This represents the lease of computing resources on a network of remote servers where applications are executed and data is stored. The application of cloud computing is very broad and growing daily because of many advantages to the users, and is driven by the increasing use of various mobile devices (laptops, tablets and smart phones) and mobile Internet access being more available. Cloud computing is applicable in education, but it implies the acceptance of these services by all involved in the educational process. Therefore, the aim of this paper is to investigate whether there is a need between our students for applications and services in the "cloud" (SaaS), the extent to which they use them and what types of applications and services are leading. The paper analyzes and interprets the results of this study which provides indications of students' willingness to "move to the cloud".

In the last couple of years "cloud computing" has increasingly been discussed. This is a relatively new trend of IT industry development, focused on users, and driven by the increasing use of various mobile devices such as laptops, tablet PCs and smart phones. Research has shown that it is one of the fastest growing sectors of the digital economy. European governments and industry plan to invest 45 billion Euros in the development of cloud computing by the year 2020 . In cloud computing networks of remote servers, storage systems (data centers and server farms) and their resources are being used upon user request. Term "cloud" is used as a metaphor for the Internet since it doesn't matter where the hardware and software resources that are used are located. For IT professionals cloud computing is a new business model and a new technology platform for developing and deploying applications, and for end-users a new and cheaper way to use applications. Cloud computing has many advantages but also some limitations, both arising from the fact that all data and applications are located somewhere on the Internet. It can be used in various activities of everyday life, including in education. In addition to providing students and teachers (usually free of charge) access to many applications and services in the cloud, which can be used in formal and informal education, cloud computing allows for greater flexibility and mobility in the use of resources for teaching and learning, greater degree of collaboration, communication and sharing of resources, and creates a personalized learning environment or virtual communities of learning and teaching.

Theoretical Framework

The cloud computing as a model for enabling ubiquitous, convenient, on-demand network access to a shared pool of configurable computing resources (e.g., networks, servers, storage, applications, and services) that can be rapidly provisioned and released with minimal management effort or service provider interaction". Gartner defines cloud computing as a „style of computing in which scalable and elastic IT-enabled capabilities are delivered as a service using Internet technologies". For everyday users of the Internet and computers, cloud computing is any online activity, such as accessing data or using a software program, which can be done form different devices regardless of the on-ramp to the Internet, as in Figure 1. In this vision, the data or software applications are not stored on the user's computer, but rather are accessed through the web from any device at any location a person can get web access.". For end-users, cloud computing means that you don't have to worry about maintaining hardware or purchase new equipment, obtaining software licenses, updating or upgrading existing software, data synchronization, etc. because all of these are included in the "cloud" service. One can say that cloud computing is the new driver of IT revolution, in which new IT services are being developed, changing the ways of access, usage, maintenance and financing services on demand. Cloud computing is characterized by scalability (extent and amount of used resources according to the needs of the application and paid on the actual use of resources), mobility and platform independency (the ability to access anytime, from any location and device). There are three types of cloud computing: Infrastructure as a Service (IaaS) is the hardware component with different forms of virtual technology rentals, platform as a service (PaaS) involves the use of the operating system and development tools in the cloud and software as a service (SaaS) which refers to the use various web-based applications that run and execute on the server; These models differ in the type and extent of resources accessed and managed by users. Connecting to the cloud and using "hidden" resources enables sharing of information always and everywhere, great application scalability, service availability anytime and anywhere, data security, storage, backup copies, and more. „The potential benefits of adopting cloud computing can be accessed from both the financial savings and resource management perspectives".

Cloud Computing in Education

According to „the potential of cloud computing for improving efficiency, cost and convenience for the educational sector is being recognized by a number of educational establishments. For some universities, the availability of an awesome computing power through cloud computing for research purposes was welcome". Many educational institutions have begun their movement to cloud computing by outsourcing their student email provision. Educational institutions are also beginning to use lower level cloud services for purposes such as data storage. This may be attractive where data security is of lower concern such as where video and audio is provided as open educational resources. Another use of cloud computing which is beginning to emerge in education is for the hosting of institutional learning management systems (LMSs) in the cloud. Outsourcing the provision of LMSs such as Blackboard or Moodle to a third party makes sense for institutions who cannot justify the costs of purchasing, maintaining and supporting the hardware and software themselves". Cloud computing is often associated with e-learning and m-learning . This refers to e-learning environment mainly distributed on the cloud, in which Open Educational Resources were produced, researched and shared by participants worldwide.

With applications in the cloud (SaaS), students and teachers can flexibly access their data via a web browser from a computer at home, school, library, student room or some other place, and achieve rapid and efficient communication, collaboration, exchange or share documents, contacts, notes, audio / video and other data. With their use students can create "Cloud-Based Personalized Learning Environment" (Figure 2) . "The first idea that comes to mind when assessing such a cloud space for learning, would be the creative potentials that could be nurtured i.e. the endless ideas, thoughts and knowledge that could be shared, created and inspired". In addition to individual applications in the cloud, bundled applications are also available (eg. Google Apps for Education or Microsoft Live@edu with Office 365 and other applications for Education) that combine tools for communication and collaboration, office tools for working with documents, and space to store and synchronize data on demand. Whereas a university computing service department may aim to achieve 99.5% availability for its educational services such as the LMS, Google offers 99.9% availability for its educational application suite and appears to outperform this target.

Using services and applications in the cloud, students and teachers can achieve mobility because their educational resources and necessary applications are available via portable computers and Internet-connected devices. For example, classes can be implemented outside the school / faculty or students can perform duties at various places.

Problem and Hypotheses

The broader problem domain of this paper is to investigate the preconditions for the implementation of cloud services and applications in higher education. This implies the acceptance and active use of such services by students and teachers. The study is focused on the use of cloud services (SaaS) for students. The reason for selecting students as a target population of research lies in the fact that students are increasingly dependent on online services for learning and assessment.

The aim of this study is to determine if students show a need for cloud services and applications (SaaS) and how often they use them. It also aims to investigate the relationship between the reported need for cloud services and their active use, since it may not always be correlated. According to goals, the following null hypotheses are posted:

1. There is no significant difference in reported need for cloud services between male and female students.
2. There is no significant difference in reported use of cloud services between male and female students.
3. There is no positive correlation between reported need for cloud services and frequency of use them.
4. There is no positive correlation between number of devices from which students access the Internet and frequency of cloud services use.

Methodology

Research began in January 2014 and lasted until mid-April 2014. The subjects of this study were students from the Some colleges. For the purpose of this research a questionnaire (consisting of three sections) was created in GoogleDocs - Forms and distributed online.

The first section collected general data about the respondent (gender, faculty, year of study) and data on the use of computers (number of computers and similar devices, frequency of accessing Internet). This was followed by eight statements in which participants estimated the frequency of situations indicating the need for cloud applications and services, based on a 4-point scale. The third section of the questionnaire contained 10 questions about the frequency of use of cloud applications and services. Here we listed cloud applications and in parentheses names of the most popular ones from categories, for respondents to be clear on what the question was about. In statements and questions in the second and third section of the questionnaire, the responses were given on a 4-point frequency scale (1 = none, 2 = rarely, 3 = sometimes, 4 = often / very often). The questionnaire was distributed through the website of the Student. The survey was anonymous, and the questionnaire was completed by 100 students. Empirical data were analyzed using descriptive statistics, and hypothesis testing was done using nonparametric tests: Mann-Whitney U test and Spearman correlation.

Results

The questionnaire was completed by 100 respondents; 58% males and 42% females. The proportion of students was 78% from the Informatics study program and 22% from other study programs; all from the college students. A vast amount of the students (90%) attended professional studies (first 3 years), and only a small proportion of students (10%) were from specialized studies (4th and 5th year).

On the question “Which devices do you use for accessing Internet and data?” respondents could select multiple answers, and distribution is shown on Figure 3. The respondents mostly use laptop computers (74%) and smart phones (67%) indicating their mobility. A lower number of users selected desktop computers at home (64%) and faculty (54%), and the smallest number used tablet computers (13 %), and ultra-portable computers (5%). Respondents reported the frequency of Internet access, and responses were grouped into three categories: weekends or a few times a week (5%), several times a day (18%), all of the time or whenever I get an opportunity (77%). Another survey by, on a population of 15-30 years, indicates that

80% of respondents use online services daily, and nearly 50% use the Internet via mobile phone.

Items with statements about frequency of situations that indicate a need for services in the cloud are grouped by category of service to which the statement relates. Respondents expressed the frequency on a 4-point scale, and the distribution of responses is shown in Table 1. These data show that the respondents expressed the greatest need for communication software to the cloud, then cloud multimedia sharing, cloud docs / office software, and the smallest need for cloud storage and file synchronization software. However, mean scores indicate that all of the needs for services in the cloud fall into the category "sometimes", with similar standard deviation.

Through the 10 questions in the final section of the questionnaire respondents expressed the frequency of the active use of various cloud services (SaaS). Question items are grouped and response distribution is shown in Table 2. Arithmetic mean of responses indicate that respondents use cloud communication software often and very often, they sometimes use cloud services for multimedia sharing and learning, and are little less likely to use cloud storage and file synchronization software and cloud docs / office software. The largest scattering in answers was regarding to using cloud services for multimedia sharing and learning.

Research analyzing cloud computing activities of online Americans also reported frequency of cloud communication services being most used, and least use of cloud storage and file synchronization software, while the cloud docs / office software use was in the middle.

Conclusion

Cloud computing represents a new model of providing IT services which includes rental of resources located somewhere in the "cloud" and is considered to be the direction of future development of the IT sector. Ordinary people are increasingly online and more work is done online, from checking e-mails and using other forms of communication, writing and editing documents and collaboration, through watching movies and videos or listening to music, up to the fact that personal documents and images are being stored on web. There is no need for installation, licensing and updating of program, and there are no maintenance costs because all programs and services are available through a web browser. Cloud computing (SaaS) is based on "on-demand self-services" with "pay as use" model, although for ordinary users and for applications in education such software is usually free of charge. Cloud computing usability in education is very broad, as recognized by many educational institutions around the world. The reasons for the worldwide introduction of cloud computing for educational establishment are mainly of a financial nature, but it should be noted that „cloud" has creative potentials because it enables that ideas, thoughts and knowledge can be created, used and shared easily. Students may create their own "Cloud-Based Personalized Learning Environment" or use m-learning and access to Open Educational Resources from the cloud. However, to achieve this, students and teachers should be willing to use services in cloud and be familiar with their advantages and limitations. The study shows that the respondents (students) are often online and at the same time using multiple computers and similar devices (tablet computers, smart phones). When using computers they are (on average) sometimes in situations that require the use of applications and services in the cloud. The largest use is noted with cloud communication software, the smallest with cloud docs / office software. Gender difference in reported need for services in the cloud, or in the frequency of use of applications in cloud is not confirmed. However, a significant correlation between the reported need for cloud applications / services and the frequency of their use is found. There is also a correlation between the number of computers and mobile devices used for Internet access and frequency of use of cloud applications / services. The students have expressed, based on the average of their answers that they "sometimes" need and use cloud applications / services, which means that they are not yet ready for a "move to the cloud". It is necessary to educate and motivate them about cloud applications and services to make them become aware of the benefits.

References

1. Gartner, IT Glossary, http://www.gartner.com/it-glossary/cloud-computing (15. 01. 2013)

2. [Cloud Computing in Education, IITE Policy Brief, UNESCO, 2010, http://iite.unesco.org/pics/publications/en/files/3214674.pdf (29. 01. 2013)

3. Horrigan, J.B., Use of Cloud Computing Applications and Services, 2008, http://www.pewinternet.org/Reports/2008/Use-of-Cloud-Computing-Applications-and-Services.aspx (26. 01. 2013)

4. Kop, R., Carroll, F., Cloud Computing and Creativity: Learning on a Massive Open Online Course, European Journal of Open, Distance and E-Learning, 2011, http://www.eurodl.org/index.php?article=457 (21. 01. 2013).

16

ICT Enabling Learning Without Limit of the Differently Abled Visually Impaired

Introduction

Eyes are the gateway to knowledge and sense of sight plays a vital role in receiving information from the outside world. The differently abled visually impaired due to lack of sight are deprived of the knowledge from the surroundings. Information and Communication Technology (ICT) paves way for the differently abled visually impaired learners to break the barriers of learning and to acquire learning beyond limits. The assistive technology for the differently abled visually impaired such as screen readers, screen magnification software and speech recognition software enable them to enter into e-learning, mobile learning and virtual learning. With the help of assistive technology the differently abled visually impaired access the web world and are enriched with learning without limits.

Senses are the gateway to knowledge and sense of sight plays a vital role in receiving knowledge from the outside world. Due to absence of sight the differently abled visually impaired are deprived of receiving information from the surrounding world. The deprivation of sight leads to manifold problems for the differently abled visually impaired such as lack of imagery of the surrounding, mobility, daily living skills, learning through the sense of sight and communication skills. These problems are rectified to a great extent through the application of ICT. The ICT stands for Information and Communication Technologies and is defined as a "Diverse set of Technological tools and resources used to communicate, and to create, disseminate, store and manage information". (Blurton, C.1999) This paper deals with Information and Communication Technology for the differently abled visually impaired, the assistive technologies available for them and ICT enabling learning without limit of the differently abled visually impaired.

Differently abled Visually Impaired

Visual impairment (or vision impairment) is vision loss (of a person) to such a degree as to qualify as an additional support need through a significant limitation of visual capability resulting from either disease, trauma, or congenital or degenerative conditions that cannot be corrected by conventional means, such as refractive correction or medication. (Arditi, A., & Rosenthal, B. 1998)

According to Persons with Disabilities (Equal Opportunities, Protection of Rights and Full Participation) Act 1995, Blindness refers to a condition where a person suffers from any of the following conditions, namely:

1. Total absence of sight; or
2. Visual acuity not exceeding 6/60 or 20/200 (Snellen) in the better eye even with correction lenses; or
3. Limitation of the field of vision subtending an angle of 20 degree or worse.

The Persons with Disabilities Act, 1995 also recognizes low vision as a category of disability and defines it as follows: "Person with low vision" means a person with impairment of visual functioning even after treatment or standard refractive correction but who uses or is potentially capable of using vision for the planning or execution of a task with appropriate assistive device".

Information and Communication Technology

ICT denotes information and communication technologies and it includes computers, broadcasting technologies (radio and television), telephony, the wireless networks, the cellular phones, the internet and the other communication systems. According to Margaret Rouse, ICT (information and communications technology - or technologies) is an umbrella term that includes any communication device or application, encompassing: radio, television, cellular phones, computer and network, hardware and software, satellite systems and so on, as well as the various services and applications associated with them, such as videoconferencing and distance learning. ICTs are often spoken of in a particular context, such as ICTs in education, health care, or libraries (Margaret Rouse 2005).

ICT is a wide range of collection of data, applications, communication systems and technologies using software. Information and Communication Technology (ICT) is referred to as all electronic technologies for collecting, storing, processing and transmitting information. (Aluko, 2004) Its application includes teleconferencing, distance learning, video conferencing, e-learning, mobile learning and virtual learning.

ICT for the Differently abled Visually Impaired

Milken Exchange on Education Technology (1999) defines ICT as computer-based tools used by people to work with the information and communication processing needs of an organization. It encompasses the computer hardware and software, the network and several other devices (video, audio, photography camera, etc) that convert information (text), images, sound, motion and so on into common digital form. Information and Communication Technology for the differently abled visually impaired includes a wide range of services, assistive technologies, special applications and modified technologies created to respond to the needs of the differently abled visually impaired. There are tools that enable easier access to technology such as computers or cell phones, making using these devices simpler; newer technology or devices designed to cater to their specific needs; and applications accessed through smart devices such as cell phones and tablets. (Vikram Singh, 2013)

Specialized assistive technologies are created to fulfill the needs of the differently abled visually impaired learners. These assistive technologies enable the differently abled visually impaired learners to explore knowledge and receive information beyond the boundaries. With the help of assistive technologies the differently abled visually impaired have access to web world, retrieve information and learn from the multiple sources of knowledge.

Assistive Technology for the Differently abled Visually Impaired

Individuals with Disabilities Education Act (IDEA), Section §300.5 on Assistive technology device spells, Assistive technology device means any item, piece of equipment, or product system, whether acquired commercially off the shelf, modified, or customized, that is used to increase, maintain, or improve the functional capabilities of a child with a disability. Assistive technology enables the visually impaired learners to learn more independently and to be on par with their sighted peer group. These technologies pave way for the differently abled visually impaired learners to cross the barriers of learning due to lack of sight or absence of sight. There are manifold varieties of assistive technologies for the differently abled visually impaired learners.

Screen reader is a software application that enables the differently abled visually impaired learners to read the information on the computer screen, such as web page, menus, icons and dialogue boxes. JAWS (Job Access with Speech) is a software which enables the differently abled visually impaired learners to read a computer screen with the help of a text-to-speech output or a refreshable Braille display. Sparsha is a toolset for the differently abled visually impaired which can translate the text on screen to Bharati Braille – a unified Braille script used to write English languages using cells containing six braille dots. Apart from English, the languages supported by Sparsha include Hindi, Bengali, Assamese, Marathi, Gujarati, Oriya, Telugu and Kannada. It has the facility to save the document, as well, so that it can be later printed using a Braille printer. (Vikram Singh, 2013)

Screen magnification software paves way for the low vision learners to access information on the computer screen by enlarging it to a readable form for them. Portable note-takers provide speech output and help the differently abled visually impaired learners to read the text with ease. These note-takers have no visual display and these can be connected to printers and computers for printing and uploading text.

Speech recognition software helps the differently abled visually impaired learners to access computer and to enter data using voice instead of using a mouse or a keyboard. The other assistive technology for the differently abled visually impaired is the Text-to-speech software which converts the written text such as, text files, web pages, and emails into audio files. These converted audio files can be played on computers, MP3 players, iPods and CD players.

ICT Enabling Learning without Limit of the Differently abled Visually Impaired

Information and communication technology open the doors of learning to the differently abled visually impaired to explore possibilities of learning from the world at large and to lead an equal and integrated life as individuals. ICT paves way for the differently abled visually impaired to convert the printed materials into digital materials hence enable them to learn the same materials which their sighted peer group uses and to have an exposure to the vast field of knowledge.

The various types of assistive technology available provide possibilities for the differently abled visually impaired learners to explore the world of knowledge from the web world and to enhance their learning. Due to lack of sight the differently abled visually impaired learners find difficulty in mobility and orientation skills, which too prevent them from having access to higher learning. The assistive technologies enable them to cross the barriers and to learn through e-learning, mobile learning and virtual learning.

The information and communication technology for the differently baled visually impaired learners paves way for them to communicate with their peers, thereby promoting collaborative and social learning environment. Assistive technology provides opportunities for them to enter into open and distance learning and to get connected to their teacher through electronic media hence have a two-way communication which allows the teachers and the differently abled visually impaired learners to interact. Through distance learning they are able to rise above time and space and to break the barriers of orientation and mobility problems.

Conclusion

Information and Communication Technology widens the horizon of the differently abled visually impaired and create possibilities for them to deepen their knowledge, to enhance their learning skills and to be confident to explore possibilities of learning beyond limits. With the help of multiple types of assistive technology available the differently abled visually impaired learners are able to learn on par with their sighted peer group and to excel in the educational arena.

References

1. Arditi, A., & Rosenthal, B. (1998). “Developing an objective definition of visual impairment.” In Vision ’96: Proceedings of the International Low Vision Conference (pp. 331-334). Madrid, Spain: ONCE.
2. Ntukidem, E. P. & Ashi, M. M (2009). Assistive technology: Gateway to independence of persons with visual impairment. *The Exceptional Child,* 11(2), 345-353.
3. Sansanwal, D.N.: Information Technology and Higher Education. UNIVERSITY NEWS, Vol. 38, No. 46, 2000.
4. Smith and Cambell (1982) quoted in Pillai, S. Swaminathan: Are Women Sustainable in InfoTech Industry? In Papa, Regina and Shanmugasundaram, Y. (Eds.). Women & Emerging Technologies, British Council Division, British Deputy High Commission, Chennai, 1996.
5. Milken Exchange on Education Technology (1999). *Will new teachers be prepared to teach in a digital age*? Santa Monica: Milken Family Foundation. Retrieved from file http://www.mf.org/puts/ME154.pdf.

6. Vikram Singh 2013, ICT for the Differently-Abled, *Learn, Out of the Box: ICT for the Differently-Abled.* Retrieved from *www.learn-outofthebox.org/2013/11/ict-for-differently-abled.html*

7. WBT Information Centre (1997). http://www.wbtic.com/primer-whatiswbt.aspx

17

Role of Emotional Management in Cognitive Perspectives

Introduction

Ultimate aim of education is to prepare students to live independence lives this objective is accomplished by helping students to acquire knowledge and skills to independently therefore today it is recognized the aspect of cognition, that are the focus of school learning, attention, memory, decision making, motivation and social functions are not only affected by emotion but intertwined within emotion process. In application of knowledge facts and logical reasoning skills learnt at school to real world situations requires emotion process. The new directions in thinking about emotions have contributed to a greater understanding of student and teacher experience of emotion and in a particular situation, an enhanced knowledge of how emotion can be managed. Emotion management is associated with favorable education outcomes however specific emotion management research still needs to occur in order to understand adaptive regulation and how it may be enhanced in the classroom. This paper concentrate to emotion management skills in addition to the role of emotional intensity and self efficacy in emotion regulation inertia for an anxiety had difficulty to manage the emotion.

Emotional management

Emotion management refers to the ways in which people influence their own feelings and expressions and the ways in which they influence other people's feelings like the strength of the anger, sadness, anxiety or discouragement control their emotion. Strong emotions are both a causes and a result of conflict. Pupil in conflict may have a variety of strong and often negative emotions-anger, distrust, disappointment, frustration, confusion, worry, or fear.

Ways to improve the emotional management

- External and internal resources.

  External and internal resources with increasing age in student's management of emotion shifts gradually from external sources in the world (for example, parents) to self-initiated, internal resources. Caregivers' help to young children, manage young children's emotion by choosing the contexts in which they behave, and provide children with information (facial cuts, narratives, and so on) to help them interpret events. With age and advances in cognitive development, students are better equipped to manage their emotion themselves. For example, adulthood student might minimize the escalation of negative emotion in an interpersonal conflict by monitoring their facial expressions (for example, avoiding uncomplimentary or looks of contempt).

- Cognitive strategies

  Cognitive strategies for regulating emotions, such as thinking about situations in a positive aspect, cognitive avoidance and the ability to shift the focus of one's attention and increase with an age.

- Self-regulation of arousal.

  Self-regulation of arousal with a greater maturity of student develops greater capacity to modulate their emotional arousal (such as controlling angry outbursts).

- Situations and relationships.

  Situations and relationships with an age individuals become more adept at selecting and managing situations and relationships in ways that minimize negative emotion.

- Coping with stress.

  Students become more capable of selecting effective ways to coping with stress depending upon their age.

Meaning of cognitive models

Cognitive science is concerned with understanding the process that the brain especially the human brain, uses to accomplish complex tasks including perceiving, learning, remembering, thinking, predicting, inference, problem solving, decision making, planning and moving around the environment the goal of cognitive model is to scientifically explain one or more of these basic cognitive process or explain how these process interact.

Advantage of cognitive model

Models over conceptual frameworks are using mathematical or computer languages, cognitive models are guaranteed to produce logically valid predictions. This is not true of conclusions based on intuitively based verbal reasoning.

A second important reason for using mathematical or computer models is that they are capable of making precise quantitative predictions.

There are many practical uses for cognitive models in a wide variety of areas. Clinical psychologists use cognitive models to assess individual differences in cognitive processing between normal individuals and clinical patients (e.g., schizophrenics). Cognitive neuroscientists use cognitive models to understand the psychological function of different brain regions. Aging researchers use cognitive models to understand the aging process and the deterioration or slow down of cognitive functioning with age. Human factors researchers use cognitive models to improve human - machine or human - computer interactions.

Decision researchers use cognitive models of decision making to predict preferences for consumer products, investment portfolios for businesses, medical choices, and military strategies. Artificial intelligence and robotic researchers use cognitive models for automated detection of dangerous targets, automated recognition of handwriting, automated recognition of faces or approach and avoidance movement behavior of robots. Researchers in social science such as economics and sociology use cognitive models to construct computerized agents in agent based models of market behavior or social network working..

Cognitive modeling in emotional management

A emotional experience is perceived relative to individuals previous affective residue ,which is akin to a specific situational emotional schema (Baumeister,et.al .2007)baumeister and colleagues introduced the emotion of an affective residue ,borrowing heavily from russel's(2003)the crux of baumeister and stimulates analysis learning and adaptation, often occurring in the aftermath of behaviour and its outcomes., automatic affective response can preserve the lessons and information from previous emotional experience, the combination previous emotional outcomes and current affect also contributes to making people start anticipating emotional outcomes and to choose their actions according to the emotions they expect will ensure "people create their affective residues from their conscious emotional states, which are used to guide subsequent similar occurrences. The affective residue acts as feedback mechanism allowing the perceived optimal outcomes with the least amount cognitive effort .Hence the name affective residue the remaining results from previous emotions are cognitively analyzed causing lessions to be extracted , framing heuristics for future behaviour ,which shapes their affective residue as well;

The affective residue is a less abstract view of russel's(2003) "attributed affect and affect regulation" both of which are intertwined with his "core affect" core affect is the consciously accessible neuro psychological state is object free and it's an integrated blend of hedonic (pleasure –pain)and arousal (sleepy-activated)values (resulls

2003) think of hedonic and arousal as the primary colors, except for emotional and they and that they are polar continues.

Nabi (2003) examines framing issues within the theoretical content of functional emotions result from evaluate appraisals made relative to personal well being which create subjective states of valenced "action readiness" these states provide feedback with cognitions, physiological changes and preceptors to create action tendencies and ultimately behaviors.

Intensity of emotion is important to functional theories, because intensity is related to motivation and affective positive as three "central intensity variables within each of the emotional classes;" a person's appraisal of an emotion including situation is based on three central variables; desirability, praiseworthiness which apply to event based emotions, agent based emotions and object based emotions, respectively.

Related to appraisal theory ,teacher belief contribute to the judgment teachers make about the behaviours in the classroom (friedman,1995).among the teacher belief theories ,teachers' sense of efficacy is found to be central to enthusiasm, persistence and resilience across the span of a teaching career(coladarci,1992;day 2005).teachers 'sense of efficacy is grounded in social cognitive theory(bandura,1983)and refers to the teachers 'belief in his or her capability to organize and execute courses of action required to successfully accomplishing a specific teaching task in a particular context (tschannen-moran, wool folk hoy,1998).several studies have found higher levels of burnout are related to lower perceptions of teacher efficacy (brouwers&tomic,1998; friedman&farber,1992).yet few studies have investigated how teachers' sense of efficacy shapes the way teachers view students' misbehavior and the accompanying emotions.

While appraisals are central to teachers 'emotional experiences in the classroom, emotion regulation and coping are considered as integral features in emotional process dynamics as well (lazarus, 2002; gross, 2002).emotion regulation refers to the process by which we influence which emotions we have, when we have ,when them and how we experience and express the (gross, 2002). it also defined theoretical conceptulation of psychological behaviour and cognitive process that enable individuals to modulate the experience and expression of positive and negative emotions (gross john, 2003).coping refers to individuals effort s to master demands (condition of harm, threat or challenge) that are apprised or perceived as exceeding or taxing his or her resources (monat&lazarus,1991). coping in the literature has been found to be effective in lowering stress levels.

Although appraisals, regulation and coping in emotional process have been studied in the past decades in psychology and health fields, there are only few studies about this issue in educational fields (sutton, 2002) Investigating teachers' appraisal about students behaviour can assist in the cognitive antecedents of teacher emotions in the classroom. The present study examined the patterns in teachers appraisals about student misbehaviors and how the appraisals contribute to their experience of emotion as well as general feeling of burnout.

Conclusion

Emotion has significant role in the managing class room for the teacher's beaviour. Teacher must have managed their emotion influence in the emotional climate on the school as well as principals and parents with who interact.

18

Multimedia Blended Learning: An Innovative Strategy in the Digital Age

Introduction

Blended learning is the integration of ICT with the classroom teaching – learning process. Multimedia blended learning combines online delivery of educational content with the best features of classroom interaction and live instruction to personalize learning and allow thoughtful reflection from student to student across a diverse group of learners. Multimedia blended instruction is slowly gaining ground as a way for students to represent the knowledge that they acquire in class with digital multiple representations foster interpretation of the information, collaborative and co-operative learning and thus preparing them with a skill set for real life work situations. The integration of multimedia in the classroom instruction instills effective lifelong learning attitude and acquisition of problem – solving skills.

Nelson Mandela quotes *"Education is the most powerful weapon which you can use to change the world.* Education is essential to build a workforce capable of underpinning a modern competitive economy. Education determines the standard of the society. In the digital era, Information Communication Technology has the power to change many aspects of everyday lives and its importance increasing day by day. With the advancement of modern technology in the world, it is more urgent to use innovative pedagogy and also to develop efficiency in the way the student learns. There is a need to renovate our teaching strategies to make the classroom teaching effective. Blended learning education program 'combining internet and digital multimedia was established the classroom forums that require the physical co-presence of teacher and students. The ultimate aim of multimedia blended learning is to provide realistic practical opportunities for learners and teachers to make learning independent, useful sustainable and every growing. This paper highlights how a relevant use of multimedia blended learning may help improve teaching, especially to better bridge the gaps between theory and practice, simulation and reality and to deal with the multiple learning perspectives of the learners.

Blended Learning in Education

Blended learning refers to a mixing of different learning environments. A blended learning approach can combine face – to face instruction with computer mediated instruction. Blended learning provides a 'good' mix of technologies and interactions, resulting in a socially supported, constructive, learning experience. Blended learning is *"a way of meeting the challenges of tailoring learning and development to the needs of individual by integrating the innovative and technological advances offered by online learning with the interaction and participation offered in the best of traditional learning"* (Thorne. 2003) Good classroom teachers have always blended their methods – reading, writing, lecture, discussion, practice and projects are all part of an effective blend. The guiding design principle of blended learning is the usage of right tool, in the right situation, for the right purpose (Dutta, 2012). As blended learning gives varieties of experience, there is no doubt that it will lead impact on knowledge management?

Strategies of Blended Learning

Flip Teaching

Flip Teaching is a form of blended learning in which students watch lectures online and work on problem set with other students in class. It allows teachers and trainers to flip through concepts, which in turn gives them more time to interact with students instead of lecturing. This is also known as reverse instruction or teaching. In flip classrooms, learners engage in activities, applying concepts and focusing on higher level learning outcomes. Thus flip teaching focuses a productive experience for the learner.

Enriched Virtual Teaching

Simulation based e-learning provides a great potential to develop practical skills in a virtual environment. It also provides the opportunity for students to engage experiment and reflect with practical skills required at a given workplace through simulated real world scenarios.

Collaborative learning

Collaborative learning directly addresses some of the generic skills such as problem solving, critical thinking and communication while encouraging team work in collaborative learning, students benefit from an active exchange of knowledge and ideas as well as having the possibility to monitor one another's work. In the modern era, collaborative learning is more digital – oriented and allows collaboration to take place without any face to face contact. Collaborative learning provides opportunities to work with people from different cultures and enhance teaming, communicative skills and global awareness.

Multimedia blended learning as obvious strategy

Dr. A.P.J. Abdul Kalam quotes, *"A good teacher prepare himself for teaching with meticulous planning and prepares the students for acquisition of knowledge."* The present fast progress of technology, education takes the shape in accordance with the concept of multimedia. Multimedia is developed with the terms of hyper text and hypermedia. Multimedia is defined as the combining of different media types such as sound, animation text, graphics and videos for the presentation of information by making use of computers (Bornman & Solms, 1993). Multimedia application design offers new insights into the learning process of the designer and forces him or her to represent information and knowledge in an innovative way (Neo and Neo 2000).

In Multimedia blended learning, the teacher is the director of the knowledge and can use the various combinations of digital media elements to create interactive educational content. It is the mixing of synchronous and asynchronous instruction. In this mixed mode, the teacher has the flexibility to incorporate the teacher centered and student-centered teaching-learning approaches through presentation, demonstration and multimedia course ware. Teacher could also add relevant curriculum content that would be unavailable or difficult to comprehend outside the digital media. This multimedia blended instruction fosters team – processing and active learning as with collaborative and cooperative methods. The student is then free to engage in learning on his or her own time and pace and encourages higher level learning, increases comprehension and retention rates, and focuses on the total development of the student in self – accessed and self – directed learning.

Impact of Multimedia Blended Learning

Moreno quotes *"A picture is worth a thousand words"*. Multimedia blended strategy is the effective instructional medium for delivering information. A multisensory experience can be created for the learners, which in turn, elicits positive attitude towards learning. Multimedia blended learning focuses to move from content towards problems to provide a more realistic approach to learning and to create an educational methodology which emphasizes real world challenges, higher order thinking skills, multi – disciplinary learning, independent learning, team work and communication skills.

In multimedia blended instruction, students can utilize the knowledge presented to them by the teacher and represent them in a more meaningful way, using different media elements enhance the use of multiple sensory modalities which would motivate learners to pay more attention to the information presented and better retain the information. Multimedia blended instruction help students to achieve high self – esteem, to increase their ability to function as self – directed learners, to learn to think effectively, and to practice problem – solving, decision making and lifelong learning attitudes into the student. In this mixed instruction, the students had to utilize their prior knowledge in other disciplines to break down the problem into component parts, and then synthesize and re-constructs a possible solution. This experience is invaluable in creating a new generation of effective problem – solvers for the current industry needs.

Conclusion

The changing role of education is currently being reinforced with the integration of multimedia blended technologies. This has led to a new paradigm in education and the evolution of new concepts in content development and a number of innovative methods in which information can be communicated to the learners. This new learning environment will undoubtedly influence the way teachers teach and students learn.

Reference

1. Anandan, K., & Raja, B.W.D. (2010). *Educational technology, New Delhi*: APH publishing corporation.
2. Bornman, H. & Solms, S.H. (1993). *Hypermedia, Multimedia and Hypertext definitions and overview.* Electronic library , 11(4/5), 259-268
3. Dutta, I & Dutta, N. (2012). *Blended learning a pedagogical approach to teach in smart classrooms.* Edutracks, 11(10), 6-10.
4. Neo, M & Neo, T.K. (2000). *"Multimedia learning using multimedia as a plat form for instruction and learning in higher education"*. Proceedings of M2USIC 2000, PJ Hilton, October 5-6, 2000, PP S3 – 1.1 – 1.4

19

Designing Principles for Future Learning Environment

Introduction

Learning Environment refers to the whole range of components and activities within which learning happens. Learning occurs best when situated in authentic contexts, environments and problems. The goal for all teachers is to provide effective instruction that leads to student learning. However, that goal is greatly dependent upon having a safe and supportive environment in which teachers can teach and students can learn. Without such an environment instructional and learning time is lost. An effective classroom environment for teaching and learning can be created by the teacher for maximizing the dedicated time for instruction and learning. Key variables include effective curriculum planning, systemic assessment, effective strategies for delivering instruction and classroom procedures for preventing and responding to student problem behavior (Colvin & Lazar, 1997). Once these components are in place instructional time can increase and learning time maximized with minimal problem behavior.

Learning environment refers to the diverse physical locations, contexts and cultures in which students learn. Since students may learn in a wide variety of settings, such as outside-of school locations and outdoor environments, the term is often used as a more accurate or preferred alternative to *classroom,* which has more limited and traditional connotations—a room with rows of desks and a chalkboard. Qualities and characteristics of a learning environment are determined by a wide variety of factors, school policies, governance structures.

Learning Environment

Learners in supportive environments have high levels of self-efficacy and self-motivation and use learning as a primary transformative force. Welcoming the learner –child, youth or adult– in an environment where they can feel safe and nurtured for is very important for the development of each individual and the society as a whole. Addressing the issue of learning environment in a comprehensive and systematic way is even more critical in countries with limited financial resources.

Learning takes place in multiple settings and the learning environment can be structured or unstructured and the learning in different environments can complement each other. Formal and non-formal education occurs mainly in structured environments in the form of institutions (schools, community centers, multimedia centers, learning villages/cities, etc.). Informal education on the other hand takes place in both structured and unstructured environments.

Major Influences on 21st Century Learning

Twenty-first century learning is at the confluence of three major influences: globalization, which increases global interdependence and competition; technology innovations that enable more engaged teaching and learning; and new research on how people learn.

Educators know that students learn best when they learn with understanding or use what they already know to derive meaning from new information. Awareness and productive use of one's own cognitive processes — metacognition is also important to learning.

However, when combined with new and sophisticated cognitive and neuroscience research on such topics as working memory, cognitive overload and executive function, these fundamental concepts become breakthrough ideas that can lead to new and better ways of teaching.

Concept of Enriched Learning Environment

An effective learning environment is developed by focusing on four dimensions of the environment.

1. **A Focus on Meaning** - Meaningful learning, growth in performance and creating processes/products that make a difference in the world, embedding meaning in the context and artifacts of the environment.
2. **Support for Each Person** - Align each person with their talents—what they like doing and what they do best, safe environment for taking risks, create alignments with values and interests of individuals, opportunities for professional growth and feedback.
3. **Structure for Each Person** - Clear performance criteria, scope, schedule, challenge and resources.
4. **Collaboration that adds Value** - Supporting others, using effective practices such as assessment and compelling goals.

The Need for New Generation Learning Environment

The teaching and learning process is a mix of formal and informal experiences that take place in a range of built environments. The primary formal settings include lecture theatres, seminar rooms, practical laboratories, IT spaces and libraries. More informal settings include cafes, learning commons and areas of serendipitous contact such as corridors and other interstitial spaces where effective learning may also take place.

Schools and educators must be well versed in core subjects, the broad range of interdisciplinary knowledge, skills and attitudes that education and business leaders call "21st century skills" and in teaching methods that engage and inspire students to learn. Examples of 21st century skills include global awareness, financial and entrepreneurial literacy, information and media literacy, civic literacy and health literacy. Students also need to acquire skills such as innovation and creativity, critical thinking and problem solving, information and media literacy, self-direction, adaptability and accountability.

In terms of teaching methods, schools must recognize that what engages this generation of learners is very different from what may have engaged previous generations. Students today have grown up in a world where mobile computers, cell phones with browsers and other personal digital devices are common tools, instant messaging, blogs and wikis are common modes of self-expression. All together, students spend an average of nearly 6.5 hours a day with media.

Six Design Principles for the 21st Century High School

The essential design principles for the 21st century high school by focusing on the relationships that matter most: those between students, teachers and curriculum. While the design principles themselves are not new, what is new is that the complexity that characterizes most education reform models has been cleared away, enabling immediate action and results.

1. Understanding of 21st Century Skills and Outcomes

Establish as a baseline that educators, students and parents must be well versed in the 21st century skills that students need to acquire to be successful. Teachers should be able to make relevant and useful choices about when and how to teach them and whether or not students are making progress toward their personal demonstration of accomplishment. Rethinking what we teach must come before we can rethink how we teach.

2. Relevant and Applied Curriculum

Offers an innovative vision of what the learning environment should be by applying what we know about how people learn and adapting the best pedagogy to meet the needs of this generation of learners. Students should be engaged in relevant and contextual problem-based and project - based learning designed to apply 21st century skills and that is provided using a multi - disciplinary approach. Curriculum should apply to students' current and future lives and leverage the power of Web 2.0 and other ubiquitous technologies.

3. Informative Assessment

Identifies the types and systems of assessments schools need to develop to fully capture the varied dimensions of 21st century learning as well as the independent role students need to take on in monitoring and adjusting their own learning. Assessments used in the classroom should increase relevant feedback to students, teachers, parents, decision-makers and should be designed to continuously improve student learning and inform the learning environment.

4. A Culture of Innovation and Creativity

Acknowledges the fuel that drives today's global economy and in turn, its importance in both student learning and the school environment. As a result, schools should create a culture that supports and reinforces innovation for student learning and leverages the creativity and ingenuity of every adult and student in their environment to solve their unique problems. Additionally, the teaching and learning environment should generate the continuous development of those skills.

5. Social and Emotional Connections with Students

Gives appropriate recognition to the personal, professional, and familial relationships that determine the health, growth, and cognitive development of a child within the family, school, and community. Specifically, each student should have a clear and purposeful connection to the social environment in school, with at least one adult who is purposefully in tune with the student's learning preferences, learning interests, and social connections.

6. Ubiquitous Access to Technology

Underscore the essential role technology plays in 21st century life and work and, consequently, the role that it must play in learning. Students and educators need 24 by 7 access to information, resources and technologies that engage and empower them to do background research, information and resource gathering and data analysis, to publish with multiple media types to wide and varied audiences, to communicate with peers and experts and to gain experience and expertise in collaborative work.

Learning and Innovation Skills

"We need people who think with the creative side of their brains—people who have played in a band, who have painted, been involved in the community as volunteers. It enhances symbiotic thinking capabilities, not always thinking in the same paradigm, learning how to kick - start a new idea or how to get a job done better, less expensively."- **Annette Byrd.**

Learning and innovation skills are those needed to solve complex problems. They include critical thinking and problem-solving skills, creativity and innovation skills, and communication skills. These areas have a long history of research. Individual cognition and problem-solving research findings have highlighted the skills that experts use in critical thinking. In addition to an extensive knowledge base of organized factual information, a key finding is that experts monitor their own thinking: they define their learning and problem-solving goals and keep track of their progress toward achieving them. There is evidence that children can be taught these skills and enhance their problem-solving performance.

Creativity and innovation are the processes of developing new perspectives and applying them to specific problems. These skills are thought to arise as problem- solvers reinterpret problems and elaborate on these new interpretations. Research has recently begun to contrast "routine experts," those who efficiently and accurately retrieve a solution for a problem, with "adaptive experts," those who continually evolve new approaches to problem situations. Traditional assessments and schooling tend to emphasize routine efficiency, but in the 21st century, routine tasks will be done by machines or be outsourced to lower paid workers. Research suggests that if learners and teachers are aware of these two different kinds of expertise, and monitor and encourage their development, students can be both efficient and adaptive.

Technology in Teaching And Learning

The infusion of information and communication technologies in teaching and learning is one of the primary drivers behind a conversation about learning environments, though many of the fundamental principles involved are equally valid in settings with little or no technology. Understanding the forces that affect learning can help educators implement environments that are appropriate for different situations, regardless of technology. That said, what makes a discussion of learning environments particularly important today is the range of opportunities that technology provides for creating new kinds of learning activities and experiences. The challenge is finding the right places for technology and using it wisely.

Learning Environments offered by academic buildings and walls and strong vestiges of this impulse to retreat from the more materially focused elements of society persist among educators and students alike. Nevertheless, technology today allows people who so choose to stay in essentially constant connection with friends, families and colleagues through social networks, communication tools and web-delivered media. Higher education finds itself in a position of balancing the value of a traditional, insulated environment with the benefits for “unbounded learning” that technology can provide.

Conclusion

Learning Environments that keep them very busy and extend the time needed to complete a degree, and the cost of commuting to campus can come into play in a slow economy. Experiences from the world of work and family accumulate for students at the same time they are pursuing their studies. The economy requires greater numbers of “knowledge workers,” and members of the workforce increasingly must update their skills to maintain levels of employability. Colleges and universities should construct learning environments that enable students with a range of cultural backgrounds to succeed. The environments they cultivate should accommodate cultural differences or set minimal standards for students—and provide remedial assistance so they can meet them.

References

1. Bransford, J.D., Brown, A.L., & Cocking, R.R. (1999). How People Learn: Brain, Mind, Experience and School. Washington, DC: National Academy Press.
2. Drucker, P. (2002). The Discipline of Innovation. Harvard Business Review.
3. Johnson, D.W., Johnson, R.T. & Stanne, M.B. (2000). Cooperative Learning Methods: A Meta analysis, University of Minnesota.
4. Reeves, D.B. (2004). Accountability for Learning: How Teachers and School Leaders Can take Charge. Association for Supervision and Curriculum Development.
5. Sawyer, R.K. (2006). Introduction: The New Science of Learning. In R.K. Sawyer, Cambridge Handbook of the Learning Sciences. New York: Cambridge University Press.

20

Mind Mapping - A New Paradigm on Science Teaching Competency in Pre Service Graduate Teachers

Introduction

Teaching is a demanding profession, requiring multi-dimensional skills, patience, commitment and continuous growth to face the challenges of the present era. Teachers must take the initiative to strengthen and improve the teaching profession on a daily basis and support its high standards. In order to bring about desirable changes in students, there has been demand for competent and committed teachers. Therefore, preparation of highly competent teachers became the priority and concern of all teachers – training institutions. Competency based education encourages each student to develop his or her own full capacity and prepares them to perform essential tasks at stated standards. Mind mapping is a strategy for helping students order and structure their thinking through mentally mapping words and concepts. Mind maps was developed by Tony Buzan as a way of helping students make notes that used only key words and images. They are much quicker to make, and because of their visual quality much easier to remember and review. Mind maps are used to generate, visualize, structure and classify ideas, and as an aid to studying and organizing information, solving problems, making decisions and writing. Mind maps provide an effective study technique when applied to written material. However before mind maps are generally adopted as a study technique, consideration has to be given towards ways of improving motivation amongst users in order to enhance science teaching competency.

This paper is an attempt to discuss the mind mapping and science teaching competency. Teaching is a demanding profession, requiring multi-dimensional skills, patience, commitment and continuous growth to face the challenges of the present era. Teachers must take the initiative to strengthen and improve the teaching profession on a daily basis and support its high standards. In order to bring about desirable changes in students, there has been demand for competent and committed teachers. Therefore, preparation of highly competent teachers became the priority and concern of all teachers – training institutions. Cognitive neuroscience is an academic field concerned with the scientific study of biological substrates underlying cognition with a specific focus on the neural substrates of mental processes. It addresses the questions of how psychological/cognitive functions are produced by the brain. Competency based education encourages each student to develop his or her own full capacity and prepares them to perform essential tasks at stated standards. Mind maps are used to generate, visualize, structure and classify ideas, and as an aid to studying and organizing information, solving problems, making decisions and writing. Mind maps provide an effective study technique when applied to written material. However before mind maps are generally adopted as a study technique, consideration has to be given towards ways of improving motivation amongst users in order to enhance teaching competency.

Mind Mapping and Teaching Competency

The teaching of science should enable a student to develop and enjoy personal interests, some of which are related to science. The student should be able to recognize and enjoy some scientific aspects of their material and made environment. The student could be encouraged by excluding in the science curriculum varied activities like science clubs, exhibition, excursions and the like teacher education, therefore has to change and adopt new techniques and methods to keep pace with the changing concepts of learning and education. Science Teaching is one of the most difficult tasks in the world. It's no secret that there is a range of learning styles. Many teachers find that their Science teaching style doesn't match the learning style of some of their students. The good news is that using Mind map to prepare and present lessons can have a powerful effect on our students. While the lesson presentation follows our natural teaching style, students can create a mind map that matches their learning style. Instead of trying to fit a mould, they can take notes that feel natural, are easily remembered and suited to their individual style. The ultimate organizational thinking tool, the easiest way to put information into our brain and to take information out of our brain. It is a creative and effective means of note taking that literally "Maps out" your thought." *TonyBuzan.* A mind map is a diagram used to represent words, ideas, tasks, or other items linked to and arranged around a central key word or idea. Mind maps are used to generate, visualize, structure, and classify ideas, and as an aid to studying and organizing information, solving problems, making decisions, and writing. The elements of a given mind map are arranged intuitively according to the importance of the concepts, and are classified into groupings, branches, or areas, with the goal of representing semantic or other connections between portions of information. Mind maps may also aid recall of existing memories. The mind map can be contrasted with the similar idea of concept mapping. The former is based on radial hierarchies and tree structures denoting relationships with a central governing concept, whereas concept maps are based on connections between concepts in more diverse patterns. By presenting ideas in a radial, graphical, non-linear manner, mind maps encourage a brainstorming approach to planning and organizational tasks. Though the branches of a mind map represent hierarchical tree structures, their radial arrangement disrupts the prioritizing of concepts typically associated with hierarchies presented with more linear visual cues. This orientation towards brainstorming encourages users to enumerate and connect concepts without a tendency to begin within a particular conceptual framework.

Role of Mind Mapping Strategies

Mind Maps organize the information in the same way your brain organizes information. This makes it very natural and easy to understand. Our brains like thinking in pictures. The smooth curves and colorful pictures that are created when mind mapping create powerful images for your brain to remember. We have two halves to our brains which think in different ways. The left half thinks linearly following direct linkages to related ideas. Our right brain likes to see the whole picture with colors and flow. A mind map caters to both sides of the brain at the same time, which makes it a very good way of storing and recalling information, presenting things to other people, and brainstorming new ideas. A mind map program gives you a lot more than basic mind mapping, including things like re-coloring of branches, reorganizing the mind map, drag and drop images and so much more. Mind maps are used all around the world, in education and in business. In education, they serve three powerful functions:

1. As a student presentation tool
2. As a pre-writing tool
3. As a teaching tool (By chunking language, mind mapping makes English more accessible to non-native English speakers. More about that later.)

Mind Mapping and Science Teaching

A mind map is a diagram used to represent words, ideas, tasks, or other items linked to and arranged around a central key word or idea. Mind maps are used to generate, visualize, structure, and classify ideas, and as an aid to studying and organizing information, solving problems, making decisions, and writing. The elements of a given mind map are arranged intuitively according to the importance of the concepts, and are classified into groupings, branches, or areas, with the goal of representing semantic or other connections between portions of information. Mind maps may also aid recall of existing memories. Especially in science teaching, Mind maps are a great tool to consolidate information from reading material, whether the information is coming from one source or multiple sources, and look at it from varied perspectives in a highly visual, interactive format. Mind mapping allows for better organization and clearer connections among concepts and topics, which, in turn, allows for more thorough examination, understanding, and presentation of subject matter. 1. Planning, 2. Organizing information, 3. Classifying, 4. Visualizing, 5. Structuring, 6. Grouping, 7. Recall, 8. Retrieval, 9. Spatial Organization, 10. Solving problems 11. Hierarchical Structuring, 12. Node Folding, 13. Generating

Effectiveness in Teaching

Buzan claims that the mind map is a vastly superior note taking method because it does not lead to a "semi-hypnotic trance" state induced by other note forms. Buzan also argues that the mind map uses the full range of left and right human cortical skills, balances the brain, taps into the alleged "99% of your unused mental potential", as well as intuition (which he calls "super logic"). However, scholarly research suggests that such claims may actually be marketing hype based on misconceptions about the brain and the cerebral hemispheres. Critics argue that hemispheric specialization theory has been identified as pseudoscientific when applied to mind mapping. Farrand, Hussain, and Hennessy (2002) found that spider diagrams (similar to concept maps) had a limited but significant impact on memory recall in undergraduate students (a 10% increase over baseline for a 600-word text only) as compared to preferred study methods (a 6% increase over baseline). This improvement was only robust after a week for those in the diagram group and there was a significant decrease in motivation compared to the subjects' preferred methods of note taking. Farrand et al. suggested that learners preferred to use other methods because using a mind map was an unfamiliar technique, and its status as a "memory enhancing" technique engendered reluctance to apply it. Nevertheless the conclusion of the study was *"Mind maps provide an effective study technique when applied to written material. However before mind maps are generally adopted as a study technique, consideration has to be given towards ways of improving motivation amongst users."*

Teaching Competency

Competency based education encourages each student to develop to his or her own full capacity and prepares them to perform essential tasks at stated standards. The component of competency based education is the competency. The term 'Competence is a generic word that represents the following three levels of human functioning' (i) Knowledge (ii) attitude and (iii) Performance Skill. A Program could be based on Competency Statement in one or more of the following components (a) its planning and design (b) its training materials (c) its training procedures and (d) its evaluation. The word Competency is taken in the broad Sense of knowledge, attitudes, Skills and behaviours that facilitate intellectual, Social, emotional and physical growth in children (Weber. 1972)

The intensive interactions with teachers, teacher educators, curriculum developers, evaluators and experts of different Categories, NCTE has identified the following ten inter – related competencies as essential for making competent teachers:

(1) Contextual Competencies

(2) Conceptual Competencies

(3) Content Competencies

(4) Transactional Competencies

(5) Competencies related to other educational activities

(6) Competencies to develop teaching – learning material

(7) Evaluation Competencies

(8) Management Competencies

(9) Competencies related to working with parents

(10) Competencies related to working with community and agencies.

Conclusion

In the teaching learning process, the functioning of the brain facilitates information processing, restoration and retrieval. The teachers should be fully aware of all the brain functions to make the teaching effective. Besides, they are fully conscious about the problems of the slow learners. Teachers have to concentrate not only on the gifted children's but also on the slow learners. By identifying each group, they can plan their teaching strategy according. The neuro scientific development have provided chance to explore the problems in learning and the causes which are all left to unknown and unable to the teachers. A trend has now come to revisit the teacher's competencies and also learning achievement among learners with special reference to cognitive neuroscience. Mind mapping is a wonderfully easy-to-learn, easy-to-use, and powerful way to engage students in the process of learning. It can be particularly useful for teachers who are working with students with different language backgrounds. Simply use "mind mapping" as a search term, and we will find ample resources to get started. The effectiveness of the teacher programme would largely depend upon the effectiveness of teacher-educator, who is expected to implement the various recommendations and reforms. It is therefore, essential for them to make themselves aware of the recent developments in the field of cognitive neuro science. This calls for an effective approach on the part of teacher education. Mind mapping can be used effectively to organize large amounts of information, combining spatial organization, dynamic hierarchical structuring and node folding. Mind maps provide an effective study technique when applied to written material. However before mind maps are generally adopted as a study technique, consideration has to be given towards ways of improving motivation amongst users in order to enhance the science teaching competency.

References

1. Buzan claims mind mapping his invention in interview. *KnowledgeBoard* retrieved Jan. 2010.
2. Beel, Jöran; Gipp, Bela; Stiller, Jan-Olaf (2009). "Information Retrieval On Mind Maps - What Could It Be Good For?". *Proceedings of the 5th International Conference on Collaborative Computing: Networking, Applications and Work sharing (CollaborateCom'09)*. Washington: IEEE. http://www.sciplore.org/publications_en.php

3. Buzan, Tony. (2000). *The Mind Map Book*, Penguin Books, 1996. ISBN 978-0452273221

4. Williams (2000) Encyclopedia of Pseudoscience. Facts on file. ISBN 978-0816033515

5. Farrand, P.; Hussain, F.; Hennessy, E. (2002). "The efficacy of the mind map study technique". *Medical Education* 36 (5): 426–431. doi:10.1046/j.1365-2923.2002.01205.x. PMID 12028392. http://www3.interscience.wiley.com/journal/118952400/abstract. Retrieved 2009-02-16.

6. Pressley, M., VanEtten, S., Yokoi, L., Freebern, G., & VanMeter, P. (1998). "The meta-cognition of college studentship: A grounded theory approach". In: D.J. Hacker, J. Dunlosky, & A.C. Graesser (Eds.), *Meta-cognition in Theory and Practice* (pp. 347-367). Mahwah NJ: Erlbaum ISBN 9780805824810

7. Dolman E.C. (July 1948). "Cognitive maps in rats and men". *Psychological Review* **55** (4): 189–208. doi:10.1037/h0061626. PMID 18870876.

8. Trade Mark 1424476, UK Intellectual Property Office, filed Nov. 1990

9. US Trademark, USPTO Trademark Application and Registration Retrieval system

21

Shifting From Traditional Teaching to Flipped Classroom Teaching

Introduction

The flipped classroom describes a reversal of traditional teaching where students gain first exposure to new material outside of class, usually via reading or lecture videos, and then class time is used to do the harder work of assimilating that knowledge through strategies such as problem-solving, discussion or debates. The traditional pattern of teaching has been to assign students to read textbooks and work on problem sets outside school, while listening to lectures and taking tests in class. Flip teaching or a flipped classroom is a form of blended learning in which students learn new content online by watching video lectures, usually at home, and what used to be homework (assigned problems) is now done in class with teachers offering more personalized guidance and interaction with students, instead of lecturing. This is also known as backwards classroom, flipped classroom, reverse teaching, and the Thayer Method. In flip teaching, the students first study the topic by themselves, typically using video lessons prepared by the teacher or third parties. In class students apply the knowledge by solving problems and doing practical work. The teacher tutors the students when they become stuck, rather than imparting the initial lesson in person. Complementary techniques include differentiated instruction and project-based learning. Flipped classrooms free class time for hands-on work. Students learn by doing and asking questions. Students can also help each other, a process that benefits both the advanced and less advanced learners. The purpose of flipping the classroom is to shift from passive to active learning to focus on the higher order thinking skills such as analysis, synthesis and evaluation. As explained in this short video, Flipping the Classroom: Simply Speaking (Penn State), students access key content individually prior to class time and then meet face-to-face in the larger group to explore content through active learning and engagement strategies. There are many permutations of what a flipped classroom will look like and depends on variables such as class size, resources, support and readiness to change. At UQ, several teachers across the faculties have already flipped their classrooms and their valuable experiences have been captured in the Case Studies section. In the flipped classroom, the roles and expectations of students and teachers change where: students take more responsibility for their own learning and study core content either individually or in groups before class and then apply knowledge and skills to a range of activities using higher order thinking, teaching 'one-to-many' focuses more on facilitation and moderation than lecturing, though lecturing is still important. Significant learning opportunities can be gained through facilitating active learning, engaging students, guiding learning, correcting misunderstandings and providing timely feedback using a variety of pedagogical strategies, there is a greater focus on concept exploration, meaning making and demonstration or application of knowledge in the face-to-face setting.

Teaching is said to be the noblest of all profession. The future of a Nation is shaped inside the classroom. It is needless to say it is in the hands of the teacher to decide the destiny of a Nation. That's why a number of Foreign countries spend more on education. However, still in some countries the practice of chalk and talk method is followed. This paper discuss about how to change from traditional teaching to flipped classroom teaching.

Educational technologies (Diagram 1) are an important feature of the flipped classroom as they can be used to: capture key content for students to access at their own convenience and to suit their pace of learning (e.g. lecture material, readings, interactive multimedia), present learning materials in a variety of formats to suit different learner styles (e.g. text, videos, audio, multimedia), provide opportunities for discourse and interaction in and out of class (e.g. polling tools, discussion tools, content creation tools), convey timely information, updates and reminders for students (e.g. micro-blogging, announcement tools), provide immediate and anonymous feedback for teachers and students (e.g. quizzes, polls) to signal revision points, capture data about students to analyse their progress and identify 'at risk' students (e.g. analytics).

Flipping in the classroom

Flipping the classroom is a "pedagogy-first" approach to teaching. In this approach in-class time is "re-purposed" for inquiry, application, and assessment in order to better meet the needs of the individual learners. Students gain control of the learning process through studying course material outside of class, using readings, pre-recorded video lectures(using technology such as Tegrity), or research assignments. During class time, instructors become facilitators of the learning process by helping students work through problems individually and in groups. There are numerous ways to flip your class. In fact "every teacher who has chosen to flip does so differently," says flipping gurus Bergmann and Sams (2012). The University of Texas at Austin, has a nice "Quick Start" guide to help you determine what kind of flip is best for your course.

Also known as "inverting" a classroom, this approach seeks to preserve the value of lecture (expertise and custom delivery), while freeing up precious in-person class time for active learning strategies. The main goal in flipping a class is to cultivate deeper, richer active learning experiences for students when the instructor is present to coach and guide them. Emphasis is on higher-order thinking skills and application to complex problems, and may include collaborative learning, case-based learning, peer instruction and problem sets.

"Flipping the classroom" has become something of a buzzword in the last several years, driven in part by high profile publications in *The New York Times* (Fitzpatrick, 2012); *The Chronicle of Higher Education* (Berrett, 2012); and *Science* (Mazur, 2009); In essence, "flipping the classroom" means that students gain first exposure to new material outside of class, usually via reading or lecture videos, and then use class time to do the harder work of assimilating that knowledge, perhaps through problem-solving, discussion, or debates.

Bloom's Taxonomy (Revised)

In terms of Bloom's revised taxonomy (2001), this means that students are doing the lower levels of cognitive work (gaining knowledge and comprehension) outside of class, and focusing on the higher forms of cognitive work (application, analysis, synthesis, and/or evaluation) in class, where they have the support of their peers and instructor. This model contrasts from the traditional model in which "first exposure" occurs via lecture in class, with students assimilating knowledge through homework; thus the term "flipped classroom."

The **flipped classroom** approach has been used for years in some disciplines, notably within the humanities. Barbara Walvoord and Virginia Johnson Anderson promoted the use of this approach in their book *Effective Grading* (1998). They propose a model in which students gain *first-exposure learning* prior to class and focus on the *processing* part of learning (synthesizing, analyzing, problem-solving, etc.) in class.

To ensure that students do the preparation necessary for productive class time, Walvoord and Anderson propose an assignment-based model in which students produce work (writing, problems, etc.) prior to class. The students receive productive feedback through the processing activities that occur during class, reducing the need for the instructor to provide extensive written feedback on the students' work. Walvoord and Anderson describe examples of how this approach has been implemented in history, physics, and biology classes, suggesting its broad applicability.

The Key Elements of the Flipped Classroom

1. Provide an opportunity for students to gain first exposure prior to class

The mechanism used for first exposure can vary, from simple textbook readings to lecture videos to podcasts or screen casts. For example, Grand Valley State University math professor Robert Talbert provides screen casts on class topics on his YouTube channel, while Vanderbilt computer science professor Doug Fisher provides his students video lectures prior to class (see examples here and here. These videos can be created by the instructor or found online from YouTube, the Khan Academy, MIT's Open Courseware, Courser a, or other similar sources. The pre-class exposure doesn't have to be high-tech, however; in the Deslauriers, Schelew, and Wieman study described above, students simply completed pre-class reading assignments.

2. Provide an incentive for students to prepare for class

In all the examples cited above, students completed a task associated with their preparation....and that task was associated with points. The assignment can vary; the examples above used tasks that ranged from online quizzes to worksheets to short writing assignments, but in each case the task provided an incentive for students to come to class prepared by speaking the common language of undergraduates: points. In many cases, grading for completion rather than effort can be sufficient, particularly if class activities will provide students with the kind of feedback that grading for accuracy usually provides. See a blog post by CFT Director Derek Bruff about how he gets his students to prepare for class.

3. Provide a mechanism to assess student understanding

The pre-class assignments that students complete as evidence of their preparation can also help both the instructor and the student assess understanding. Pre-class online quizzes can allow the instructor to practice Just-in-Time Teaching (JiTT; Novak et al., 1999), which basically means that the instructor tailors class activities to focus on the elements with which students are struggling. If automatically graded, the quizzes can also help students pinpoint areas where they need help. Pre-class worksheets can also help focus student attention on areas with which they're struggling, and can be a departure point for class activities, while pre-class writing assignments help students clarify their thinking about a subject, thereby producing richer in-class discussions. Importantly, much of the feedback students need is provided in class, reducing the need for instructors to provide extensive commentary outside of class (Walvoord and Anderson, 1998). In addition, many of the activities used during class time (e.g., clicker questions or debates) can serve as informal checks of student understanding.

4. Provide in-class activities that focus on higher level cognitive activities

If the students gained basic knowledge outside of class, then they need to spend class time to promote deeper learning. Again, the activity will depend on the learning goals of the class and the culture of the discipline. For example, Lage, Platt, and Treglia described experiments students did in class to illustrate economic principles (2000), while Mazur and colleagues focused on student discussion of conceptual "clicker" questions and quantitative problems focused on physical principles (2001). In other contexts, students may spend time in class engaged in debates, data analysis, or synthesis activities. The key is that students are using class time to deepen their understanding and increase their skills at using their new knowledge.

Conclusion

Flipping is still in the early stages, with much experimentation about how to do it right. Its most important popularizers are not government officials or academic experts, but Aaron Sams and Jonathan Bergmann, a pair of high school chemistry teachers in Woodland Park, Colo., who wrote a book called "Flip Your Classroom: Reach Every Student in Every Class Every Day," drawing almost completely on their own experience. It hasn't been rigorously studied (most people cite only this one research paper.) Flipping's track record in schools, while impressive, is anecdotal and short. But many people are holding it up as a potential model of how to use technology to humanize the classroom.

References

1. Berrett D (2012). How 'flipping' the classroom can improve the traditional lecture. *The Chronicle of Higher Education*, Feb. 19, 2012.
2. Anderson LW and Krathwohl D (2001). *A taxonomy for learning, teaching, and assessing: a revision of Bloom's taxonomy of educational objectives.* New York: Longman.
3. Lage MJ, Platt GJ, and Treglia M (2000). Inverting the classroom: A gateway to creating an inclusive learning environment. *The Journal of Economic Education* 31: 30-43.
4. Pashler H, McDaniel M, Rohrer D, and Bjork R (2008). Learning styles: Concepts and evidence. Psychological Science in the Public Interest 9: 103-119.
5. Walvoord BE, and Anderson VJ (1998). *Effective grading: A tool for learning and assessment.* San Francisco: Jossey-Bass.

22

Significance of Mental Health in Learning Without Limit

Introduction

Mental health of the learner is very important for efficient learning and proper development of Personality. A Child is born in a home where he remains in the formative years of his infancy. The impressions and experiences which a child has in these formative years leave permanent and indelible impressions on his mind. From the point of view of Psycho analysis, the early childhood experiences are very important for the future development of personality. A healthy individual is not only physically healthy but also mentally healthy. The modern concept of health extends beyond proper functioning of the body. It includes a sound, efficient mind and controlled emotions. Health is a state of being hale, sound or whole in body and mind. Hence, man is an integrated Psychometric unit whose behaviour is determined by both physical and mental factors. Learning is a complex phenomenon which needs positive emotions to learn more information. Emotions determine both the quality and quantity of one's learning. Negative emotions inhibit unlimited learning. Positive emotions accelerate it.

Needs of unlimited learning

In this Competitive world, the learners are in need of leaning without limit. Today, the world is much smaller thanks to technology. Class room learning gives us wider field of learning which is either language oriented or subject oriented. At the same time, the learners should have good mind to face the global competitions. A mentally healthy person can achieve his goal easily all over the world. Today learner is expected to be knowledge in all the fields of education. So the learner is in the position to learn more information from either in the class room or out of his class room. The learner should have the values of education. Information can be collected by the learner anywhere in the world. But the real value of education can be achieved by the learner through his experience and through his real teacher. Of course, a teacher is learner's second parent; he can give real value of education in the class room. A good learner has to learn the real values like kindness, duty discipline, character and service. These values give social maturity to the learner and they stimulate the involvement in learning without limit. A change in behaviour may occur because of stimulation (experience (or) practice) or because of nature growth or because of fatigue. The change in behaviour that occurs due to nature growth is known as maturity. The learner should have broad mind and behavioural maturity to enrich his learning. Whenever the learner tries to learn lot of information from other resources, he has to attain learning capacity and behavioural aspects.

Different types of unlimited learning resources

We can classify the unlimited learning resources in two terms as inner school resources and outer school resources of learning. The learner spends more time in his student hood days in the school. In the school campus, he learns a lot through his class room, library, play ground and his peer groups. Out of school campus, he can also learn by many resources like mobile, on line e-text books, face books etc. To learn, he can use the different types of method of learning like personal learning, blended learning, native learning, collaborative learning, cooperative learning, problem based learning and team learning. The learners who have thirst of unlimited learning enable to reach their potential through increased access to educational resources and experts that extend learning beyond the capacities or limitations of their school or community. They engage in rich compelling learning experiences that develop deeper knowledge and skill development especially the problem solving creativity and critical thinking skills so highly desired for our world today. They empower to take responsibility for their own educational destinies and to explore knowledge with an unfettered curiosity. Thus they are creating a new generation of lifelong learners. Today learners without limited have access to a rich and varied set of digital tools and resources that provide them with gate ways to new learning experiences that are not bound by their class room walls or ever the boundary lines of their town or city. The world is now their school. These digital learning experiences are so engraining and compelling that they ignite a new insatiable curiosity for more and more knowledge. Curiosity that is filled by the real world context of the experience and the opportunity to collaborate with peers and experts. Each learning experience is carefully tailored to meet the specific needs of the learner. The personalization potential of technology is realized. So the learner without limit has wider unlimited opportunities to learn in the world. At the same time he has to get a positive mental attitude to learn lot.

Role of mental health in learning without limit

According to Ivey and Simek Dowing (1980) the person who acts intentionally has a sense of capability. He can generate alternative behaviour in a given situation and approach a problem from different vantage points. The intentional and fully functioning individual is not bound to one course of action but respond in a moment of course of changing life situations and look forward to longer term goal.

According to Jahoda (1950), the mentally healthy person is one who actively masters his or her environment, demonstrates a considerable unity or consistency of personality and is able to perceive self and world realistically.

According to Bernard (1970), the adjustment of individual of themselves and the world at large, with maximum of effectiveness, satisfaction, cheerfulness and socially considerate behaviour and the ability of facing and accepting the realities of life.

Characteristics of a mentally Healthy person

A mentally healthy person is one who

(i) Is able to live joyfully and peacefully

(ii) Is not disturbed by mental conflicts

(iii) Has a true self appraisal of his strength and weakness.

(iv) Understands the intricacies of practical life and is very pragmatic his approach.

(v) Is emotionally stables and socially matures.

(vi) Has high degree of frustration tolerance such an individual has necessarily good physical health and mental health are inter related.

Therefore, a mentally healthy person will have positive emotions like love affection and health, joy and humour. These positive emotions will bring to learners personal and social adjustment, self motivation, involvement, self education and thirst of unlimited learning.

A mentally healthy person won't have negative emotions like fear, hostility, anger, anxiety and guilt. It is unfortunate that these negative emotions are part and parcel of our life. But it is fortunate that they have constructive component in them.

An unlimited learner must be able to bank upon this positive component learning to live with these negative emotions. This can be done by not allowing the negative emotions to grow beyond bounds.

Conclusion

Learning that is stressful, painful and dreary can't hold a candle to learning. It has to be joyful, relaxed and engaging. High emotional stress can cause barriers to learning. Mental health has positive emotions state of learners which helps to learn more effectively and even they can be motivated to engage with unlimited learning activities. Hence a learner who has a thirst of unlimited learning has physically and mentally health and he can achieve in learning in all the ways of his life. Mental Health hazards significantly increased in numbers and complexity, but they have also affected the physical efficiency of learners causing a variety of psychometric disorder. Thus mental health is now recognized as an important aspect of learners total development and mental health is accepting as integral part of the learning programmers.

Reference

1. The strategies of self control used by personal who work with adolescents "Dissertation abstract".
2. Journal of American College of Health (2005)
3. The mental health needs of today's College students challenges and recommendation. Helder publications.
4. Thinklin. T, Ridells Wilson.A (2005) support for students certain mental health difficulties in higher education.
5. The students prospective British Journal of Guidance and Counseling.

23

The Use of Digital Library Services in A Blended Learning Environment

Introduction

University libraries nowadays, are innovating to support the learning activities of academic communities, specifically by using ICT and Web technologies. These might include conducting library tutorials via mobile podcast; interacting with library users and marketing library services via Library 2.0 tools such as Face book and Blogs, and developing electronic repositories. Universities' library websites provides evidence of a wide range of innovation particularly in digital library services. Many university libraries have augmented their offerings to include digital services such as digital references, and the provision of digital resources. The Open University of Tamil Nadu is an example where the library has innovated by using Blogs, Twitter and mobile podcasting to provide tutorials and to interact with users. Many university libraries, such as International Islamic University Malaysia and University of Malaya, are currently using Face book to interact with their users. Although university libraries, such as in Malaysia, have made various attempts to encourage students to utilize their collections and services. With today's choices and convenience of access to information available over the Internet, students are inclined to retrieve information from the Internet. The status of libraries in academia is therefore open to debate. Some libraries view their role as increasing while others claim they are at professional cross-roads [1]. University libraries should be the main source of information to university communities. At the same time, learning environments have evolved to include distance, online and blended settings. The emergence of BL has raised new issues and challenges as libraries consider how to better.

Definition of Digital Libraries

Numerous terms are used by authors to denote the concept of digital libraries. According to E.A. Fox the digital library may be defined as the "New way of carrying out the functions of libraries encompassing new types of information resources, new approaches to classification and cataloguing, intensive use of electronic systems and networks and dramatic shifts in intellectual, organizational and electronic practices". Larsen defines, "A digital library as a global virtual library the library of thousands of networked electronic libraries".

Blended Learning

No single, reliable definition of blended learning exists, or evens a universal agreement on the term itself. Blended Learning is a term increasingly used to describe the way e- learning is being combined with traditional classroom methods and independent study to create a new, hybrid teaching methodology. It represents a much greater change in basic technique than simply adding computers to classrooms; it represents, in many cases, a fundamental change in the way teachers and students approach the learning experience. It has already produced an offshoot – the flipped classroom– that has quickly become a distinct approach of its own. There is not yet a consensus about the meaning of BL and definitions reflect varying complexity. One of the simplest and most widely used is that of a combination of F2F and online learning [2]. This is later extended to include "the thoughtful integration" [3] of F2F and online learning, thus identifying the importance of pedagogical design in learning.

Complexity arises with BL at different levels. The teacher must not only understand the strengths and weaknesses of the two different environments and how to make meaningful connections between them [4] but also be able to respond to different settings, for example the discipline and its learning outcomes, the institutional and community context, and of course, the students and their needs and expectations.

The flipped Classroom

The "flipped" classroom, a more recent coinage, refers to classes that are structured almost exclusively around a reversal of expectations for lectures and homework. Students are expected to watch lectures online at home, and do homework while they are in class.

Most of these universities are offering face-to-face (F2F) learning opportunities while some offer a mixture or blended learning (BL).

Components of blended learning

1. Classroom facilitator: In-person classroom activities facilitated by a trained educator.
2. Supported by on-line study materials: Online learning materials often including pre-recorded lectures given by that same instructor.
3. Independent Study: Structured independent study time guided by the material in the lectures and skills developed during the classroom experience.

Blended Learning Model

A course created in a blended learning model uses the classroom time for activities that benefit the most from direct interaction. Traditional education (especially at the college level) tends to place an emphasis on delivering material by way of a lecture, while in a blended learning model lectures can be videotaped ahead of time so the student can watch on their own time. The classroom time is more likely to be for structured exercises that emphasize the application of the curriculum to solve problems or work through tasks.

Role of teachers in Blended Learning

The word "facilitator" has emerged as an alternative to "teacher," bringing with it a slightly different focus. The facilitator places an emphasis on empowering students with the skills and knowledge required to make the most of the online material and independent study time, guiding students toward the most meaningful experience possible. Facilitators focus on four key areas.

1. Development of online and offline course content.
2. Facilitation of communication with and among students, including the pedagogy of communicating content online without the contextual clues students would get in person.
3. Guiding the learning experience of individual students, and customizing material wherever possible to strengthen the learning experience.
4. Assessment and grading, not unlike the expectations for teachers within the traditional framework.

Changing role of University Libraries in Digital Environment

The role of the library, and especially their digital library services, is becoming more important in BL environments. University libraries nowadays have augmented their digital services and have incorporated the use of ICT into various library operation and services provision. Digital library services consist of the provision of various customer and information services and access to various sources [5]. While university libraries have becoming increasingly digital, their future role and challenges is well articulated in concepts such as blended librarianship and the Web 2 library. The vision of blended librarianship [6] was one of an increasing integration of services and practice in to the teaching and learning process. This included the challenges of improved support for academic staff but also, reaching out to students by integrating the library into their learning spaces. The concept of Library 2.0 [7] reinforces the blended nature of future libraries by describing the ubiquitous library which supports learners by overcoming current physical limitations through blending flexible 'best of breed' systems to communicate, collaborate and learn online. There has been very little reported research on integration of digital library services into BL environments and this has mostly occurred in the United Kingdom. Some key issues and challenges which have been identified are the importance of universal access and responding to the needs of different learners, enabling teachers to embed their own pedagogy rather than a systemic approach, moving away from 'spoon-feeding' and encouraging online resource discovery by students, the need for strong collaboration between library and academic staff and a commitment to teaching and learning as well as technical development [8, 9]. However, a factor which may influence the success of blended approaches is access to and use of ICT's within a country [10], more commonly known as the issue of the digital divide. This is mainly regarded as the lack of physical access to ICT infrastructure and equipment and has been predominantly associated with geographic isolation (for example, rural districts) and also with weak economies, both within the United States and developing countries.

Limitation of Blended Learning

Digital Divide

Chan and Ibrahim [11] adopted a more comprehensive definition of the digital divide. They defined it as a situation whereby societal members are stratified by possession and usage of knowledge, access to ICT-based knowledge, access to means of acquiring the knowledge (e.g. computer and the Internet) and, subsequently, by possession of income and wealth acquired through the knowledge. The authors described multiple projects that the government has taken to close the digital divide including the development of a multimedia super corridor, and telecasters which provided community access to computers, and computer literacy programmes in rural areas. McMahon and Bruce argued that giving physical access is a simplistic approach to addressing a digital divide. Their research identified facets of information literacy that were also essential. These began with basic literacy skills and the ability to understand English, because it is a global language and widely used on the Internet.

1. Accessibility

Accessibility and connectivity was the main factor that either encouraged or discouraged students to utilize digital library services. Students used the digital library because it could be accessed anytime anywhere. The library is easily accessed from home, from office, from anywhere. The students are mostly working adult, so the digital library is an advantage for them. Accessibility and connectivity was an issue especially for those who live in rural areas.

Constraints

Speed

The constraint of using the digital library is in term of the internet speed. For those who live very far (from cities), the line is slow. Language barriers Language was identified as another constraint to using the digital library by students. Most resources and e-books available in the digital library were available in English.

Conclusion

Digital Library is the electronic library, which the information is stored in the digital form. With the advancement and new technology in the field of information librarians need to improve new skills using the new technology and it requires reorientation of traditional skill of librarian ship information professional and librarians must acquire the new skills as networking and web based technologies, on live searching of electronic database CD-ROM Products e-journals etc. In Multi- Disciplinary Knowledge and Skills are required if information professionals have to survive.

Reference

1. Bell, S. J., & Shank, J. D. (2007). Academic librarianship by design: A blended librarian's guide to the tools and technique, Chicago: ALA
2. Graham, C. (2006). Blended Learning Systems, Definitions, current trends and future directions. In C. Bonk & C. Graham (Eds.), The handbook of blended learning: Global perspectives, local designs. San Francisco: John Wiley and Sons.
3. Garrison, R., & Kanuka, H. (2004). Blended learning: Uncovering its transformative potential in higher education. Internet and Higher Education, 7 , 95-105.

4. Gerbic, P. (2009). Including online discussions within campus-based students' learning environments. In E. Stacey & P. Gerbic (Eds.), Effective blended learning practices: Evidenced-based perspectives in ICT-Facilitated Education,(pp. 21-38). Hershey, PA: Information Science Reference

5. 165-174.[13] Norasieh, M. A. & Yanti Idaya Aspura, M. K. (2009, November). "Understanding digital library services in the virtual learning environment in higher education" . Paper presented at the meeting of the International Conference on Teaching & Learning in Higher Education, Kuala Lumpur.

6. Bell, S. J., & Shank, J. D. (2007). Academic librarianship by design: A blended librarian's guide to the tools and technique. Chicago: ALA.

7. Casey, M. (2005) Working towards a definition of Library 2.0,. Retrieved August5,2009,fromhttp://www.librarycrunch.com/2005/10/working_towards_a_definition_o.html

8. Currier, S. (2002). INSPIRAL. Digital library services and online learning environments: Issues for integration. In P. Brophy, S. Fisher & Z. Clarke (Eds.),

9. Roberts, S., & Davey, J. (2002). VLEs and information services: Redefining distance learning and the role of information services within the virtual learning environment.

10. Hawkins, S. (2005). Beyond the digital divide: Issues of access and economics. The Canadian Journal of Information and Library Science,

11. Chan, G., & Ibrahim, M. (2008). Conceptualising the network society in Malaysia, Asian Journal of Social Science, 36, , 773 - 791.

24

Emerging Computer Paradigm

Introduction

Computers have become an essential part of life. We need computers everywhere, be it for study and work, research or in any such field. As the use of computers in our day-to-day life increases, the computing resources that we need also go up.

Cloud computing is the new technology that has various advantages and it is an adoptable technology in this present scenario. The main advantage of the cloud computing is that this technology reduces the cost effectiveness for the implementation of the Hardware, software and License for all. This is the better peak time to analyze the cloud and its implementation and better use it for the development of the quality and low cost education for all over the world. Cloud computing is becoming an adoptable technology for many of the organizations with its dynamic scalability and usage of virtualized resources as a service through the Internet. Cloud computing is growing rapidly, with applications in almost any area, including education. Especially in the universities where the uses of computers are more intensive and what can be done to increase the benefits of common applications for students and teachers. In this paper, we discuss how to influence on cloud computing and influence on this technology to take education to a wider mass of students over the country. We believe cloud computing will surely improve the current system of education and improve quality at an affordable cost.

Education or Learning is an important component of life and No human beings are able to survive properly without education. Now a days, there are lots of paradigms for getting knowledge or learn something. Cloud Computing is a new paradigm that provides an appropriate pool of computing resources with its dynamic scalability and usage of virtualized resources as a service through the Internet. The resources can be network servers, applications, platforms, infrastructure segments and services. Cloud computing deliver services autonomously based on demand and provides sufficient network access, data resource environment and effectual flexibility. This technology is used for more efficient and cost effective computing by centralizing storage, memory, computing capacity of PC's and servers.

Cloud computing applications provide flexibility for all educational universities, schools and institutions. The cloud platform in institutions' campuses provides effective infrastructure and deployment model for their dynamic demands. The benefits of cloud computing can support education institutions to resolve some of the common challenges such as cost reduction, quick and effective communication, security, privacy, flexibility and accessibility.

What is Cloud Computing?

The term "cloud" in cloud computing is the communications network or a network combined with computing infrastructure. It is an Internet-based computing technology, where shared resources such as software, platform, storage and information are provided to customers on demand. Cloud Computing is a computing platform for sharing resources that include infrastructures, software, applications, and business processes. Cloud Computing is a virtual pool of computing resources. It provides computing resources in the pool for users through internet.

Need For Cloud Computing

The cloud computing works on the cloud - so there are large groups of often low-cost servers with specialized connections to spread the data-processing chores among them. Since there are a lot of low-cost servers connected together, there are large pools of resources available. So these offer almost unlimited computing resources. This makes the availability of resources a lesser issue. The data of the application can also be stored in the cloud. Storage of data in the cloud has many distinct advantages over other storages.

The cloud computing applications also provide automatic reconfiguration of the resources based on the service level agreements. When we are using applications out of the cloud, to scale the application with respect to the load is a mundane task because the resources have to be gathered and then provided to the users. If the load on the application is such that it is present only for a small amount of time as compared to the time its working out of the load, but occurs frequently, then scaling of the resources becomes tedious. But when the application is in the cloud, the load can be managed by spreading it to other available nodes by making a copy of the application on to them. This can be reverted once the load goes down. It can be done as and when needed. All these are done automatically such that the resources maintain and manage themselves.

Characteristics of Cloud Computing

1. Infrastructure as a service (IaaS)
2. Software as a service (SaaS)
3. Platform as a service (PaaS)
4. Self Healing, Multi-tenancy, Service-oriented ,
5. SLA Driven(service-level agreements.)
6. Virtualized, Flexible

Benefits of Using Cloud Computing

1. Low cost , Improved performance , Instant software updates

2. Improved document format compatibility
3. Benefits for students, Benefits for teachers , End user satisfaction
4. Data security

One of the most interesting applications of cloud computing is educational cloud. The educational cloud computing can focus the power of thousands of computers on one problem, allowing researchers search and find models and make discoveries faster than ever. The universities can also open their technology infrastructures to private, public sectors for research advancements. The efficiencies of cloud computing can help universities keep pace with ever-growing resource requirements and energy costs. Students expect their personal mobile devices to connect to campus services for education. Faculty members are asking for efficient access and flexibility when integrating technology into their classes. Researchers want instant access to high performance computing services, without them responsibility of managing a large server and storage farm. The role of cloud computing at university education should not be underestimated as it can provide important gains in offering direct access to a wide range of different academic resources, research applications and educational tools.

Conclusion

Cloud computing is a powerful new abstraction for large scale data processing systems which is scalable, reliable and available. Cloud computing as an exciting development is a significant alternative today's educational perspective. Students and administrative personnel have the opportunity to quickly and economically access various application platforms and resources through the web pages on-demand. This automatically reduces the cost of organizational expenses and offers more powerful functional capabilities. There will be an online survey to collect the required data for the use of cloud computing in the universities and other governmental or private institutions in the region. This will help us review the current status and probable considerations to adopt the cloud technology. Beginning with the outsourcing of email service seems attractive. The gradually removal of software license costs, hardware costs and maintenance costs respectively provides great flexibility to the university/corporate management.

In this paper we discuss cloud computing based information. Describe its definition and some benefits. Cloud based education will help the students, staff, Trainers, Institutions and also the learners to a very high extent and mainly students from rural parts of the world will get an opportunity to get the knowledge shared by the professor on other part of the world. Even governments can take initiatives to implement this system in schools and colleges in future and we believe that this will happen soon.

References

1. Educause (2010). Cloud Computing. Retrieved Oct 10, 2010, from
2. "Effective use of cloud computing in educational institutions", Tuncay Ercana, WCES-2010
3. "the utility of cloud computing as a new pricing – and consumption - model for information technology", David C. Wyld, Department of Management, Southeastern Louisiana University, Hammond, LA USA, International Journal of Database Management Systems (IJDMS), Vol.1, No.1, November 2009
4. Cloud Computing Issues and Benefits Modern Education, By D.Kasi Viswanath, S.Kusuma & Saroj Kumar Gupta, Madanapalle Institute of Technology and Science Madanapalle, Chittoor.

25

Pedagogical Styles and Approaches of Online Team Teaching in Higher Education

Introduction

A team teaching online environment has the potential to help more efficiently meet the needs of online learners and provide greater satisfaction for instructors in higher education. A well-trained pair of instructors can complement each other, meeting student needs in a timely manner, as well as providing students with the opportunity to view topics from different perspectives .Higher education professionals gain more in-depth feedback about their work. Specific strategies for a successful online team teaching experience includes how to create a successful online learning community; achieve effective course management; provide systematic, in-depth assessment of student learning and provide timely feedback. Methods to improve upon one-another's teaching strengths will be introduced as well as building community between peer co-teacher and students. This paper highlights the models of online team teaching in higher education.

Over the last few years, there have been tremendous developments in teaching learning technologies to academics to enhance the teaching and learning environment using technology. New communication and information technologies have become major resources for teaching and learning in higher education. Online team teaching is one of the most modern techniques in the field of educational technology. Online teaching strategies that help students take more responsibility for their own learning and enhance the process of teaching for learning. Online team teaching offers an opportunity for better education to a large group of students through a team of teachers in higher education. The goal of online team teaching is the improvement of teaching through a better utilisation of a group of teachers. The theoretical design for online team teaching is based on the cooperative planning.

Online Team Teaching

Team teaching, whether online or on the ground, presents some unique challenges as well as opportunities. Students can derive the benefit of the multiple perspectives and teaching styles brought by two instructions, while instructions may appreciate the intellectual stimulation of the collaboration as well as the prospect of sharing some of their duties and workload (Mishra R C, 2005). However, instructors who have experience with team teaching know that being half of a two-member team doesn't necessarily mean doing only half the work. Moreover, the difficulties involved in coordination can be legion.

Even though colleagues aren't together in a physical classroom setting, they occupy the same online classroom space, and can easily trip over each other as well. Once teaching begins, differences in teaching style and approaches will invariably appear, so it's best to discuss the pedagogical approach as well as practical procedures before the course begins. The minimum students required for team-teaching is fifteen. **Tisha Bender (2003)** formulates the three basic models of online team teaching: Shared responsibility, Division of labour, and Primary- secondary.

Shared Responsibility Model

In the shared responsibility model, both instructors do everything; that is, each of them shares the responsibility for all activities in the class. Online, this means that both read and responds to all discussions and assignments. Students will know which instructor is which in the discussion forum, because instructors' name will appear next to their comments. Assignment can be graded by consensus or by averaging. However, unless instructors have an online grade-book, one of instructors will have to take charge of notifying students of grades and passing along the corresponding comments by e-mail. An instructor can sign both names to the grade and add comments.

In some situations the instructors may decide that the shared responsibility model is the best approach. The students have to be asked to send any e-mailed queries to both instructors. Each instructor must assiduously read all discussion threads in the class. If one instructor has more comments than the other on a particular topic, that's fine, but the other should make at least a few responses to the same topic. In introductory messages, the instructor has to clearly state the procedures for students to contact him and to submit assignments. For grading and evaluating student work and participation, the instructor has to work out a procedure that his co-teacher can easily follow. If the instructor is meeting with his co-teacher online, the instructor will need a way to smoothly exchange any e-mailed assignments and to maintain record keeping as well.

Division of Labour Model

The division of labour model involves just what the name suggests: The two instructors divide their responsibilities according to a prearranged plan. Like the shared responsibility model, division of labour also requires a great deal of planning and co-ordination, but it is generally easier to implement. The division of labour may be arranged by weeks; by topics; by types of class activities; or by a combination of these factors. Some activities can be handled separately by each of the two instructors, while other activities are a joint effort.

To make the division of labour model most effective, each instructor contributes something to the overall effort. This contribution should start with the selection of texts and planning of class activities. Each instructor has to decide how the classroom responsibilities divided up, and syllabus should be arranged so that students know who has the primary responsibility for any particular activity. Introduction during the first week of class is carried out jointly with the instructor's co-teacher. The students have to send any queries to all the instructors. This will ensure that each instructor is kept "in the loop". Even if the discussion responsibilities are divided up by week, a instructor not assigned to that duty in a particular week can read the discussion. The "off-duty" instructor might want to make a comment as well, and he or she can best do so after the other instructor and the students have had their say. Divide up grading of assignments is done as evenly as possible but in alternating cycles so that neither instructor loses track of students. In other words, Joe grades assignments 1 and 3, while Mary does 2 and 4. Each instructor should cc the other on any elephant-mailed evaluation comments to a student. Each instructor should have copies of all grades and comments. If there is no central grade book online, the two instructors need to keep identical records. This may mean that, after each grading turn is taken, the instructor who did the grading e-mails a list of grades to the other.

Primary-Secondary Model

In the primary-secondary model, one instructor assumes the primary or dominant role in managing the class. This approach is necessary when one instructor cannot participate in the class to the same extent as the other, yet is still making an active contribution. For example, one instructor may have less Internet access or more workload issues than the other or one instructor may feel less expert in certain areas of course content. To make the primary-secondary model as effective one, each instructors is to be fully aware of the responsibilities he or she has agreed to take on. They work this out by going over the week-by-week activities of the course. They balance the workload to each person's satisfaction. If one instructor cannot participate online as much as the other, for instance, let him or her take on more of the record-keeping duties or slightly more of the grading of assignments. The students are to be indicated the respective responsibilities for each instructor, but ask students to cc each instructor on any e-mail correspondence sent to the other. If one instructor does not have as much uninterrupted web access as the other, the partner with good access does the posting. Students need to be reminded about this practice to avoid confusion about the two instructors' contributions.

Conclusion

The use of several simple strategies can also help ensure that online learning is a valuable and stress-free experience for students. Online Team-teaching can offer students a wider knowledge base from which students can draw, offers a more varied personality base with which they can be compatible, and can expose students to a variety of assessment methods and learning techniques (Shapiro & Dempsey, 2008). Planning, communication, and organization can help and make online team teaching experience is a collegial one for instructors. Exposure to new approaches, new methods, and new philosophies can help even the most experienced teacher keep "green and growing."

Reference

1. Mishra R C. (2005).Teaching of Information Technology.A.P.H Publishing Corporation. New Delhi.P-264.
2. Shapiro, E. and Dempsey, C. (2008). Conflict resolution in team teaching: a case study in interdisciplinary teaching. *College teaching, 56* (3). 157-162.
3. Tisha Bender.(2003).Discussion- Based online teaching to enhance student learning. Stylus publishing.virginia.P-143.
4. Vijaya Kumari Kaushik, &Sharma S R.(2004).Modern Media and Education. Anmol publications, Pvt. Ltd. New Delhi.
5. http://www.interneteducationinfo.com/internet-education-facts-and-benefits.php
6. http://jolt.merlot.org/vol7no3/scribner-maclean_0911.htm

26

The Sky is Not the Limit – The Super Highway Beyond the Horizon Learning Without Limits

Introduction

The most important of educational principles is the understanding that each child's potential for learning is limitless. Learning without limits can produce high academic attainment and enhanced capacity to learn for everybody which will result in skilled personalities or human resource development. Constructivism transforms today's classrooms into a knowledge-construction site where information is absorbed and knowledge is built by the learner. Constructivist learning theory says that all knowledge is constructed from a base of prior knowledge. Children are not a blank slate and knowledge cannot be imparted without the child making sense of it according to his or her current conceptions. Therefore children learn best when they are allowed to construct a personal understanding based on experiencing things and reflecting on those experiences. Constructivist learning environments promote the learner to gather, filter, analyze, and reflect on the information provided and to comment on this knowledge so that it will result in individualized comprehension and private learning. This type of learning will reduce the dissemination of false data, prejudice, and atrocities among diverse groups and help build a moral, scientific, information society in the new millennium. The guiding principle of transformability can only be achieved through what teachers and young people do together in what is necessarily a joint enterprise. Be it developmental or social as suggested by Piaget and Vygotsky respectively, learning is the central activity for humans in search for understanding the causes and effects of natural phenomena, the progress of social events, and the meaning of life and the learning becomes unlimited. By using such teaching- learning approaches we can better introduce our children to the world that God has created for us, and lead them to think about the miracles that are all around us. This paper has discussed the new approaches and strategies in education required for the present and future generation for unlimited learning and the scope of a super-journey beyond the sky because 'The Road to Knowledge is Always under Construction and Never Ending'.

The quality of education is a hot topic of discussion amongst educators, educational administrators and politicians. Countless studies have been conducted in recent decades to determine how students' academic achievements can be maximized. One method sounds like a simple generalization but can turn around the classroom environment irrespective of the child's home life or family financial situation. Positive student engagement, among other things, seeks to make the child an active participant in his learning and enjoy learning activities. Whenever experiences stimulate mental activities that lead to meaningful learning, this is active learning. Mentally active learning of ideas-and-skills can occur in a wide variety of thought-stimulating activities, ranging from direct learning (of ideas that are explained in a web-page, book, lecture, video, tv or radio show,...) to learning by discovery (as in doing an experiment and then trying to discover your own explanations for what has been observed), or in design projects and other kinds of problem solving where the learning cannot be defined as either direct or discovery. All of these thought-stimulating activities can produce active learning, because educationally productive mental activity can occur

— with or without physical activity in which you "do" something — during a wide variety of mentally-active experiences. Active learning is the product of constructivist approach of teaching. This promotes Self-Regulated Learning in Young Children. It is important to underline the role of collaborative and peer-assisted learning in Constructivist Approach.

Constructivism- Meaning / Definition Of Constructivism

1. Constructivism is basically a theory — based on observation and scientific study — about how people learn.
2. It says that people construct their own understanding and knowledge of the world, through experiencing things and reflecting on those experiences.
3. When we encounter something new, we have to reconcile it with our previous ideas and experience, maybe changing what we believe, or maybe discarding the new information as irrelevant. To do this, we must ask questions, explore, and assess what we know.
4. Constructivism is an approach to teaching and learning based on the premise that cognition (learning) is the result of "mental construction."
5. In other words, students learn by fitting new information together with what they already know.

Characteristics of Constructivist Teaching

1. The learners are actively involved.
2. The environment is democratic.
3. The activities are interactive and student-centered.
4. The teacher facilitates a process of learning in which students are encouraged to be responsible and autonomous.

Benefits of Constructivism

1. Children learn more, and enjoy learning more when they are actively involved, rather than passive listeners.

2. Education works best when it concentrates on thinking and understanding, rather than on rote memorization. Constructivism concentrates on learning how to think and understand.
3. Constructivist learning is transferable. In constructivist classrooms, students create organizing principles that they can take with them to other learning settings.
4. Constructivism gives students ownership of what they learn, since learning is based on students' questions and explorations, and often the students have a hand in designing the assessments as well. Constructivist assessment engages the students' initiatives and personal investments in their journals, research reports, physical models, and artistic representations. Engaging the creative instincts develops students' abilities to express knowledge through a variety of ways. The students are also more likely to retain and transfer the new knowledge to real life.
5. By grounding learning activities in an authentic, real-world context, constructivism stimulates and engages students. Students in constructivist classrooms learn to question things and to apply their natural curiosity to the world.
6. Constructivism promotes social and communication skills by creating a classroom environment that emphasizes collaboration and exchange of ideas. Students must learn how to articulate their ideas clearly as well as to collaborate on tasks effectively by sharing in group projects. Students must therefore exchange ideas and so must learn to "negotiate" with others and to evaluate their contributions in a socially acceptable manner. This is essential to success in the real world, since they will always be exposed to a variety of experiences in which they will have to cooperate and navigate among the ideas of others.

Constructivist Learning Design

In this model, teachers implement a number of steps in their teaching structure.

They:

1. develop a situation for students to explain
2. select a process for groupings of materials and students
3. build a bridge between what students already know and what the teachers want them to learn
4. anticipate questions to ask and answer without giving away an explanation
5. encourage students to exhibit a record of their thinking by sharing it with others, and
6. Solicit students' reflections about their learning.

Educational Design

This helps to build a learning environment that is inclusive, humane and enabling for everybody, a place free from the damaging effects of fixed ability thinking and practices.

What Teachers Can do.

1. Create an end-of-the-year academic goal for the class, or a specific goal for each student. Pick a goal that is challenging but achievable. Tailor classroom activities to reaching that goal. Adapt the teaching strategies according to the learning style of the child. Teachers can use ICT to support their pedagogy.
2. Encourage students regularly and remind them of how each specific task is getting them closer to their goal. Monitor student achievement throughout the year and talk privately with kids who are falling behind, let them know that you care about their success, and they will too.
3. Encourage students to ask questions, discourage any judgement that could result from a question. Make learning cool by reminding kids of how the things they learn in the class will be relevant to achieving future academic and career goals.
4. Engage in activities that include the following instructional tools: group activities and assignments, long-term projects,

hands-on activities, lessons and activities that draw from students' backgrounds and interests. Group activities will allow students to support and encourage each other, hands-on activities will give them confidence, long-term projects will give them a sense of tracking their own progress, and incorporating their lifestyle into lessons will create a sense of relevancy for the students.

How Schools Can Help

1. Increase parental involvement. Engage parents in a casual manner, being too technical will alienate them. Talk to them about their child's qualities before you address any problems that you want to bring up with them. Contact them regularly, even if just to tell them their child is doing great. Ask their opinion on lesson plans or ways to further engage students.
2. Make school safety a priority. Students will learn better in an environment they feel safe in. Be consistent in your enforcement of school disciplinary action. Don't allow one student to be punished more harshly than another for the same infraction. Make sure parents have access to counselors, support staff and school security. Support a violence prevention program to teach students more productive ways to handle their anger. Contact the local police department to see if any of their officers could volunteer time to talk to students about non-violent alternatives. Students easily recognize the authority of officers, which is why they are good speakers to use.
3. Offer extracurricular activities. Students will stay out of trouble and harm's way if they are engaged in positive activities in a safe environment. Extracurricular activities will also help to become more comfortable with the school grounds and consider it a place of comfort and positivity. They will have an opportunity to explore interests outside of the classroom.

What Parents can do

Parental support is directly linked to student engagement in learning. Therefore, schools must break down any barriers that impede parental involvement and work diligently to increase parental interaction at school and with their children's schoolwork. Schools can do this by creating a welcoming and inviting environment at the school for parents, providing opportunities for parents to collaborate with the school and/or teachers to identify support needs of the students, and keeping the lines of communication open. The parents do not have to be in the schools to be involved in their child's learning; they can offer substantial support from home by reinforcing the importance of completing homework or attending classes.

Conclusion

People come into education – to make a difference for children. To make a deep difference we have to organize education differently. It describes learning in an atmosphere of deep humanity, care and transforms people. It requires teachers who are passionate, committed to life-long education and long-standing concerns about the impact of ability on young people's learning in schools. Teachers must have profound faith in the capacity of every child to be a passionate and engaged learner. Teachers must build their pedagogy around a belief that the future is in the making of the present. Teachers are the Creators of Tomorrow's Innovators. So they must be equipped with all the essential skills necessary for the ever changing world. Teachers must make a unique and irreplaceable contribution to the Learning without Limits. Teachers can help to strengthen and ultimately transform young people's capacity to learn through the choices they make. This shows the way towards a new and liberating view of human development. In other words there is no limit for learning and it can be life-long which will take us beyond the horizon.

References

1. Hart, S., Dixon, A., Drummond, M.J. and McIntyre, D. (2004) *Learning without Limits.* Maidenhead: Open University Press
2. Swann M., Peacock A., Hart, S. and Drummond, M.J. (2012) *Creating Learning without Limits.* Maidenhead: Open University Press
3. http://www.asa3.org/ASA/education/teach/active.htm
4. http://en.cyclopaedia.net/wiki/Without-Limits

27

Awareness of Educational Media Among Higher Secondary Teachers of Thiruvannamalai District and their Perception of Media Based Education

Introduction

Perception refers to "the way in which man senses or becomes immediately aware of his environment". Although knowledge about the world is gained through the senses, sensory impressions themselves are not enough to given a suitable understanding of the object perceived. It is the brain that receives and interprets them, which then become organized into meaningful understanding. Thus any given perceptual event is the result of multiple sensory messages. Perceptual events do not occur in isolation, they are continuous. As result of constant sensory stimulation, experiences are arranged and rearranged, shuffled and reshuffled, selected and reselected and organized into a convenient combination of patterns. This process finally leads the formation of concept. In general, understanding of the things and events of the world is based on sensory experiences and the physical objects, as the human beings known them are products of their own sensory perceptions. The present study aims to find out the awareness of educational media among Higher Secondary teachers of Thiruvannamalai district and their perception of media based education. A samples of 200 samples selected randomly were studied. A questionnaire method of survey was used to find out the awareness of educational media among Higher Secondary teachers. The data were collected by using questionnaire as an instrument. Primary data were collected by conducting direct structured interview using questionnaire. All the respondents were asked the same questions in the same fashion and they were informed the purpose of study. t-test, One way ANOVA analysis, correlation analysis were applied to test the hypotheses. The findings and observations are the result and outcome of the interpretations made during the study of analysis. The result found that the average level of awareness of educational media among Higher Secondary teachers.

"Audio – visual aids are the different types of tools that appeal to the senses of learning and vision and are used in classroom for presentation of abstract information". Almost every educational reformer has expressed deep concern over excessive use of words that carry the shadow of meaning but not the substance. Several educationists have suggested making education realistic. About three centuries ago, Comenius (1976) prepared first "visualized" text book which contained some 150 pictures. "let the pictures be a source of delight to the children and let them become familiar with them before they enter school" was his theory. Later Rousseau (1712-1778) criticized the teaching of his days and condemned the liberal use of words by teachers. According to him the teaching process must be directed to the learner's natural curiosity. Rousseau's theory was put into action by Pestalozzi (1756-1827) in his 'object method'. His idea was to base instruction on sense perception. Although attempts on the use of concrete aids were made sporadically, intensive development in audio – visual education has been going on successfully of using motion films and by 1929 sound films was produced. Today it has been proved beyond doubt by research and classroom experience that audio-visual aids can contribute effectively in learning. These materials may be used to convey meaning without complete dependence on verbal symbols or language. Some audiovisual activities like filed trip, demonstrating an experiment etc. are in the nature of process or experience. Some like motion film or filmstrip need a projector to handle it. Some others like chart need no equipment and can be directly used. Experiences of this type will be classified under visual category. Magnetic tape or disc recordings belongs to audio category, hence 'a-v' aids designated in common usage means both process and material things.

The present era is an information technology era. Now-a-day the students are more aware of latest technological advancement. In olden days, teachers generally used oral method of teaching as well as they used black board for writing purpose. But these things were not given much more concentration to the students. Teachers faced a lot of problems to create attention among the students.

Number of researchers found that in comparing, Audio and Video method of teaching will attract the students as well as to motivate the students to concentrate more. Based on the concept, the present researches focus to know the teachers awareness educational media.

In the present technological world, a lot of Audio Visual aids are designed and used by the teachers to teach the subjects effectively. Generally, computers, Television, LCD's (Liquid Crystal Display) and OHP (over Head Projector) are the common educational media used by the teachers for teaching. Computers play an important role to access any kind of latest information within a short time as well as any individual can search any type of information throughout the globe. It is very easy to learn new informative technique when compared to the traditional methods. Efforts are also very less using this technique. Both teachers and students are able to know up to date information easily. Considering all this advantages educational media are very important for students and teachers to learn.

Even though teachers used these aids but there is a necessity to measure the teachers awareness of educational media and their perception of media based education. Only by knowing the teachers can enhance their method of teaching. In this concept, the present research title is significant and needed for the study.

Review of Literature

Rama and Kumar (2007) described in detail, various dimensions of LAN to internet in education through educational media. They pointed out the local area network (LAN) to provide the concept of integrated learning, system where by a central file server can provide random access and interactivity in learning WAN promote the concept of integrated learning system where by a central file server can provide random access and interactivity in learning. Wide Area Networks (WAN) concept would be needed for multi campus as inter institutional environment when internet and intranet faculties would be needed larger band width, fiber optic lives for the internet and intranet enable to transmit full video broad casting. Internet provides information and instructional services within organization. An internet would be capable of communication between the organization faculty, library students and other seminars, transforming sessions, research presentation, guest lectures, silent development course of orientation programmes and can be held of interests since the www is accessible through the internet only if may be installed to extend seminar, short and long term courses along with a variety of extracurricular activities in addition.

Kumar (2007) reported that the recent innovation in information technology have revolutions the mean of instruction within and outside institution. LAN (Local Area Network) brought in the concept of integrated learning system where by a central file servers can provide random access and interactivity in learning. The internet and intranet enable them to transmit full view broad casting. Intranets provide information and instructional services within organization.

Bansal and Chaudhary (2008) found that interactive radio has a great potential to support learning at a distance. Being an easily accessible and cost effective medium, IGNOU (Indira Gandhi National Open University) now started an interactive radio project for the students of management and bachelor preparatory programme. The objective of the project was to interact within the students in their own language and share experiences with them the effectiveness interactive radio instruction was evaluated and reported in this paper.

The students appreciated interactive radio sessions as effective inputs to accomplish the course objectives. Besides students enrolled with other institutions and enlightened public also participated in the session. The study revealed that student's participation in the interactive radio sessions was higher than the teleconferences and face to face personal contact sessions. The project can be replicated in other areas also, with systematic planning, implementation and monitoring.

Shivanekar (2008) reported that powerful computer networks enabling access to the data bases may however turn information into a real utility after an integrated service of e-mail and conferencing, advertising and news, information access to a range of key database and so on. To link every school in the nation, every public library, every university and every other educational or cultural institution to one massive communication network meeting all the communication and information differentiate needs of all the members may be called education utility.

Jamtshio (2008) discussed the distance education course for in service primary at the National Institute of Education (NIE) in Samtse, Bhutan. It is the fast and the only distance education, teacher have same syllabus and appear for the same term-end examination. The distance learners attend compulsory residential contact programme. The distance education programme needs systematic planning and monitoring to impart knowledge and skills to the teachers.

Baheerathan M, (2008) studied the awareness of educational media among the teachers of mathematics at high school level in Tanjavur district. He reported that the internet awareness among the students of mathematics at high school level is not sufficient. Also he found that the gender of the teachers and the locale and the management of the schools where they are working caused no significant difference in respect of their awareness of educational media.

Singh (2008) took up a study to see the effectiveness of educational media in teaching mathematics. He found that students significantly higher than those taught through the conventional method.

Jeyamani (2009) developed a computer assisted instruction (CAI) package in physics for class XI students. The experimental group received, CAI and after the experiment it was found that the experimental group performed better on the post test. The differences were insignificant in terms of sex and medium of instruction.

Gunawatdena (2009) discussed the use of technology for quality improvement in the distance education programme. The study is based on data gathered for teacher education programmes, which has implication for other open universities too.

Huang and Aloi (2010) investigated the impact of using interactive video in teaching general biology. Biology undergraduate students using a computer-assisted interactive videodisc system which included dissection simulations performed significantly better than students who had not used the computer-aided instruction.

Kalimuthu (2010) developed a video programme on environmental pollution in biology for higher secondary students and investigated whether students in higher secondary schools, who are taught environmental pollution in biology by the video method, achieve more than those who are taught by the traditional method. The major findings were that the higher secondary students taught through the video programme learnt more of the concepts on environmental pollution than those who were taught by the lecture method. The higher secondary students improved their performance in environmental pollution after viewing the video programme.

Wagh (2011) developed a multi-media instructional system for remedial measures for class VIII students, in fractional numbers. The multi-instructional system contains charts, flash cards, film-strips, audio-cassettes, assignments, and a self-learning programme. The results revealed that the Traditional Instructional System (TIS) and the (MIS) remedial approaches both helped students in improving their performance on all the six computational skills in fractional numbers.

Beerman, Brown and Evans (2011) found that there was a significant benefit of new technologies, as opposed to traditional texts, and hence it is better to allow students to learn in their own style and at their own pace. An additional argument is that CD-ROM provides media and visually rich material that is more likely to correspond effectively with students' individual learning styles.

Senthil Kumar K, (2011) studied the educational media knowledge of higher secondary chemistry students. He found that the media knowledge possessed by the first year higher secondary students is not high. Also he reported that, the girls have relatively high media knowledge when compared to boys in general.

Objective

To find out the awareness of educational media among Higher Secondary teachers of Thiruvannamalai District and their perception of Media based Education of the entire and its sub samples.

Methodology

The methodology adopted for the study is explained in detail. The sampling technique, size of the sample, variables of the study, description of the tool used and administration of tool are elaborated.

Method of Data Collection

The investigator personally distributed the questionnaires to each member of the randomly selected sample. They were requested to answer the items in the booklet as per the instructions provided at the beginning of each questionnaire. Confidentiality of response was assured. The questionnaires were collected by the investigator from the teachers. The responses were scored as per the scoring key of the respective questionnaire. Then the results were tabulated, analysed and discussed.

Sample

The investigator prepared a representative random sample of Higher Secondary teachers in different schools at Thiruvannamalai District. A sample of 200 teachers was finally selected.

Data Collection

Primary data, required for the present research work were collected by conducting direct interviews using questionnaire. All the respondents were given sufficient information about the study.

These respondents were provided with the same questionnaires. They were also informed that they have to answer in the same fashion.

Statistical Tools for Analysis

The following tools statistical tools were used for the analysis of data. t-test, ANOVA analysis and correlation analysis.

Analysis and Interpretation

Table 1

Showing Mean, SD and F-test for respondent about educational media awareness among Higher Secondary teachers on the basis of Academic qualification

Academic qualification	N	Mean	SD	F-value	Level of Significance
M.A. B.Ed.	54	72.26	9.37	3.24	0.01
M.Sc. B.Ed.	48	72.89	8.84		
M.Com. B.Ed.	98	69.00	7.08		
Total	200	71.78	8.58		

Hypothesis : Teachers do not differ in their educational media awareness among higher secondary teachers on the basis of Academic qualification.

The calculated F-value (3.24), which is significant at 0.01 level, confirms that there is a significant difference in their educational media awareness among higher secondary teachers on the basis of Academic qualification. Hence the stated hypothesis is rejected.

Table 2

Showing Mean, SD and t-test for respondent about educational media awareness among Higher Secondary teachers on the basis of Designation

Designation	N	Mean	SD	t-value	Level of Significance
PG Teachers	132	72.08	9.22	2.34	0.01
BT Teachers	68	69.33	5.18		

Hypothesis: Teachers do not differ in their educational media awareness among higher secondary teachers on the basis of Designation.

The calculated t-value (2.34), which is significant at 0.01 level, confirms that there is a significant difference in educational media awareness among higher secondary teachers on the basis of Designation. Hence the stated hypothesis is rejected. So PG Teachers have high level of educational media awareness than BT teachers.

Table 3

Showing Mean, SD and F-test for respondent about educational media awareness among Higher Secondary teachers on the basis of Type of Institution

Type of Institution	N	Mean	SD	F-value	Level of Significance
Govt.	58	70.31	4.09	3.42	0.01
Govt. Aided	68	71.30	9.56		
Self-Financing	74	74.29	9.75		
Total	200	71.78	8.58		

Hypothesis : Teachers do not differ in their educational media awareness among higher secondary teachers on the basis of Type of Institution.

The calculated F-value (3.42), which is significant at 0.01 level, confirms that there is a significant difference in their educational media awareness among higher secondary teachers on the basis of Type of Institution. Hence the stated hypothesis is rejected.

Table 4

Showing Mean, SD and F-test for respondent about educational media awareness among Higher Secondary teachers on the basis of Teaching Experience

Teaching Experience	N	Mean	SD	F-value	Level of Significance
Below 10 years	67	69.20	9.64	3.62	0.01
11 – 20 years	88	71.75	4.19		
Above 20 years	45	75.00	8.60		
Total	200	71.78	8.58		

Hypothesis : Teachers do not differ in their educational media awareness among higher secondary teachers on the basis of Teaching experience.

The calculated F-value (3.62), which is significant at 0.01 level, confirms that there is a significant difference in their educational media awareness among higher secondary teachers on the basis of Teaching experience. Hence the stated hypothesis is rejected.

Table 5

Showing Mean, SD and F-test for respondent about media perception evaluation among Higher Secondary teachers on the basis of Academic qualification

Academic qualification	N	Mean	SD	F-value	Level of Significance
M.A. B.Ed.	54	92.42	9.69	3.42	0.01
M.Sc. B.Ed.	48	92.24	9.24		
M.Com. B.Ed.	98	99.00	8.24		
Total	200	91.81	7.24		

Hypothesis : Teachers do not differ in their media perception evaluation among higher secondary teachers on the basis of Academic qualification.

The calculated F-value (3.42), which is significant at 0.01 level, confirms that there is a significant difference in their media perception evaluation among higher secondary teachers on the basis of Academic qualification. Hence the stated hypothesis is rejected.

Table 6

Showing Mean, SD and t-test for respondent about media perception evaluation among Higher Secondary teachers on the basis of Designation

Designation	N	Mean	SD	t-value	Level of Significance
PG Teachers	132	92.26	9.48	2.22	0.01
BT Teachers	68	98.42	5.36		

Hypothesis: Teachers do not differ in their media perception evaluation among higher secondary teachers on the basis of Designation.

The calculated t-value (2.22), which is significant at 0.01 level, confirms that there is a significant difference in media perception evaluation among higher secondary teachers on the basis of Designation. Hence the stated hypothesis is rejected. So BT Teachers have high level of media perception evaluation than PG teachers.

Table 7

Showing Mean, SD and F-test for respondent about media perception evaluation among Higher Secondary teachers on the basis of Type of Institution

Type of Institution	N	Mean	SD	F-value	Level of Significance
Govt.	58	90.24	4.29	3.92	0.01
Govt. Aided	68	91.29	9.29		
Self-Financing	74	94.65	9.36		
Total	200	91.81	7.24		

Hypothesis : Teachers do not differ in their media perception evaluation among higher secondary teachers on the basis of Type of Institution.

The calculated F-value (3.92), which is significant at 0.01 level, confirms that there is a significant difference in their media perception evaluation among higher secondary teachers on the basis of Type of Institution. Hence the stated hypothesis is rejected.

Table 8

Showing Mean, SD and F-test for respondent about media perception evaluation among Higher Secondary teachers on the basis of Teaching Experience

Teaching Experience	N	Mean	SD	F-value	Level of Significance
Below 10 years	67	99.22	9.24	3.94	0.01
11 – 20 years	88	91.24	5.29		
Above 20 years	45	95.21	7.21		
Total	200	91.81	7.24		

Hypothesis : Teachers do not differ in their media perception evaluation among higher secondary teachers on the basis of Teaching experience.

The calculated F-value (3.94), which is significant at 0.01 level, confirms that there is a significant difference in their media perception evaluation among higher secondary teachers on the basis of Teaching experience. Hence the stated hypothesis is rejected.

The above table shows correlation between educational media awareness and media perception evaluation among Higher Secondary teachers. Result shows that there is a positive and significant correlation between educational media awareness and media perception evaluation.

Suggestions

The following suggestions are arrived from the research findings. Research found that use of educational media will contribute more in student's achievement. Also the result reveals that use of awareness educational media increases the memory power, concentration. Further it sharpens the intelligence. Apart from that it reduces misconception in learning. So, the present research suggested that in all schools and colleges, the students advised to use of educational media compulsory. The education department forms a rule for that and advises the educational institutions make a step to establish separate infrastructure for this one. Also the Government take a step to use media based teaching effectively students in their academic. This will definitely help the students to be a good learner imbibing the concepts.

Conclusion

The present study awareness of educational media among Higher Secondary teachers of Thiruvannamalai district and their perception of media based education. For that the researcher framed some objectives. On the basis of objectives, a questionnaire is framed. After framing the questionnaire, these are circulated to the selected samples. 200 samples were selected randomly. The responses were collected and coded using computerised. To test the hypotheses and characteristics of the data, some standard statistical tools were used. The statistical tools such as t-test, F-ratio and correlation were used. From the analysis the result concluded that the Higher Secondary teachers have favourable of educational media and their perception of media based education.

Reference

1. Agostinho, Hedberg and Lefoe (2008), "Advanced Educational Technology", New Delhi : Knishka Publishers distribution.
2. Baheerathan M, (2008) "Teach the Internet in a week". New Delhi: Prentice Hall of India Private Limited.
3. Bansal and Chaudhary (2008) "The Internet invasion of how wills the teachers educator cope" New Delhi: Journal of higher education".
4. Beerman, K., Brown, G., & Evans, M. (2011). Interactive CD study modules in food science and Human Nutrition: Assessing Technology-Enhanced study programs. *Journal of Educational Multimedia and Hypermedia, 7(4): 365-374.*
5. Charag (2011), "Practice Experiences of CD-Rom based language learning", British Journal of Educational technology, vol.30, page 153-175, Oxford Blackwell.
6. Coneia (2010), "Computer and language learning", International Journal, page no 15-68.
7. Fetterman (2008), Asia and the Pacific programme of educational in Innovation for development (APEID), page 15-82 UNESCO Regional offices for education in Asia and the Pacific.
8. Gunawatdena (2009), "Quantitative Techniques and Operations Research" Thiruvananthapuram : Yamuna publications.
9. Hexel, Marcellus and Berwoull (2008). "The concept and problem of Networking in educational research" The experience of Ernesa, Networking in educational research. Proceeding of the Boleswa Education Research Symposium, University of Swaziland.

10. Huang, S. D., & Aloi, J. (2010). The impact of using interactive video in teaching general biology. *The American Biology Teacher, 53(5): 281-284.*

11. Jamtshio (2008) "Living in the information age" Vadodara: Premise and Implication for school education programme, Challenges in School Education.

12. Jeyamani (2009). "The concept and problem of Networking in educational research" The experience of Ernesa, Networking in educational research. Proceeding of the Boleswa Education Research Symposium, University of Swaziland.

13. Johnson (2009), "Education, Its Philosophy, Psychology and Technology" Thrissur : Breeze publications.

14. Jonasson (2008), "Mastering the Internet", USA: International Journal of Information Technology and Communication.

15. Kalimuthu, T. (2010). Developing a video programme on environmental pollution in biology for higher secondary students. *Fifth Survey of Research in Education, Vol. II, p.1377.*

16. Koeppen and Andre (2011), "Quantitative Techniques and Operations Research" USA: Yamuna publications.

17. Kumar (2007) "A Study of Utilisation of Internet by the Students of Higher Education", M.Ed Dissertation, Annamalai University.

18. Lee (2009), "Third survey of researcher in education and development", Baroda.

19. Medina (2011) "Cognitive and Affective Attitude of Teachers Towards Computer", Experiments in Education, 30 (2), pp.7-12.

20. Rama and Kumar (2007) "Cognitive and Affective Attitude of Teachers Towards Computer", Experiments in Education, 30 (2), pp.7-12.

21. Senthil Kumar K, (2011): "New Approach to Information Technology Education", Compendium on Information Technology on Science Education.

22. Shivanekar (2008). "Introduction of Educational Technology", New Delhi, Sterling Publishers Pvt. Ltd.
23. Singh (2008) "Introduction to educational technology, Sterility Publishers", New Delhi : Private Limited.
24. Stefansdottir (2007) "The Internet Complete Reference; Second Edition", New Delhi: Tata McGraw-Hill Company Limited".
25. Teles and Rylands (2011) "Living in the information age" Vadodara: Premise and Implication for school education programme, Challenges in School Education.
26. Wagh, S. K. (2011). Development of a multimedia instructional system for remedial measures in fractional numbers. *Fifth Survey of Research in Education, Vol. II, pp.1299.*

28

Designing Learning Environment Tomorrow

Education is the foundation of our nation. It is one of the pillars of society and a tool of building our nation. The global is changing very dramatically and quickly and it is unavoidable to produce our young generation to compete with technology world. To achieve this we have to modernise our learning environment with new tools and strategies. Nowadays most of the percentage of our teaching – learning method is a traditional one. Even though our government takes many steps and form educational commissions to improve our teaching – learning method, there is no change or improvement in our learning methodology. Our 'sit and get' approach to learning is not an effective way to reach our goals. There are only two basic purposes for educating children. One is, making more value to them, and the second is making more value to others. But we are failed to create valuable children. Because schools in our country is really like a factory and the faculties are the workers and the students are the products. The factory opens with the ringing bell sharply at 8.30 AM and the workers starts to produce the mark scoring machines and Xerox machines as a product and the factory closes with a long bell after 4.00 PM and over time goes for X and XII students. In the year ending the quality of the product was tested through examinations and labelled.

Another problem is Homework. When we handle it properly it will be an important tool of success. The values of homework are Responsibility, Independence, Perseverance, Time management, self reliance and resourcefulness. But what we are doing? In most of time the assignments are used as punishments. We are asking them to copy the content from the text books, in the class work note and then it in the homework note. If we were giving project work means, it is only for the parent and beneficial to stationeries shops.

The ingestion of the compulsory study leads to the production of mentally depressed and physically weak children which makes an unhealthy society and nation. Most of our children hate our school system because of its boredom traditional method. Our only goal is to get centum result and scoring centum marks. So, development life skills, moral values, social integration etc are loss, and these leads to the production of weak generation. So, to avoid this and to develop positive attitude on learning and to develop interest towards the education we have to design the tomorrows learning environment with educational technology.

Our education system need to improve the quality of education through Information technology, when it integrated into the curriculum it revolutionizes the learning process. The technology integration in the curriculum improves students learning process and their outcomes. Technology help to make ease of the students and teachers roles and relationships. Students alone take responsibility for their learning outcomes. Here the teacher acts as a guide and facilitator. The teachers have to be trained in using the technologies and implement in their teaching methods. If the students learn by using these technology based learning, they can become creators and critics instead of just consumers.

The technology integrated curriculum is essential for today's students to have

1. Personal and social responsibility

2. Planning, critical thinking, reasoning and creativity
3. Strong communications skills
4. Cross – cultural understanding
5. Visualizing and decision making
6. Knowledge in using the technology

By adopting Modern Learning Methods (MLM) can facilitate the learning.

1. Collaborative learning
2. Integrated learning
3. Blended learning
4. Flipped model class room
5. Using interactive technology
6. ICT in education etc

The suggestions for Teachers in designing the learning environment.

1. The teacher has to play new role of mentoring, coaching and helping students in their studies rather than spoon feeding in the class room.
2. The teachers can guide and coach the students to improve the ways of learning, promote their ability and skills of applying their learning in real situations
3. Developing self – learning habits at their own pace and time
4. Diagnose the learning problem of students and the teachers can prepare learning material according to them to overcome their problem
5. Students are having individual differences in their learning process. On the basis of this the teacher have to create the learning environment according to their pace and time individually
6. They can interact with individual students or a small group of students according to their learning ability. Through this

they can help and facilitate students learning in an effective manner

7. The teacher while planning any lesson, should think of the method or using technology, results in making class instruction dynamic and effective
8. The teachers have to deliver their teaching with concern of students. They should avoid to deliver their lectures without any concern of students and they have to change their attitude in completing the syllabus and the aim of showing centum result by squeezing the children
9. The methods of evaluation system also have to reform. The works given for FA should be modified. The teachers have to choose the projects for the students should be appropriate to their ability. It should include realistic task that generalized the students learning and its application in new situations and not burden to parents.
10. The teachers should be the role model of the children. They should rich in good behaviour, humanism and moral values.

The suggestions for Parents in designing the learning environment.

1. The parents should have the awareness on education. They should know that education is not the amount of information that is put into the brain but the primary tool to achieve the power of mind. They should avoid treating the child as a miniature of adult.
2. Mostly the middle class educated parents were only comparing their children with others. They want to mould them what they wish to be. They feel proud to show that their children were engaged with extracurricular activities throughout the day, weak, month and the year. But they are forgetting to realize that they are fail in creating a physically and mentally healthy child. So, that only after their school education most of the children becomes opposite to their parents. So, the parent should give importance to their children's decisions. They should be a friend, guide and counsellor to their children.

3. They should change their attitude that the school, which makes the children engaged throughout the day i.e., giving heavy homework, is the best school. They can avoid pulling them into the Tuition centers. They should accept their child's capacity of learning and facilitate them easy learning methods and spend at least an hour per day and chat with them about their that day's experience .
4. They should realize that the marks are not the yard sticks to measure their child's knowledge and wisdom and have to change their attitude that the centum scoring children were brilliant and others were not.
5. They should consider their child's opinions, and respect them. They should create their mind set to accept the real status of their children. This makes the children, mentally free and they can achieve what they want to be and they desire.
6. Parent should give importance to their physical and spiritual development. They should give importance in promoting the behavioural qualities humanism and they should be a role model

The suggestions for Administration in designing the learning environment

1. The management plays an important role in enhancing quality in education
2. The management should support and adopt the changes, suggestions and recommendations given by the government
3. Quality of education depends upon the quality of teachers and the quality of infrastructure. So, the management should introduce the modern technology inventions and discoveries which enhance the personality of the children.
4. The management should take care in creating a valuable child instead of producing the best product of their school.
5. The management should update the faculties by giving in-service training and encourage the best teachers by recognising them and honouring with rewards and awards

and this will help them to be active, innovative and work with interest.

6. The management should give importance in promoting the humanism, moral values, ethics, life skill and social skills of the children.
7. The management should consider the income of the parents, intelligence and creativity of the student and facilitate their fee structure. They can encourage the innovative children by adopting them and provide the facilities to develop their research attitude.
8. Parent should give importance to the physical and spiritual development of their children. They should give importance in promoting the behavioural qualities humanism and they should be a role model.

The suggestions for Government in designing the learning environment

1. The government should recognise that the teachers are the backbone of educational system and architects in designing the new nation which have to compete with this Technology Era.
2. They should begin to modernise the education system from the primary level. They should insist the school, first to change the learning environment of KGs'. All of us know that the physical development of the children is not fulfilling at the age of three. But we are compelling to read, write and to do the sums. We are breaking the fingers of the sapling by giving written works. We are stealing their childhood happiness. So, the government should restrict all these things and should limit their study hours and school hours. The infrastructure of the classrooms should be modified. They are keeping the name of Kinder Garden and are not following the Frobel's thoughts.
3. Then the study hours of primary level. Up to Third standard it is enough to develop the Reading, writing, speaking skills

and doing simple maths like knowing the numerals, tables' additions, subtractions, multiplications and divisions. Along with this the basic of computer science. Instead of giving free bags, books, notebooks, writing materials ect., to them it is best to provide them desktops. Now the government is implementing the ABL method. The bitter truth we have to accept is that there is no use of it. Most of the children at Sixth standard in government schools not able to read and write, but exceptions are there, but it is rare. They are not even known the alphabetic. So, the teaching – learning methodology should be changed and Modern Learning Method should be introduced.

4. From Fourth standard the science and social science can be introduced. The science subject should be teaches by learning and doing method. It should be alive. The social science should teach by using smart board, because we can use pen drives, modems to connect internet etc. There should be at least one spacious smart class room per primary school which can be utilised for all sections. This will reduce the burden of teaching and the children can actively take part in this. Instead of giving assignments the projects can given for them according to their individual differences. Through this method the teacher will have enough time to plan and think the method of teaching using technology which results in making class instruction dynamic and effective. Along with this we should give importance for moral education and games. Through this we can make a strong basement, and create physically and mentally healthy children.

5. For secondary and Higher secondary education the system should be completely modernized. The modern teaching techniques should be handled according to their level. Learning by doing methods, Seminars, team teaching methods can be followed. Importance should give for extra-curricular activities, life skills and research in science and technology. When the Public examination system is completely abolished mean, then automatically the production of mark scoring

machines will be stopped. Yearly once compulsory exhibitions should be conducted in each and every school and prizes should be distributed for the innovations.

6. The government should reduce the burden of teachers. Nowadays the teachers in the government schools are concentrating in completing the Records and not in teaching. They are telling that their superiors are giving the first preference for the record completion. So, they have to concentrate in doing the office works. The government should minimize the non academic work of teachers.
7. Instead of conducting eligibility test for recruiting teachers, they can create quality teachers by selecting the students by conducting eligibility test for the Teachers education and to give recognition for the colleges with modernized infrastructure and well equipped classrooms. The government should strictly follow rules and regulations without any compromise. During teaching practice the students are not taking practice in teaching but being as a teacher. The teachers were going in medical leave and in many schools due to insufficient teachers, the trainees are compelled to handle the subjects other than their major subjects and insist to complete the syllabus and to complete the official works of their Guide teacher. So, the aim of teaching practice is not achieved. The curriculum for the teacher education also should be reformed according to the school curriculum.

Conclusion

There is an old saying,

I hear I forget

I see I remember

I do I understand

Yesterday and today's teaching learning method is based on I hear and I see. But tomorrow's learning environment should designed as I do I understand. For this the education should integrated with technology. Technologies will increase the teaching learning process.

Tomorrow will be an era of Technology. So, making the student cantered learning as a technological cantered learning we can promote our standard equal to the standard of developed countries and construct a progressive and prosperous nation.

29

Edu-Digital Skill

Introduction

To excel in today's digital world, students need to know how to use technology to explore, acquire knowledge, analyze and evaluate information, test ideas, and draw conclusions. We believe the following sets of skills are essential for the 21st century and we've developed digital learning solutions that help students develop these skills:

1. Technology Operations and Concepts: Students understand how to use technology systems safely, effectively, and productively.
2. Critical Thinking and Problem Solving: Students are able to interpret, analyze, and evaluate new information. They can solve non-familiar problems in conventional and innovative ways.
3. Communication and Collaboration: Students listen effectively and can formulate and disseminate their own thoughts and ideas. They are able to effectively work with others to accomplish a common goal.

4. Creativity and Innovation: Students are confident at brainstorming, developing new ideas, and acting on their creative ideas to make them tangible.
5. Research and Information Fluency: Students are able to gather and evaluate information. They can communicate using the most effective forms of media.
6. Digital Citizenship: Students practice safe, legal, and ethical online behaviour. They understand cultural and societal issues related to technology and etiquette.

Digital literacy and 21st-century skills

Digital literacy requires certain skill sets that are interdisciplinary in nature. Warshauer and Matuchniak list information, media, and technology; learning and innovation skills; and life and career skills as the three skill sets that individuals need to master in order to be digitally literate, or the 21st-century skills. In order to achieve information, media, and technology skills, one needs to achieve competency in information literacy, media literacy and ICT (information communicative technologies). Encompassed within Learning and Innovation Skills, one must also be able to be able to be exercise their creativity and innovation, critical thinking and problem solving, and communication and collaboration skills. In order to be competent in Life and Career Skills, it is also necessary to be able to exercise flexibility and adaptability, initiative and self-direction, social and cross-cultural skills, productivity and accountability, leadership and responsibility. Eshet-Alkalai contends that there are five types of literacies that are encompassed in the umbrella term that is digital literacy.

1. Photo-visual literacy is the ability to read and deduce information from visuals.
2. Reproduction literacy is the ability to use digital technology to create a new piece of work or combine existing pieces of work together to make it your own.
3. Branching literacy is the ability to successfully navigate in the non-linear medium of digital space.

4. Information literacy is the ability to search, locate, assess and critically evaluate information found on the web.
5. Socio-emotional literacy refers to the social and emotional aspects of being present online, whether it may be through socializing, and collaborating, or simply consuming content.

Use in education

Schools are continuously updating their curriculum for digital literacy to keep up with accelerating technological developments. This often includes computers in the classroom, the use of educational software to teach curriculum, and course materials being made available to students online. Some classrooms are designed to use smart boards and audience response systems. These techniques are most effective when the teacher is digitally literate as well.

Teachers often teach digital literacy skills to students who use computers for research. Such skills include verifying credible sources online and how-to cite web sites. Google and Wikipedia are used by students "for everyday life research."

Educators are often required to be certified in digital literacy to teach certain software and, more prevalently, to prevent plagiarism amongst students.

Digital natives and immigrants

Marc Prensky invented and popularized the terms "digital native" and "digital immigrant." A digital native, according to Prensky, is one who was born into the digital age. A digital immigrant refers to one who adopts technology later in life. These terms aid in understanding the issues of teaching digital literacy, however, simply being a digital native does not make one digitally literate.

Digital immigrants, although they adapt to the same technology as natives, possess a sort of "accent" which restricts them from communicating the way natives do. In fact, research shows that, due to the brain's malleable nature, technology has changed the way today's students read, perceive, and process information. This means that today's educators may struggle to find effective teaching methods for digital natives. Digital immigrants might resist teaching digital literacy because they themselves weren't taught that way. Prensky believes this is a problem because today's students are "a population that speaks an entirely new language" than the people who educate them.

Digital visitors and residents

In contrast to Marc Prensky, Dave White from the Department for Continuing Education at the University of Oxford has been publicising his concept of digital visitors and residents. Briefly, the concept is that visitors leave no online social trace where as residents live a portion of their lives online. These are not two separate categories of people but rather a description of a continuum of behaviours. It is probable that many individuals demonstrate both visitor and residential behaviours in different contexts. Dave White has developed a mapping tool which explores this concept.

Digital writing

Digital writing is a new type of composition being taught increasingly within universities. Digital writing is a pedagogy focused on technology's impact on writing environments; it is not simply using a computer to write. Rather than the traditional print perspective, digital writing enables students to explore modern technologies and learn how different writing spaces affect the meaning, audience, and readability of text. Educators in favour of digital writing argue that it is necessary because "technology fundamentally changes how writing is produced, delivered, and received."[10] The goal of teaching digital writing is that students will increase their ability to produce a relevant, high-quality product, instead of just a standard academic paper.

One aspect of digital writing is the use of hypertext. As opposed to printed text, hypertext invites readers to explore information in a non-linear fashion. Hypertext consists of traditional text and hyperlinks that send readers to other texts. These links may refer to related terms or concepts (such is the case on Wikipedia), or they may enable readers to choose the order in which they read. The process of digital writing requires the composer to make unique "decisions regarding linking and omission." These decisions "give rise to questions about the author's responsibilities to the [text] and to objectivity."

Use in society

Digital literacy helps people communicate and keep up with societal trends. Literacy in social network services and Web 2.0 sites helps people stay in contact with others, pass timely information and even sell goods and services. This is mostly popular among younger generations, though sites like LinkedIn have made it valuable to older professionals. Digital literacy can also prevent people from believing hoaxes that are spread online or are the result of photo manipulation. E-mail frauds and phishing often take advantage of the digitally illiterate, costing victims money and making them vulnerable to identity theft. Research has demonstrated that the differences in the level of digital literacy depend mainly on age and education level, while the influence of gender is decreasing(Hargittai, 2002; van Dijk, 2005; van Dijk and van Deursen, 2009). Among young people, in particular, digital literacy is high in its operational dimension (e.g. rapidly move through hypertext, familiarity with different kinds of online resources) while the skills to critically evaluate content found online show a deficit (Gui and Argentin, 2011).

Building on digital literacy is the concept of digital creativity which is the expression of creative skills in the digital medium. This can include programming, web sites and the generation and manipulation of digital images.

Social networking

With the emergence of social networking, one who is digitally literate now has a major voice online.[13] The level of digital literacy needed to voice an opinion online today compared to the Internet before social networks is minute. Websites like Facebook and Twitter, as well as personal websites and blogs have enabled a new type of journalism that is subjective, personal, and "represents a global conversation that is connected through its community of readers." [14] These online communities foster group interactivity among the digitally literate. Social networks also help users establish a digital identity, or a "symbolic digital representation of identity attributes."[15]

Without digital literacy or the assistance of someone who is digitally literate, one cannot possess a personal digital identity.

The digital divide

Digital literacy and digital access have become increasingly important competitive differentiators. Bridging the economic and developmental divides is in large measure a matter of increasing digital literacy and access for peoples who have been left out of the information and communications technology (ICT) revolutions. Scholar Howard Besser contends that the digital divide is more than just a gap between those who have access to technology and those who don't. This issue encompasses aspects such as information literacy, appropriateness of content, and access to content. Beyond access, a digital divide exists between those who apply critical thinking to technology or not, those who speak English or not, and those who create digital content or merely consume it. Research published in 2012 found that the digital divide, as defined by access to information technology, does not exist amongst youth in the United States. Young people of all races and ethnicities report being connected to the internet at rates of 94-98%.There remains, however, a Civic Opportunity Gap, where youth from poorer families and those attending lower socioeconomic status schools are less likely to encounter opportunities to apply their digital literacies toward civic ends.

Community Informatics overlaps to a considerable degree with digital literacy by being concerned with ensuring the opportunity not only for ICT access at the community level but also, according to Michael Gurstein, that the means for the "effective use" of ICTs for community betterment and empowerment are available. Digital literacy is of course, one of the significant elements in this process. The United Nations Global Alliance for ICT and Development (GAID) seeks to address this set of issues at an international and global level. Many organizations (e.g. *Per* Scholars for underserved communities in the United States and Interconnection for underserved communities around the world as well as the U.S.) focus on addressing this concern at national, local and community levels.

Digital citizenship (nine components)

1. Digital access: full electronic participation in society.
2. Digital commerce: electronic buying and selling of goods.
3. Digital communication: electronic exchange of information.
4. Digital literacy: process of teaching and learning about technology and the use of technology.
5. Digital etiquette: electronic standards of conduct or procedure.
6. Digital law: electronic responsibility for actions and deeds.
7. Digital rights and responsibilities: those freedoms extended to everyone in a digital world.
8. Digital health and wellness: physical and psychological well-being in a digital technology world.
9. Digital security (self-protection): electronic precautions to guarantee safety.

Global impact

Government officials around the world have emphasized the importance of digital literacy for their economy. According to Hot Chalk, an Online resource for educators: "Nations with centralized education systems, such as China, are leading the charge and implementing digital literacy training programs faster than anyone else. For those countries, the news is good."Many developing nations are also focusing on digital literacy education to compete globally. Economically, socially and regionally marginalized people have benefited from the ECDL Foundation's ECDL / ICDL programme through funding and support from Corporate Social Responsibility initiatives, international development agency funding and non-governmental organisations(NGO's).The Philippines' Education Secretary Jelly Lapus has emphasized the importance of digital literacy in Filipino education. He claims a resistance to change is the main obstacle to improving the nation's education in the globalized world. In 2008, Lapus was inducted into Certiport's "Champions of Digital Literacy" Hall of Fame for his work to emphasize digital literacy.[23]

Use in the workforce

Those who are digitally literate are more likely to be economically secure.[24] Many jobs require a working knowledge of computers and the Internet to perform basic functions. As wireless technology improves, more jobs require proficiency with cell phones and PDAs (sometimes combined into smart phones).White collar jobs are increasingly performed primarily on computers and portable devices. Many of these jobs require proof of digital literacy to be hired or promoted. Sometimes companies will administer their own tests to employees, or official certification will be required. As technology has become cheaper and more readily available, more blue-collar jobs have required digital literacy as well. Manufacturers and retailers, for example, are expected to collect and analyze data about productivity and market trends to stay competitive. Construction workers often use computers to increase employee safety. Job recruiters often use employment Web sites to find potential employees, thus magnifying the importance of digital literacy in securing a job.

Bibliography & Web sites referred

1. Jenkins, Henry (2009). *Confronting the Challenges of Participatory Culture: Media Education for the 21st Century.* Cambridge, MA: The MIT Press.
2. Selfe, Cynthia L. (1989). Redeûning literacy: The multi-layered grammar of computers. In Gail E. Hawisher & Cynthia L. Selfe (Eds.), Critical perspectives on computers and composition studies (pp. 3–15). New York: Teachers College Press
3. Warschauer, Mark; Tina Matuchniak (2010). "New Technology and Digital Worlds: Analyzing Evidence of Equity in Access, Use, and Outcomes". *Review of Research in Education* 34: 179–225. doi:10.3102/0091732X09349791.
4. "How College Students Seek Information in the Digital Age".
5. Prensky, Marc. "Digital Natives, Digital Immigrants". *On the Horizon.* MCB University Press. Retrieved 30 November 2011.
6. Carr, Nicholas. "Is Google Making Us Stupid?". Retrieved 30 November 2011.

7. http://firstmonday.org/ojs/index.php/fm/article/view/3171/3049
8. http://www.youtube.com/watch?v=0sFBadv04eY
9. http://www.youtube.com/watch?v=x9IMObcyKbo
10. WIDE Research Center Collective. "Why Teach Digital Writing?". Retrieved 30 November 2011.
11. Beers, Kylene (2007). *Adolescent Literacy.* Portsmouth: Heinemann.
12. McAdams, Mindy. "JEP: Hypertext". Retrieved 30 November 2011.

30

Empowering Digital age Learners in Creating innovative future Through Blended Learning in Higher Education

Introduction

Today's digital age learners are tomorrow's nation builders as well as policy makers. Therefore the education imparted to them must be innovative and updated in the digital era. Educational institutions are becoming increasingly aware that today's generation learners is different with the widening of success to education and greater exposure to technology, today's learners are not only much more diverse but more wired as well. Higher education leaders have the challenge to position their institutions for the twenty-first century. Added to this, the 21st century workplace also poses knowledge and skill demands that are different from the previous century. Educators have been cautioning that unless the challenges posed by this new education landscape, are addressed, they can result in dire consequences. Bored with traditional methods, this new generation learners may withdraw from studies and go in search of activities that are, more engaging and interactive. The need to revolutionize approaches to learning and teaching is therefore now more urgent than ever. This paper is to highlight the importance, benefits, models, new approaches and techniques of blended learning and how it is suitable for the digital age learners to empower them with advanced learning skills. The term Blended Learning has become a corporate buzzword. Blended Learning provides a 'good' mix of technologies and interaction, resulting in a socially supported, constructive, learning experience. The purpose here is to explore the concept of blended learning in a comprehensive yet coherent manner.

Higher education institutions must address changing expectations associated with the quality of the learning experience and the wave of technological innovations. It is beyond time that higher education institutions recognize the untenable position of holding onto past practices that are incongruent with the needs and demands of a knowledge society. The greatest possibility of recapturing the ideals of higher education is through redesigning blended learning. Blended learning is more than enhancing lecturers. It represents the transformation of how we approach teaching and learning. It is a complete rethinking and redesign of the educational environment and learning experience. Blended learning is a coherent design approach that openly assesses and integrates the strengths of face-to-face and online learning to address worthwhile educational goals. When blended learning is well understood and implemented, higher education will be transformed in a way not seen since the expansion of higher education in the late of 19th and 20th century. The challenge now is to gain a deep understanding of the need, potential, and strategies of blended learning to approach the ideals of higher education.

Blended Learning – An Overview

E-Learning has had an interesting impact on the learning environment. Although it represents tremendous potential in the way it could revolutionize learning and development, it has rapidly evolved into a concept of blended learning which, like its name suggests, blends online learning with more traditional methods of learning and development.

Blended learning is the most logical and natural evolution of our learning agenda. It suggests an elegant solution to the challenges of tailoring learning and development to the needs of individuals. It represents an opportunity to integrate the innovative and technological advances offered by online learning with the interaction and participation offered in the best of traditional learning. It can be supported and enhanced by using the wisdom and one-to-one contact of personal coaches. One of the most important factors in creating blended learning, solutions is to recognize where it fits in the broader context of organizational learning and development. The potential of blended learning is almost limitless and represents a naturally evolving process from traditional forms of learning to a personalized and focused development path.

Meaning and Definition of Blended Learning

Recognizing true blended learning is not obvious. Blended learning is the thoughtful fusion of face-to-face oral communication and online written communication that are optimally integrated such that the strengths of each are blended into a unique learning experience congruent with the context and mended educational purpose. Although the concept of blended learning may be intuitively apparent and simple, the practical application is more complex. Blended learning is not an addition that simply builds another expensive educational layer. It represents a restructuring of class contact hours with the goal to enhance engagement and to extend access to Internet-based learning opportunities. Most important, blended learning is a fundamental redesign that transforms the structure of, and approach to teaching and learning.

Blended learning emerges from an understanding of the relative strengths of face-to-face and online learning. This opens a wide range of possibilities for redesigning learning that goes beyond enhancing the traditional classroom lecture. Attaining the threshold of blended learning means replacing aspects of face-to-face learning with appropriate online learning experiences such as labs, simulations, tutorials and assessment. Blended learning represents a new approach and mix of classroom and online activities consistent with the goals of specific courses or programs. Blended learning brings into consideration a range of options that require revisiting how students learn in deep and meaningful ways.

Blended learning environment combines traditional face-to-face instruction with computer-mediated or online instruction. The term has become a corporate buzzword during the past few years (Lamb, 2001) Recently the American Society for training and Development identified blended learning as one of the top ten trends to emerge in the knowledge delivery industry in 2003 (cited by Rooney, 2003). As noted by Barbian (2002), Marc Rosenberg, author of E –Learning Strategies for Delivering knowledge in the Digital Age (2001) , has argued that "the question is not what we should blend.... rather the question is what are the ingredients that are to be Blended?". The key assumptions of blended learning designs are:

1. Thoughtfully integrating face-to-face and online learning.
2. Fundamentally rethinking the course design to optimize student engagement.
3. Restructuring and replacing traditional class contact hours.

Blended Learning in Higher Education

Blended Learning in Higher Education provides a vision and a roadmap for higher education students to understand the possibilities of organically blending face-to-face and online learning for engaging and meaningful learning experiences. Blended Learning provides an organizing framework to guide the exploration and understanding of the principles and practices needed to effect the much needed transformational changes in higher education. It also provides practical examples and organizational support structures required to fuse a range of face-to- face and online learning to meet the quality challenges and serve disciplinary goals effectively and efficiently.

The transformation of teaching and learning in higher education is inevitable with the use of Web-based communications technology (Newman, Couturier & Scurry, 2004). Fundamental redesign based on blended approaches to teaching and learning represent the means of address the challenges associated with providing a quality of learning experience. Although the catalyst for change in teaching and learning has been technology, it is the need to enhance quality standards that is drawing attention to the potential of blended approaches. Technology is an enabling tool. Because blended learning is an approach and design that merges the best of traditional and Web-based learning experiences to create and sustain vital communities of inquiry, many higher education institutions are quietly positioning themselves to harness its transformational potential.

Blended learning is at the center of an evolutionary transformation of teaching and learning in higher education. However, transformational growth can only be sustained with a clear understanding of the nature of the educational process and intended learning outcomes. The higher education there is an expressed focus on opportunities for learners to construct meaning and confirm understanding through discourse. At the core of this process is a community of inquiry and supports connection and collaboration among learners and creates a learning environment that integrates social, cognitive, and teaching elements in a way that will precipitate and sustain critical reflection and discourse. Blended learning opens the possibility of creating and sustaining a community of inquiry beyond the classroom.

Blended learning for Higher Education Learners will be

1. Highly interactive with practice exercises and activities
2. Less expensive, more flexible and more effective
3. Meeting the learners expectations for utilizing technology in learning skills
4. Developing independent learning skills
5. Offering increased flexibility and convenience
6. Providing better success to those with learning difficulty
7. Enhancing technical savvy

Six Models of Blended Learning

Blended Learning can be group into six distinct models based on the difference in teacher roles, physical space, delivery methods and scheduling. The six models of blended learning are:

* Face –to-face Driver
* Rotation
* Flex
* Online Lab
* Self-Blend
* Online Driver

1. *Face –to-face Driver:* Teacher deliver the content face-to-face and use online as a supplement.
2. *Rotation:* Within in a given course, the students rotate on a fixed time schedule between a self paced online learning and sitting in a classroom with a face-to-face teacher.
3. *Flex*: An online platform delivers most of the content. The teachers provide onsite as need support to the students in person through tutoring or small group sessions.
4. *Online Lab*: An online lab delivers entire course through online but under bricks and motor location. Often students who learn through online lab also take traditional courses.
5. *Self-Blend*: Students choose remote online courses to supplement their curriculum.
6. *Online Driver*: Through an online platform the teacher delivers the entire curriculum. Students work remotely or face-to-face check-in are available or mandatory.

Benefits in Blended Learning

1. Face to face learning is interactive and enjoyable.
2. Opportunities to learn from each other collaboratively in online mode.
3. There is collaboration in content as well as the mode of delivery which is innovative in nature.
4. Save time and paper, and provide feedback quickly to each learner.

5. Critical thinking is fostered.
6. Creative thinking processes are developed within a meaningful context.
7. Encourage lifelong learning.
8. Encourage learning across the curriculum by blending the boundaries of knowledge.
9. Research attitude in ignited and initiated.
10. Team work and collaborative leaning is fostered.
11. Proper utility of useful ICT resources.

Importance of Blended Learning

Learning requires some sort of experience to take place in learning environment which may be quite different for each learner in that we have to consider differences in (Banathy 1968):

1. Interest spans
2. Needs
3. Aptitudes
4. Achievements
5. Variations of time needed to master a specific learning task
6. Abilities to deal with abstractness or concreteness
7. Degree to which a learner needs to be guided
8. Abilities to deal with complexities
9. Abilities to manipulate objects (such as equipment or machines)
10. The degree to which imagination can be involved
11. Degree to motivate creativity
12. Problem solving differences.

Blended Learning: Trends and Innovative Approaches

Trends come and go, but quality education will last a lifetime. In Blended Learning, attendees learn what best practice blended learning trends are, and how they can help support personalization of learning for each unique student. Effective blended learning approaches are beneficial for both students and teachers. They share ideas for how to use these strategies to support student engagement and achievement, particularly in higher education. Learners gain knowledge about many blended learning topics, including:

1. Emerging blended learning techniques
2. Teaching and learning in an increasingly mobile world
3. How blended learning can boost achievement
4. The impact of blended learning on professional development

Conclusion

The term blended has many specific meanings based upon the context in which it is used. Blended Learning refers to a mixing of different learning environments in teaching and learning process. Blended Learning gives learners and teachers a potential environment to learn and teach more effectively than any other method of teaching. It offers learners the opportunity "to be both together and apart." A group of learners can interact at anytime and anywhere because of the benefits that computer-mediated educational tools provide. Blended Learning provides a 'good' mix of technologies and interaction, resulting in a socially supported, constructive, learning experience. Blended learning holds promise for every individual learner. Blended learning has been implemented in various formats in schools and higher education institutions in order to build and create a new revolution in this present digital age society. So practicing and applying blending learning in higher education for the present and future generations will no wonder take our educational system to its peek and which in turn is the vision and mission of every literary nation.

Reference

1. Anthony G. Picciano, Charles D. Dziuban, Charles R. Graham. (2005). *Research Perspectives in Blended Learning, Volume 2;* Mc Graw-Hill, New York.

2. Curtis J. Bonk, Charles R. Graham. (2008). The Handbook of Blended Learning: Global Perspectives, Local Designs, Australia.

3. Deanie French. (2010). *Blended Learning: An Ongoing Process for Internet Integration,* UK.

4. Helen Beetham, Rhona Sharpe. (2009). Rethinking Pedagogy for a Digital Age: Designing for 21st Century Learning; Mc Graw-Hill, New York.

5. Kaye Thorne. (2003). *Blended Learning: How to Integrate Online & Traditional Learning;* Kogan Page Publishers, Business & Economics-148 pages.

6. Randy D. Garrison, Norman D. Vaughan. (2008). *Blended Learning in Higher Education: Framework, Principles and Guidelines*; Jossey – Bass Publication, San Francisco.

7. Rooney, J.E. (2003). *Blended Learning Opportunities to enhance educational programming and Meetings.* Association Management, 55(5), 26-32.

31

Learning Without Limit

Creating Learning without limits builds on the learning without limit study by exploring the wider opportunities for enhancing the learning capacity of every child that become possible when a whole staff group works together to create an environment free from the limiting effects of ability labels and practices. When staff group replace the fatalism of ability labels with a more hopeful, powerful and empowering view of learners and learning. Learning process has continuity and is carried over through various steps. Limitless learning is achieved if we have curiosity to learn and effort to know about it. Mere, curiosity doesn't help a person learn and at the same time just effort doesn't get us effective learning. Learning has to be achieved through interest not as a burden.

Learning Definitions

Smith gives the following verdict, "In short, the learning process involves a motive or drive, an attractive goal and a block to the attainting or the goal. All these are essential".

Woodworth: "Any activity can be called learning so far as it develops the individual (in any respect, good or bad) and makes him alter behavior and experience different from what that would otherwise have been".

Gardner Murphy

"The term learning covers every modification in behavior to meet environmental requirements".

Kingsley and Garry

"Learning is the process by which behavior (in the broader sense) is organized or changes through practice or training".

An overview of above definitions may clearly reveal that learning may be turned as a process or its outcome in which necessary changes in the behavior of the learner are brought through experience. Here it has been also emphasized that although changes in behavior are also brought out by the factors other than experience yet all such changes in behavior are not associated with the process and product of learning.

Natures of Learning

1. Learning can find from all living things.
2. It is continuous.
3. Learning from practice of self experience.
4. Gradual process.
5. Learning includes Mental and Physical activities.

Learning Theories

Pavlov's	-	Classical Conditioning
Skinner's	-	Operant Conditioning
Thorndike's	-	Trial and Error
Kohler's	-	Insight Learning

In all these theories there is one common thing that education is must for everyone. Learning is one's life is to get knowledge, habits, behavior practices and abilities and activities. One gets more information by learning in the school. Knowledge and activities will be different and new if a child gets good learning. In my view there are three types or learning as in English Grammar Personal Pronouns.

I Person	-	Self
II Person	-	Others- Known
III Person	-	Others from Unknown

in the same way, " learning self" – is I Person "Learning from others" is II person. "Learning from anybody or incidents from books and media". – is III Person.

I Person – Self Learning

Self learning through activities by us. Child realizes the nature of heat by touching it. Not just in childhood, we have self learning when a person tries to cook. He finds his own recipe to achieve a better taste. Due to old age some happens automatically. This will not come under learning. All the activities improve and become better only due to learning from our Childhood.

II Person

Man is a dependent. He gets learning by meeting people and from their speech, activities and decision making. In this regard he follows good things and neglects the bad things, following and understanding his own ethics. Child understands languages by speaking with others and hearing others. Child tries to walk by seeing others walk, in this way all the activities we find the intense learning.

III Person

Man gets learning from unknown persons for examples. From Conversation and seeing incidents. He changes his way of life from the above things. All these aspects of learning vary with time period. Initially, when man without any prior knowledge sparked fire with the help of two stones was just co-incidents without any scientific hypothesis. That was a first person learning inferred from co-incidence (knowledge acquired himself). As, time pass by we have social life, man tried to speak and create languages. Those dialects and languages are shared with other person. This followed second person learning. Then later people started to write and communicate through books and stories. In our culture stories are the main attraction for us to learn. A small concept to be understood rather than telling it bluntly in technical terms if we could enhance interest by sharing it through a story, then an effective fun learning is achieved. Books and stories will come under third person learning. Now, technology has taken us places, we have movies to tell us stories instead of books. Visualization was considered an effective tool to learn rather than letters. If a student could visualize the letters in book, he achieves a complete understanding of the concept so that he could remember it for a long time. Now presently we have a complex world of learning as the social media has taken us so close that we could learn in seconds from other end of world. Now through technology we feel we are so close at least virtually. In all these period of time, learning got various forms, but always what made a person to learn (i.e, to read a book, to listen to a conversation, to accept and understand ideology etc..) is curiosity to learn and effort to make it happen.

Books

Books dominate in every one's life. By reading the variety of books the contents changes the life and faces all challenges.

From above three levels or learning life of a person improves.

"What we have learnt is handful, and what we have to learn is vast".

Present scenario

Technology based Education through Computer.

Educate

Educate provides some of the following Channels.

1. Virtual classrooms through two-way videoconferencing.
2. Educational broadcast with or without interactive facilities,
3. Virtual classrooms through computer conferencing – both real time as well as asynchronous,

4. Digital storage and retrieval of educational software at convenience, and
5. Internet supported interactive learning.

For making effective use of EDUSAT, scientific principles and practices of interactive learning have to be adopted.

Conclusion

A Teacher must update his/her learning day to day. He must try to know new things. He must have knowledge in all worldly affairs. Updating of knowledge is from reading books, newspapers and Media. This will help a teacher to give innovative thoughts to the students. Learning should be encouraged out of scope. Learning can be entertaining if we could have piano learning session in between two informative class sessions. It relaxed our mind and improves capacity to learn more. In this competitive world a teacher also must be enriched with all the modern technologies. Then only the teaching will be effective and purposeful. Particularly teacher educators must be informative and well versed in modern technologies. All these can be achieved only if someone has a real interest to learn.

References

1. P.Sambasiva Rao., D.Bhaskara Rao "Techniques of Teaching Psychology. Sonali Publications, 2006.
2. Clifford T.Morgan, Richard A.King, John R.Weis and John Schopler, "Introduction to Psychology"-7th Edition. Tata McGraw Hill Book Co. New Delhi, 1993.
3. Ernest R.Hillgard, Richard C.Atkinson, Rita L.Atkinson, "Introduction to Psychology" 6th Edition, oxford IBH publishing Co.Pvt Ltd., New Delhi, 1975 .
4. Baron.A.Robert, Psychology, Pearson Education Vth Ed., 2002.

32

Techno-pedagogy in Teaching Learning Process to Progress the Education

Introduction

In this article the authors give explanation about technology and the techniques used in it. Educational Technology as the means of development application and evaluation of three different things: techniques, system and aids to improve the process of learning. Also give important to teaching learning process through technology. Multimedia approach has come out of researches and experiments in educational technology that have been undertaken in order to improve the process of teaching learning. The teacher education institutions should prepare in service teachers to keep with the technology utility in the class room. Technology is not only an essential tool for teachers in their day to day work, but it also offers then opportunities for their own professional development. Educational technology was used in proper way then it can enhance the learning and interest of students. Finally the authors discussed various technologies equipment which are used in education and explained mobile technology in detailed.

The word technology is derived from the Greek word "technical" meaning art or skill and login meaning science or study .Thus technology is the science of study of an art or skill. A systematic way of applying the technique to achieve the objectives is an important as the use of technical equipment for the same. Man is always on the lookout for inviting new innovations in all walks of life. Human life has improved tremendously as a result of the growth in science and technology. Education is a social institution that has also been influenced by technological developments. Educational technology is a system in education in which machines, materials, media, men and methods are interrelated and work together for the fulfillment of specific educational objectives. Educational technology is a communication process resulting from application of scientific method to the behavioral science of teaching and learning. The communication may or may require the use of media such as radio, films, television broadcasts, cassettes, etc.

Definition of Technology

According to Hierra .A (1973) "Technology is the set of instruments and skills which are used to satisfy the needs of community".

Objectives of Techno-pedagogy

1. To create awareness about the use of technologies in research
2. To make famous with basic of information and communication technology.
3. To acquire facts of computers languages and software packages for education.
4. To expand programming skill in computer languages for education.
5. To develop skill in operation of different software packages in education.
6. To develop skill in utilizing intranet and internet.
7. To exploit technology for solving educational problems.

Teaching and Learning process

Teaching is a pivotal aspect in the process of education. In comparison to education, teaching is narrower in scope and is associated with only 3R's.Reading, Writing and Arithmetic. Teaching is an agent-The source, human or material that tries to produce learning. Teaching is goal or target that is to be achieved through the process of teaching.

Learning is an enrichment of experiences in learning there is an interaction of the environment with the organism. Teaching would be worthless and meaningless if learning is not produced. Learning is a process by which behavior is originated or changes through practice and teaching. We all have our own interpretations on how we learn or teach. These interpretations are influenced by our unique epistemological beliefs. As individuals, lecturers or learners, we bring with us different epistemological approaches that stem from our past unique learning experiences and educational value systems (Laurillard, 1993; Negroponte, 1995; Rossette, 1987.) Therefore, we could have different yardsticks, or perspectives, on what is considered to be effective learning and teaching.

Pedagogy

Technology has also shaped pedagogy, or the art of teaching. Today, instructors can create and supplement their lessons in exciting ways. For example, online video conferencing enables teachers to talk directly with experts who are unable to visit a classroom in person. Interviews with such figures can be incorporated into lessons with the assistance of presentation software such as Microsoft PowerPoint.

Communication continues to improve as the result of technological advances. Teachers can use email, texting, instant messaging, video chats and more to make themselves more available to students who need help with their schoolwork. Tutors can provide extra assistance in a similar manner. As a result, students can get the help they need outside of the classroom easier than ever before.

The number of pedagogical possibilities that technology opens up increases every year. Teachers can create review exercises online to help their students learn their lessons and prepare for exams. Instructors can create online forums and blogs where students, outside of the classroom setting, can discuss what they are learning.

Examples could be multiplied, and the way teachers teach will no doubt continue to change as new software is created and other advancements are made.

Techno-pedagogy in Teaching and Learning process

The term technology enhanced learning is used extensively throughout the educational world; it is the latest in an assortment of terms that have been used to describe the application of information and communication technologies (ICT) to learning and teaching. Unlike other terms such as e-Learning or on-line learning, technology enhanced learning implies a value judgment: the word "enhancement" suggests an improvement or betterment some way. However, it is rare to find explicit statements about its meaning. Although there any many examples of innovative uses of technology in learning and teaching it is not clear whether these actually enhance student learning. More readily observed is the use of technology to support or replace existing teaching practices, with limited evidence to confirm any enhancements to the status quo. To date there has been an over-emphasis on technological manifestations and this has led to the omission of pedagogical considerations (Beetham, H. & Sharpe, R., 2007; Kirkwood, 2009).

Enhancement of Learning and Teaching

1. Emphasizing learning rather than technology;
2. Mainstreaming the role of technology in normal analysis, planning, design, implementation and evaluation processes;
3. Developing staff-ensuring that professional development opportunities are evidence-based and include scholarly and academic illiteracies appropriate to the digital age;
4. Enhancing other core processes through use of technology, e.g. Student selection, enrolment, and assessment.

Enhancement of students learning

1. Evidencing the role of technology in meeting the needs of diverse learners and ensuring parity of learning experience

by developing student scholarly/ academic illiteracies. Engaging with students as partners;

2. Research is encouraged to inform decision-making and build capacity by identifying new opportunities for enhancement of the student learning experience.
3. Increased flexibility and accessibility of provision:
4. Technology has a role in increasing accessibility and flexibility above and beyond benefiting individuals with particular needs. It is important in supporting student transition and progression, including addressing equality and diversity, Welsh-medium learning, and fostering lifelong learning.

Importance of technology

1. Technology was originally intended to serve as a means of improving efficiency in the educational research.
2. It can help to improve memory retention, increase motivation and gradually deepen understanding.
3. Technology can also be used to promote collaborative learning including role playing, group problem solving activities and articulated objects.
4. It is helpful for critical thinking.
5. It is used Generalist (broad) competencies.
6. Technology competencies enable expert work.
7. Technology is used for decision making.
8. It is used in handling of dynamic situation.
9. It helps to communicating effectively.

E-learning

E-learning is self-paced. E-learning is used in the research to develop ICT based resources. Interactive learning material can be provided to the researcher. Through E-learning researcher can learn how to prepare Questionnaire. Web-based learning materials can be given from time to time where ever needed.

Digital library

Digital library is a library in which collections are stored in digital formats (as opposed to print, microform, or other media) and accessible by computers. The digital contents may be stored logically, or accessed remotely via computer networks. A digital library is a type of information retrieval system. Researcher can use this library for their research.

Learning through Computer

The computer's ability to perform logical operations is a major characteristic and must surely be central to any compute application. In the context of learning the rapid response to a learner action is of particular benefit as there can be quick reinforcement of good ideas which the learner has and any miscoreeptions may be corrected many motor skills can only be least by directive of the equipment concerned. Commonly used terms of computers in education are Computer Assisted Instruction (CAI), Computer Assisted Learning (CAL), Computer Assisted Training (CAT), Computer based Training (CBT), Computer Managed Instruction (CMI), Computer Managed Learning (CML).

Internet and web technology

Internet and web technology play a significant role in this area. Special mention has to be made on the applications of search and Meta search engines. Search engines are special sites on the Web that are designed to help people find information stored on the other sites and a Meta search engine that searches information from almost all the search engines linked to that engine and gives the entire list of searched information.

Multimedia Approach to Teaching-Learning Process

The word Multimedia may split into two words Multi and Media which means many and Techniques or methods respectively. Multimedia approach uses a number of media devices techniques in the teaching learning process. Multimedia approach has come out of researches and experiments in educational technology that have been undertaken in order to improve the process of teaching-learning.

Educational Games

Through technology we may also play educational games, gaming simulations and other interactive applications can be participatory and gain immersive experience and add a layer of motivation to learning, engaging users, and can bring scenarios to classroom educators could not otherwise.

Audio learning

Audio learning can take place through listening to audio. Podcasts can be downloaded of relevant lectures, interviews, or overviews of the latest research. For example, participants may download an audio (or video) podcast of a session prior to attending a session.

Assessment

Assessment through answering multiple choice questions can enable both learners and educators to test knowledge and skills. For example, educators can conduct pre-assessments prior to face-to-face sessions to enable them to determine learners' level of knowledge and plan their sessions accordingly. Learners can identify areas in which they require more training.

Recording Information

Recording Information Mobile devices provide numerous ways to input information through touch, stylus and voice. This allows learners to build up a series of personal notes, observations, collection of evidences and reflections of progress. These can be useful to prompt future recall, build a portfolio, or for assisting comprehension and reflection.

Uses of Techno-pedagogy

1. Creativity
2. Critical-thinking ability
3. Problem-solving ability
4. Mind of independence
5. Self-learning ability

6. Desire to learn
7. Knowledge and skills to learn

The changing face of the classroom

Technology is entering into abstract all subjects. It is supposed to be used as tool where and when considered useful Technology will be real part of the curriculum by supporting software developed by integrating Technology into standard learning material by offering Technology module cases and by integrating the use of Technology in the different subject areas. The face of the classroom is changing. The teacher education institutions should prepare in-service teacher to keep up with the technology utility in the classroom. Technology is not only an essential tool for teacher in their day to day work, build also offers them opportunities for their own professional development.

Teaching through Technology in the Modern period

The challenges of the modern world as emerged from a global approach of scientific. Knowledge, democratic ideas and demands on personality require that teaching methodology must undergo revolutionary changes to meet the mew aspirations and needs of the society. In order to make the best use of our resources inventory is essential that all personnel engaged in the educational enterprise and especially the teachers understand adequately the dynamics and mechanism of educational technology and provide the best possible education to the students.

Advanced Mobile Devices

Advanced mobile devices such as “smart” cellular telephones are very popular among people primarily because they are wireless and portable. These functionalities enable users to communicate while on the move. The popularity of these devices is therefore a consequent of their ability to function at multiple levels. Moreover, the intense commercial competitiveness in the mobile device industry is forcing manufacturers to be very innovative, constantly striving to introduce new features that can give them a competitive edge. Against this backdrop, visionary educators, designers and developers should begin to consider the implications of these devices for the modern teaching and learning environment. In such an environment, contents and services can be relayed to a university student by personal wireless mobile devices. This will add another layer to the personal computer-based model of teaching and learning. This also means e-learning will take place in conditions that will be radically different from those educators and learners are familiar with. Providing university students with services, content instruction and information outside the traditional learning space is becoming more acceptable among education providers who predicate their services on the routine use of advanced information and communication technologies.

Mobile Learning

The educational potential of mobile devices in the executive education sector remains largely untapped, although this is not the case in the education sector as a whole. Few executive education providers have harnessed the true potential of mobile devices for learning, and yet ironically it is a device that the majority of senior executives bring with them to the classroom. At present, the focus for the majority of those who are exploring this seems to be techno-centric on technology and devices rather than learning design. The real potential lies in focusing on the needs of the user and designing the learning experience accordingly where the individual is empowered to learn in a whole new way. Thus it consists of the practice implementation, knowing your mobile learner, getting information, choosing technology, costs, pedagogy, content, support, evaluation.

Mobile Learning Practice as a Learning Style

Mobile devices such as clickers or smart phone can be used to enhance the experience in the classroom by providing the possibility for professors to get feedback. An easy way to display your student's work is to create a web page designed for your class. Once a web page is designed, teachers can post homework assignments, student work, famous quotes, trivia games, and so much more. In today's society, children know how to use the Mobile and navigate their way through a website, so why not give them one where they can be a published author. Just be careful as most districts maintain strong policies to manage official websites for a school or classroom. Also, most school districts provide teacher web pages that can easily be viewed through the school district's website in their *mobile phone*. Streamed video websites can be utilized to enhance a classroom lesson (e.g. United Streaming, Teacher Tube, etc.)

Class blogs, Wireless and wikis for mobile-learning

There are a variety of Web tools that are currently being implemented in the classroom. Blogs allow for students to maintain a running dialogue, such as a journal, thoughts, ideas, and assignments that also provide for student comment and reflection. Wikis are more group focused to allow multiple members of the group to edit a single document and create a truly collaborative and carefully edited finished product. Noisy classrooms are a daily occurrence, and with the help of microphones, students are able to hear their teachers more clearly. Children learn better when they hear the teacher clearly. The benefit for teachers is that they no longer lose their voices at the end of the day.

Electronic books and World mapper

The Horizon Report mentions that e-books have taken hold strongly in the consumer sector and the time for mass adoption across campuses. This trend has been strongly enabled by the explosion of tablet computing, which can augment text with interactive experiences, support classroom note-taking and research activities, and allow readers to interact socially. This trend will totally change our perception of what it means to read. World mapper is a geographic visualization site which helps the K-12 social studies teachers to get maximum utility, in particular from the animated maps that combine geographic and demographic data, in some cases along chronological timelines.

Mobile Computing in Technology

The Horizon Report defines mobile computing as "network-capable devices students are already carrying" (e.g., smart phones, iPod Touch, net-books). The portability of these devices and easy wireless access to the Internet makes mobile computing devices ideal pedagogical conduits for a variety of teaching and learning activities of education. Using Mobile Technologies to Promote Children's learning, as follows:

Encourage "anywhere, anytime" learning:

Mobile devices allow students to gather, access, and process information outside the classroom. They can encourage learning in a real-world context, and help bridge school, afterschool, and home environments.

Reach underserved children:

Because of their relatively low cost and accessibility in low-income communities, handheld devices can help advance digital equity, reaching and inspiring populations "at the edges" that is children from economically disadvantaged communities and those from developing countries.

Improve 21st-century social interactions:

Mobile technologies have the power to promote and foster collaboration and communication, which are deemed essential for 21st-century success.

Fit with learning environments:

Mobile devices help to overcome many of the challenges associated with larger technologies, as they fit more naturally within various learning environments.

Enable a personalized learning experience:

Not all children are alike; instruction should be adaptable to individual and diverse learners. There are significant opportunities for genuinely supporting differentiated, autonomous, and individualized learning through mobile devices.

Value of Mobile Learning

Tutors who have used Mobile-Learning programs and techniques have made the following value statements in favor of Mobile -Learning.

1. It is important to bring new technology into the classroom.
2. Devices used are more lightweight than books and PCs.
3. Mobile learning can be used to diversify the types of learning activities and the students partake in a blended learning approach.
4. Mobile learning supports the learning process rather than being integral to it.
5. Mobile learning can be a useful add-on tool for students with special needs.
6. Mobile learning can be used as a 'hook' to re-engage disaffected youth.

Uses of mobile learning

1. Mobile learning can happen anywhere, any time
2. Learning is more user-centred as Mobile technology is bridging tool.
3. Mobile learning increases motivation and engagement with learning.
4. Mobile learning makes the learning process quicker, easier and more attractive.
5. Mobile learning is Potentially a more rewarding learning experience

Findings

The findings of this paper show that the global position of the technology in education. Through techno-pedagogy the teacher can make the class more effective and the student can participate with the teacher as active learner. The mobile learning takes place in the global level education as informal education. Thus the development of global trends of mobile learning and technology is very high in modern research practice and the learning style also modernized in the present situation. So techno-pedagogy in teaching learning process will help to progress the education.

Recommendations to the Educational Institutions

The educational institutions will provide the facilities to the learners to use mobile technology and other technology equipments in their learning environment. Also they provide the advance network (wifi) for collecting the information from web and also the information's and the keynotes are sent to them by SMS or MMS. This help the students to participate whole heartedly in their learning and the learning take place informally.

Conclusion

Technology Concerns a host of issues including pedagogical theory, choice of land ware or software, methods of use and evaluation of effectiveness. Technologies are not single technologies but complex combination of hardware and software. These technologies may employ some combinations of audio channels, computer code, data, graphics, video or text. Technology, inventory properly used, can enhance the learning and interest of student. Evolution of new technologies will be necessitated to maximize development of learning in modern research practice. Thus in the present investigation the authors concluded that techno-pedagogy's are very necessary in teaching learning process to progress the education.

References

1. Hierra, A. (1973). Essentials of educational psychology (2nd ed.) New Delhi: J.C. Aggarwal VIKAS Publication House PVT LTD.
2. Laurillard, D. (1993). Rethinking university teaching. New York, NY: Routledge.
3. Negroponte, N. (1995). Being digital. New York, NY: Knopf.
4. Rossett, A. (1987). Training needs assessment. Englewood Cliffs, NJ: Educational
5. Technology Publications.
6. Beetham, H. & Sharpe, R. (2007). Rethinking Pedagogy for a Digital Age: Designing and Delivering E-Learning, UK: Routledge; New edition. ISBN 0203961684, 9780203961681

7. Kirkwood, A.(2009). E-learning: you don't always get what you hoped for Technology. Pedagogy and Education, 18(2), 107-121. doi:10.1080/14759390902992576

8. http://www.slideshare.net/jamesclay/the-future-of-learning-is-mobile

9. http://www.jisc.ac.uk/whatwedo/topics/mobilelearning.aspx

10. http://www.upsidelearning.com/blog/index.php/2011/02/01/whatismobilelearning.htm

33

A Study on The used-less Usage of Technology That is useless, as useful

Introduction

This paper heralds the availability of numerous technological tools which is used less and thereby, considered as useless. For the past two decades it is very clear, that the technology has advanced rapidly in the field of learning any foreign language with Internet, ICT (Information Communication Technology), VLE(Virtual learning environments), CALL (Computer Assisted Language Learning), digital media and software. It is evident that in every step of our lives the significance of technology is seen which are bountiful. More funds are spent on the improvement of the student learning process. Inspite of the availability of Web-based language teaching and learning activities, the use of technology still remains unexplored. The researches still recommend the teachers and the students to make use of the existing endless choice of multimedia, software, applications and devices to improve their learning process. Further it is not needed for any advanced tool to facilitate the language learning process. It is a challenge still, for the teachers as well as the learners to acquaint themselves with the recent technology that is already available. The aim of this paper adds a dimension to the English learning in the educational environments through the available sources and it makes the study of language enjoyable.

English language teachers must be innovative, imaginative, supportive, resourceful and adaptive and have scrupulous knowledge of the subject and advocate new techniques to change socio, economic status of the learners. Technology that is used in various fields has been so flourishing and advantageous for the teachers to reach some particular goals especially in education and for those who are learning a foreign language. Teaching English depends on the potential brilliance, expertise and proficient knowledge of English teachers. The liability of an English teacher in present context has remarkably changed because of various factors such as social, cultural, economic and technology developments across the globe. Over a decade, interactive, multi-media courseware has enabled the various linguistic skills and the intellectual and sensory activities involved in language use to be integrated in a single platform. However, language teachers are progressively sentient of the potential benefits of technology, one challenge they face is how to accomplish effective technology-based language tasks. Many professionals feel uncertain on how to take advantage of the Web to bring part of the world into the digital classroom, especially when working with young learners. Teachers are often over whelmed by a large quantity of sites and materials which often exceed the linguistic level and the technological abilities of their students. Deciding how to use and integrate systematically those materials within a more traditional methodology demands an extra effort many full-time teachers cannot afford. Many learners are now techno – savvy as the in that case, the faculty must also adapt the use of technology and multimedia based learning resource to transmit the functional learning of English in class room. So, we limit our focus on ICT (Information Communication Technology), VLE (Virtual learning environments), CALL (Computer Assisted Language Learning), digital media and software in order to reduce convolution. In this modern epoch students are growing with a glut of electronic media use and this differentiates them from previous generations of students whose learning experiences were dominated by text in books and journals.

Need for the study

This paper proposes a test and hoard data to check the effectiveness of the task-based approach within the modern medium of technology in English language teaching. Some problems and challenges still exist in language learning. Possibilities provided by the Internet for educational purposes have been attracting more attention in recent studies devoted to the problems of using Information and Communication Technologies (ICTs), VLE(Virtual learning environments), CALL (Computer Assisted Language Learning), digital media and software in education. This tendency is fed by the development of Internet infrastructure and technologies, by their increasing availability and use, and by the ongoing search for new ways to improve educational quality through the use of technology. When these technologies are used correctly in the classroom, it allows students to experience situations and circumstances which they have dreamt about it twenty years ago.

Objectives

1. To improve the effectiveness of the technology tools on the students' learning progress
2. To create teaching materials which cater to different students who have different learning styles
3. To demonstrate a high level of technical awareness for the learners with opportunities for building knowledge, integrated with academic and linguistic skills
4. To review technology in English language and literature learning activities and internet communication tools in use
5. To promote effective and efficient learning and explore the boundless possibilities in the language technology.

Expected Outcomes

The paper expects that this hi-tech teaching will enhance the learners to communicate effectively and become proficient in all the skills. This kind will enable them to be competent in the global market. As it doesn't require a separate place for their enhancement and it could be done during mobility. It helps the learners to employ their time in a suitable way as it is not time consuming. The learners will become a potent and comprehend the essentials that he requires through ICT.

Review of Related Literature

An extensive work and effort have been put in review of literature, where both Indian studies and global studies in using technology to teach English language has been done, the major findings were been consolidated as below:

Many new technologies have been acknowledged with a great deal of enthusiasm, but their real significance as educational tools has continued to be questionable. From the study it is established out that "Technology also may affect the way we teach, the way we learn and affect teachers choice of teaching and learning styles as put forward by Watson (2010, p. Teachers may face a conflict of teaching and learning styles. Older teachers generally teach in person and proceed in a logical or step-by-step basis. In contrast, modern students inclined to jump around from one idea or thought to another and expect sensory-laden milieu as a matter of course. They also want instant results and recurrent rewards, whereas many teachers regard learning as slower and serious and consider that students should just keep quiet and listen.

The need to persuade the development of teachers' digital proficiency has been documented by many researchers. Beavers (2001) and Hope (1998) state that although much technology has been positioned in schools and colleges (such as computers, educational software etc.) not many teachers make use of this technology in their classrooms. This is a result of various factors among which the lack of proper education of teachers (Ward, West and Isaac, 2002) of the pedagogical and methodological principles underlying the effective use of digital technologies to successfully provide rich learning experiences to their learners by using the new types of media.

Many digital training materials have been created, but the developed materials are not widely and effectively used by teachers in the learning process. There are many reasons for this: no access to the Internet, slow Internet, and lack of compensation for creating media, and so on.

Impediment for Using ICT in the Classroom

Becta classified the barriers based on whether they refer to individual (teacher-level barriers), such as lack of confidence, shortage of time, and resistance to change, or to the institution (school-level barriers), such as lack of effective training in solving technical problems and lack of access to resources [14]. Balanskat et al. Another group of researchers refer to the barriers as those pertaining to two types of conditions: material and non-material. As Pelgrum classifies, the material conditions refer to the insufficient number of computers or copies of software [16]. The non-material barriers refer to teachers' insufficient ICT knowledge and skills, the difficulty of integrating ICT in instruction, and insufficient teacher time.

The most important barriers are teachers' use of ICT were insufficient number of computers, lack of free time for learning and lack of classroom time for students to use computers. Lack of personal confidence and insufficient access to the ICT resources were the key barriers for majority of the surveyed teachers. Some other factors which were more internal to the teachers such as resistance to change and lack of awareness of the benefits of the ICTs for learning Other factors such as ICTs not being considered as important enough to be a priority, contentment with current approaches and lack of confidence to integrate ICTs in the curriculum were reported by the teachers as well.

The findings disclose that teachers still have difficulty in using assured applications such as MS Excel. The virtually limitless opportunities of access to information in an educational context can pose a real danger of information overload if the teachers do not have the skills in filtering information for relevance, or are incapable to establish a coherent organizing principle. It is no longer for teachers to give excuses as technology is evolving rapidly. It is time for all to equip and learn the required skills. Positive attitude motivates individuals use ICT effectively and further upgrade the needed skills.

Suggestions

This term paper suggests that, the equipment which is already in persistence must be used efficiently by the language teachers to promote the student to the next level of learning. There is no necessitating for additional new technology. The used-less technology can be used as useful by the language trainers at the right time.

Alan Waters (Waters & Hockly, 2012):

"Technology is not a magic bullet. ... Depending on context and how it's used, technology can be effective or not, just like any other teaching tool"..

Providing the necessary tools and access to technology, combined with constant support and training, language teachers will be more willing to integrate technology into their teaching contexts. New technology is not only a subject in and of it, but can also be applied to any subject, enhancing the learning experience and equipping students to join an increasingly global workforce. The use of ICT in language learning not only involves pedagogical changes for teachers but also involves environmental and pedagogical changes for learners who are traditionally used to face-to-face teaching in classrooms. Although an increasing number of learners have access to online technologies and use ICT for personal interactions, they find it challenging to use ICT in an educational context. Many learners hesitate to take an online language course because they can only conceive of learning a language in the presence of a teacher and peers and cannot imagine learning to speak at a distance. Although many online language courses include spoken elements and oral interactions with the teacher, learners are often unsure how such elements would work and whether they could actually learn using ICT resources in the physical absence of the teacher. Often students are more willing to listen to audio materials, watch video materials, and take self-tests online as a supplement to face-to-face interaction and communication in a language course. Examples could be: Cloud computing, open source, connectives, Webinar, Nptel Programme

Conclusion:

It is a dispute still, for the teachers as well as the learners to acquaint themselves with the recent technology that is already available. If the available resources are used useful and nothing can be assumed as useless.

Reference

1. Sean Kennedy and Don Soifer, 2013, "Technology-Driven Innovations for Teaching English Learners", "Journal of Lexington Institute", Lexington Institute, Vol 1., Pg.NO.44
2. Beavers, D. (2001) "Professional development outside the workshop box". In *Principal Leadership, 1 (9),* pp. 43-46.
3. Hope, W. C. (1998) "The next step: integrating computers and related technologies into practice". In *Contemporary Education, 69 (3),* pp. 137 - 140.
4. Baek, Y. et al. (2006). What makes teachers use technology in the classroom? Exploring the factors affecting facilitation of technology with a Korean sample. Computers & Education, 50(1), 224-234.
5. Chester, S. (1987). *Use of Computers in the Teaching of Language*, Houston: Athelstan Publications
6. Brierley, B. (1991). *Computers as a Tool in Language Teaching (Ellis Horwood Series on Computers and Their Applications),* New York: Ellis Horwood.
7. Sabourin, C. (1994). *Computer assisted language teaching: Teaching vocabulary, grammar, spelling, writing, composition, listening, speaking, translation, foreign languages*, Montreal, Canada: Infolingua.
8. Boswood, T. (1997). *New Ways of Using Computers in Language Teaching (New Ways in Tesol Series II),* California: Teachers of English to Speakers of Other Languages.
9. Beatty, K. (2003). *Teaching and Researching Computer-Assisted Language Learning (Applied Linguistics in Action),* New York: Pearson ESL.
10. Lee, C., George Jor, G., & Lai, E. (2005). *Web-based Teaching and English Language Teaching: A Hong Kong Experience*, Hong Kong: The Chinese University Press.

11. Szendeffy, J. (2005). *A Practical Guide to Using Computers in Language Teaching*, East Lansing: University of Michigan Press/ESL.
12. Warschauer, M., & Kern, K. (2000). *Network-based Language Teaching: Concepts and Practice*, Cambridge University Press.
13. Arnó Macià, E., Soler Cervera, A., & Rueda Ramos, C. (2006). *Information Technology in Languages for Specific Purposes: Issues and Prospects*, Berlin: Springer.
14. Tsou, W., Wang, W., & Tzeng, Y. (2006) Applying a Multimedia Storytelling Website in Foreign Language Learning. *Computers and Education, 47*(1), 17-28.
15. Felix, U. (2005). Analysing recent call effectiveness research—towards a common agenda. *Computer Assisted Language Learning, 18*(1-2), 1-32.
16. Padurean, A., Margan, M. (2009). "Foreign Language Teaching Via ICT". Revista de Informatica Sociala, vol. VII nr. 12, ISSN 1584-384X.
17. Rozgiene, I, Medvedeva, O., Straková, Z. (2008). "Integrating ICT into Language Learning and Teaching: Guide for Tutors". Johannes Kepler Universität Linz, Altenberger Straße 69, 4040 Linz

34

The Role of open Educational Resources (Oers) in Enhancing The Teaching and Learning Process

Introduction

Open Educational Resources (OER) are educational materials and resources offered freely and openly for anyone to use and under some license to adapt, copy and redistribute. OER can include course syllabi, presentation slides, image collections, animations, videos, textbooks, research papers and self-assessments. OER have the potential to advance the delivery of education by increasing the availability of relevant learning materials, reducing the cost of accessing educational materials and stimulating the active engagement of teaching staff and students in creating learning resources. OER are any resources avail-able at little or no cost that can be used for teaching, learning or research. OER typically refers to electronic resources, including those in multime-dia formats and such materials are generally released under a Creative Commons or GNU licenses or similar license that supports open or nearly open use of the content. OER can originate from colleges, uni-versities, libraries, archival organizations, government agencies, commercial organizations such as publishers or faculty or other individuals who develop educational resources they are willing to share. The central to the idea of OER is openness in the creation, sharing and reuse of learning & teaching materials with barriers of cost or access for the student or end-user reduced as much as possible. The present paper emphasizes on the meaning of OER, Open Licenses and distribution models, the role of OER in teaching and learning process, OER content repositories and advantages and disadvantages of OER in teaching and learning process.

"Open Educational Resources (OER) describes any educational resources (including curriculum maps, course materials, textbooks, streaming videos, multimedia applications, podcasts, and any other materials that have been designed for use in teaching and learning) that are openly available for use by educators and students, without an accompanying need to pay royalties or license fees". - Neil Butcher, A Basic Guide to Open Educational Resources (OER)

OER are educational materials and resources offered freely and openly for anyone to use and under some license to adapt, copy and redistribute. OER can include course syllabi, presentation slides, image collections, animations, videos, textbooks, research papers and self-assessments. The term "Open Educational Resources" was first adapted at *UNESCO's 2002 Forum on the Impact of Open Courseware for Higher Education in Developing Countries.* OER have the potential to advance the delivery of education by increasing the availability of relevant learning materials, reducing the cost of accessing educational materials and stimulating the active engagement of teaching staff and students in creating learning resources. A wealth of public domain and fair use learning materials are currently available via the internet that faculty can repurpose for use in their classes to replace some of the books required for purchase by students. OER are any resources avail-able at little or no cost that can be used for teaching, learning or research. OER typically refers to electronic resources, including those in multime-dia formats and such materials are generally released under a Creative Commons or similar license that supports open or nearly open use of the content. OER can originate from colleges and uni-versities, libraries, archival organizations, government agencies, commercial organizations such as publishers or faculty or other individuals who develop educational resources they are willing to share. In January 2007 the OECD (ORGANISATION FOR ECONOMIC CO-OPERATION AND DEVELOPMENT) identified over 3000 open courseware courses available from over 300 universities worldwide.

Meaning and Definitions of OER

The term OER is largely synonymous with another term: Open Courseware (OCW), although the latter may be used to refer to a specific, more structured subset of OER. An Open Courseware is defined by the OCW Consortium as 'a free and open digital publication of high quality university-level educational materials. These materials are organized as courses and often include course planning materials and evaluation tools as well as thematic content'. OER has emerged as a concept with great potential to support educational transformation. Importantly, there is *only* one key differentiator between an OER and any other educational resource: its *license.* Thus, an OER is simply an educational resource that incorporates a license that facilitates reuse and potentially adaptation, without first requesting permission from the copyright holder. The central to the idea of OER is openness in the creation, sharing and reuse of learning & teaching materials with barriers of cost or access for the student or end-user reduced as much as possible.

"OER are teaching, learning and research resources that reside in the public domain or have been released under an intellectual property license that permits their free use or re-purposing by others. OERs include full courses, course materials, modules, textbooks, streaming videos, tests, software, and any other tools, materials, or techniques used to support access to knowledge"- William and Flora Hewlett Foundation

"OER as digitized materials, offered freely and openly for educators, students and self-learners, to use and re-use for teaching, learning and research. OER includes open access to both the content and the technology such as Open Software, Open Standards and Open Licenses to distribute the material".

"Free sharing of software, scientific results and educational resources reinforces societal development and diminishes social inequality. From a more individual standpoint, open sharing is claimed to increase publicity, reputation and the pleasure of sharing with peers" -Jan Hylen, OECD Centre for Educational Research and Innovation.

Open Licenses and Distribution Models

OER main rule is to open access to an educational content by sharing it according to various free models of distribution. Models of distribution over the Internet mainly rely on the type of license the producer is going to choose to diffuse its work. Using an Open License model does not mean the author is going to lose his rights. It is exactly the opposite. Open Licenses help the owner of any Open Content to protect it, by defining conditions under which the material can be used, modified and distributed. Will you allow commercial use of your training material ? Should I mention the source if I use it ? Can I distribute a new version of your work under any type of license ? All this depends on the type of Open License chosen by the Author. Two different types of licenses used by OER producers are recommended by the OER dgCommunity:

Creative Commons licenses (CC licenses)

This is a non-profit organization devoted to expanding the range of creative work available for others legally to build upon and share. The organization has released several copyright licenses known as Creative Commons licenses. Globally, a CC license answers two different questions: *do you allow commercial use of your work ? : Do you allow modifications of your work?* For the second question, the answer can be Yes, No or under "Share Alike" (Which means the licensor permits others to distribute derivative works only under a license identical to the one of the original work). This mechanism is also known as copy left.

GNU license

GNU licenses are widely used to license Free and Open Source Software (FOSS) as well as Documentation. The GNU General Public License (GNU GPL), a widely used free software license, was originally written by *Richard Stallman* for the GNU project. The GPL is the most popular and well known example of the type of strong copy left license. Another interesting GNU license is the Free Documentation License (FDL). GNU FDL or simply GFDL, is a copy left license for free documentation, designed by the Free Software Foundation (FSF) for the GNU project.

The Role of OER in Teaching and Learning Process

OER are teaching and learning materials that are freely available online for anyone to use, whether you are an instructor, student, or self-learner. OER can exist as smaller, stand-alone resources that can be mixed and combined to form larger pieces of content or as larger course modules or full courses. These definitions locate OER online, but it is arguable that any resource used for teaching and learning that can be freely accessed is an OER. It is usually safe to assume, however, that OER refers to online materials in most contexts. They can range from single file resources (reading lists, image files, video clips), through meaningfully structured collections as single units (sometimes called 'learning objects') to textbooks and whole courses. These last two types of resource, open textbooks and whole courses *(Massive Open Online Course (MOOCs))* have their own advocates and models for application. The currently most used definition of OER is: *"Open Educational Resources are digitized materials offered freely and openly for educators, students and self-learners to use and re-use for teaching, learning and research."*

The main aspect is that the object is usable to improve education. The following classification shows parallels to other initiatives:

1. **Learning resources:** Currently, the main research field is how to make learning objects (specific digital objects created for learning purposes) available and re-usable. This includes multimedia documents, simulations but also simple html web resources.

2. **Articles, textbooks and digital equivalents:** This class of resources contains typical objects provided by libraries, such as articles, papers, books or journals.

3. **Software tools** are used for different purposes, such as producing / authoring learning resources but also for communication and collaboration. Objects of this class are usually referenced as Open Source or Free Software (OSFS).
4. **Instructional/didactical designs and experiences:** Educators are highly dependent on successfully planning and designing their learning experiences – this class of resources includes access to instructional designs, didactical plans such as lesson plans, case studies or curricula. It also includes one of the most valuable resources: sharing experiences about materials and lessons between colleagues. This class of objects is also called Open Educational Practices.
5. **Web assets:** This class of objects regards simple resources (assets) like pictures, links, or short texts which are not usable on their own in a learning context but can be used to support or illustrate a certain topic. In many ways, these are objects found by Google or similar search engines.

OER Content Repositories

Many new initiatives have been launched during the past five years in the field of OER. The following are the list of the websites related to OER content repositories.

1. Common Content : www.commoncontent.org
2. Wikiversity : www.en.wikiversity.org
3. Connexions : www.cnx.org
4. The OpenCourseWare Consortium (OCW) : www. ocw consortium. org
5. OER Commons : www.oercommons.org
6. The Open Training Platform – UNESCO : www. opentraining platform.org
7. OpenCourse.org : www.OpenCourse.org
8. Merlot : www.merlot.org
9. Carnegie Mellon Open Learning Initiative : www.cmu.edu/oli

10. The Open Learn Initiative : www.openlearn.open.ac.uk
11. OER search engines : www.learn.creativecommons.org/projects/oesearch
12. OpenContentOnline : www.opencontentonline.com
13. Curriki : www.curriki.org
14. Commonwealth of Learning (COL) : www.col.org
15. The William and Flora Hewlett Foundation (WFHF) OER Initiative : www.hewlett. org/ Programs/Education/OER/
16. Center for Open and Sustainable Learning (COSL) : www. oslo.usu.edu
17. Open Learning Content Observatory Services (OLCOS): www. olcos.org
18. ccLearn - the education division of Creative Commons : www.learn.Creative commons.org
19. Eduforge : www.eduforge.org
20. China Open Resources for Education (CORE) : www. core. org.cn
21. Western Cooperative for Educational Telecommunications (WCET): www.wcet.info
22. International Institute for Educational Planning (IIEP)- OER useful resources : www.oerwiki.iiep-unesco.org/index. php? title=OER_useful_ resources
23. 80 OER-Tools for Publishing and Development Initiatives : www.oedb.org/library/features/80-oer-tools

MOOCS (Massive Open Online Courses)

MOOCs are recent development that is reshaping the trend of higher education on the web. It represents an emerging methodology of online teaching, based on the philosophy of connectives. This term was coined by George Seimens and Stephen Downs in 2008. 'Massive' here refers to the large number of students that can be engaged in an online course and its 'openness' is associated with the software used, registration to anyone who has access to web, open curriculum, learning resources and assessment. Pedagogically it characterizes an open, constructivist and connectivity approach of knowledge production, even though these courses provide a structured curriculum, learners are permitted to be autonomous and self organize their participation according to their learning needs, prior knowledge and skills, and common interests. The first generation MOOCs were referred to as cMOOCs since they aimed at maximizing connections between learners, whereas those emerged in 2012 are termed as xMOOCs, sine they adapted a behaviouristic and top-down style of teaching. Some of the MOOC providers are *EDx, courseera, Open Courseware (http://ocw.mit.edu), Udacity, Futurelearn and OpenUpEd.*

Advantages of OER

The following are the advantages of OER in teaching and learning process :

1. ***Innovative teaching method :*** Fosters pedagogical innovation and relevance that avoids teaching from the textbook
2. ***Revised and Latest :*** OER materials are often more up-to-date than textbooks purchased on a multi-year replacement cycle.
3. ***ICT Application :*** Many higher education institutions are looking to shift to a one-to-one computing environment, where every student has a tablet, laptop or other device.
4. ***Collaboration and Partnerships :*** OER provide a foundation to collaborations with other group. Importantly, they also create powerful partnering opportunities at the classroom level by enabling educators to see, develop, share and reuse quality OER to meet their students' unique requirements and needs.
5. ***Exchanging the knowledge:*** OER enables knowledge sharing for the benefit of all students and educators by widening access to high quality resources.
6. ***Cost Savings and Efficiency :*** By sharing and reusing educational materials, the costs for content development can be cut dramatically and allow educators to make better use

of available resources. The minimal funding for professional development and training to develop content can be far less than the recurring costs for printed materials. OER are a cost-effective way to provide digital content.

7. ***Concern about the Quality :*** OER quality improves over time by enabling continuous improvement of online and other digital learning resources by professional peers.

8. ***Support for Independent Learning :*** OER help students access additional learning resources, enhance supplemental materials in support of academic plans, become better prepared, learn independently and pursue learning guided by personal interest. OER offer students access to high-quality material that may be more engaging and in-sync with their own interests.

9. ***OER encourage adaptability enabling users to:*** Translate content into a local language, adapt content to specific learning needs, connect with collaborators at other institutions.

10. ***Benefits of OER for Faculty :*** Use openly licensed materials to build our own resources, license our own OER so others can use it, promote our work to a global audience.

11. ***Benefits of OER for Students :*** Provide supplemental learning materials for courses, determine what classes or program to enroll in and better prepared for classes.

Disadvantages of OER

The following are the disadvantages of OER in teaching and learning process :

1. The quality of OER materials can be inconsistent.
2. There is no common standard for review of OER accuracy and quality.
3. Need of proper way to check accuracy of content.
4. Customization necessary to match departmental and/or college curriculum requirements.

5. Technical knowledge is necessary for the accessing the OER.
6. Need of supportive & compatible software and hardware to access the OER.

Conclusion

Open Educational Resources (OER) are educational materials and resources offered freely and openly for anyone to use and under some license to adapt, copy and redistribute. OER has emerged as a concept with great potential to support educational transformation. OER is simply an educational resource that incorporates a license that facilitates reuse, and potentially adaptation, without first requesting permission from the copyright holder. The central to the idea of OER is openness in the creation, sharing and reuse of learning and teaching materials with barriers of cost or access for the student or end-user reduced as much as possible. OER movement encourages the creation of free, high-quality content for community college courses to replace commonly used textbooks. In higher education institution can create sustainable academic resources for students and provide professional development opportunities for faculty by promoting the use of OER.

Bibliography

1. Neil Butcher (2004), A Basic Guide to Open Educational Resources (OER), Edited by Asha Kanwar (COL) and Stamenka Uvalic´-Trumbic´ (UNESCO) ,Commonwealth of Learning 1055 West Hastings, Suite 1200, Vancouver, British Columbia, Canada V6E 2E9.
2. Smith, M. S., & Casserly, C. M. (2006, September/October). The Promise of Open Educational Resources. Change , 8-17.
3. T. Iiyoshi & M. S. V. Kumar, (Eds.), Opening Up Education (135-148): Cambridge, MA: MIT Press.
4. Thomas Bekkers (2004), Open Educational Resources (OERs), dgCommunity of the Development Gateway Foundation.
5. UNESCO. (2004), Second Global Forum on International Quality Assurance, Accreditation and the Recognition of

Qualifications in Higher Education: “Widening Access to Quality Higher Education”: Background Document, Paris: UNESCO.

6. Wenger, E. (1998, June), Communities of Practice: Learning as a Social System, The Systems Thinker.

35

Digi-class for Tomorrow

Introduction

Education, a road to success, a way to flourish, a formula for development, a weapon to win. One can achieve victory through many factors but education is something which gives endless victory and satisfaction. But to achieve it (education), the path followed should be very systematic and diplomatic. For a country to develop, it should have people who are determined to take quality education. This is very true and we believe in this since many decades. But the education system that we had around four to five decades before is not same as today's education. Many changes are evident from the input as well as the output that is got from the present generation. Earlier it used to be very monotonous where teacher centered education was followed and the students had very less possibilities and opportunities to express their views and creative talents. It was only to teach but nothing was tested at the level of application. To be very precise no ground work was done on this. Strategy of applying the skill learnt for the sake of problem solving was not known to the then generation. Major change was experienced only when child centered education was introduced and learner was considered as the major part of teaching learning programme. In fact, teacher also plays a major role as a guide. But teacher role is very much to bring out the hidden talents in the students.

Why is digital technology essential in education?

The means to fulfill the present requirement is by including technology in present education. This has been started and the process of universalizing is into action. It is not just using computers during teaching or learning but also to bring innovation by using this computer technology. Information and communication technology is something which is already in picture. ICT tries to pick up every kind of student and present education. This is one of the best of many modern techniques as it overcomes the difficulties faced by the conventional classroom teacher due to individual differences. But again the preparation of programmes for different groups of students based on their ability is a task for the teachers.

Today's education is not same as yesterdays. Similarly today's will not be the same as tomorrow's education. There is a need for updating of modern skill time to time. Young people of today should be prepared for emerging digital society of tomorrow. More emphasize on the need for the education system to embrace technology and foster digital literacy at an early stage to create next generation of informed and responsible participants.

Educating a digital society is the way forward. Actual teacher should have sound knowledge about the latest technology. The present generations that are in need of education are way ahead in terms of ability to use digital technology. Teacher should be very enthusiastic in acquiring new digital skills. This would be one way to help all groups of students. Slow learners would be category of students who will be very much favored by this technique of using digital technology during teaching. Proper and effective adaptation of these digital skills would help both students as well as children.

Following are the major aspects to be kept in mind while preparing materials using digital technology

1. Involvement of both course creator and the teacher.

Here course creator means one who builds the syllabus. It should be combined effort of both of them during whole stages of course building implementation.

2. Arranging the content in educationally sound sequence

   Arranging in Simple to complex or concrete to abstract manner, as this is for all category of students.

3. Content analysis

   Breaking the existing content into manageable units for the learner. Every unit should accomplish specific objectives. This helps the learners to have easy access over the content.

4. Teacher can standardize the content by making a common course framework by making flowcharts/course maps. This should be done only after the thorough analysis of content, setting the goals to be achieved after the completion, structure and size of lesson.
5. Adapting to the technique of presenting the content with the help of PowerPoint presentations would help to some extent but not for all the units.
6. Use of audio/ video presentation of the lesson, which would make learning
7. Making of interactive exercises and different brain storming activities, other than theoretical content. These activities ensure the involvement of children.
8. Providing the learning material in a language level that is easy and appropriate for the learner community. Use of shortcuts, acronyms etc would be helpful for slow learners.
9. Making content on the screen in such a way that it would be easy for the learners to scroll and learn without difficulty.
10. The teacher should decide as of how the students would navigate, when the content is presented. And this should not be a barrier for later on assessment.
11. The material can be presented to the students either in printed form or can be downloaded.

Training is regarded as key to success, as long as digital education is concerned. If this digital technology is to be applied in full fledged manner among the present generation, teacher should be taught about the use of this technology in fruitful way. For getting maximum benefits from digital learning, the cost for it is extending facilities for the teachers to standardize the digital content using modern technology. Providing proper training for teachers to do this with confidence and motivation is very essential. It is to be remembered that teachers remain central to the learning process as they should plan, prepare, assess and provide follow up activities to the children. Mere use of technology in class rooms would not change the teaching learning process. It is a technique that is for enabling the teachers to transform their teaching practices and thereby impacts on student's achievement.

Merits of Using Digital Technology

1. It improves teacher's confidence and motivates them to learn new technology.
2. It enables the teacher to bring in required changes in teaching process.
3. It ensures effective participation of teacher in teaching learning process.
4. It widens the subject knowledge among teachers as they have to thoroughly analyze the content before presentation.
5. Narrow thinking and conventional method of teaching can be now forgotten as this digital age is all about broadening the horizon of knowledge using skill and creativity.
6. Teacher can create more of learner centric environment.
7. This method keeps the teachers updated.
8. It provides exposure to mixed effectiveness for the students because even difficult/abstract concept could be put across the students using pictures, PowerPoint presentations, simulations etc.

Demerits of Adapting Digital Technology in Present Day Education

1. It is difficult to provide training to all the teachers, as it requires wide coverage.

2. Government should take initiative of providing no cost training to all the teachers.
3. Every school should have the minimum facility of providing digital classes to the students, which is usually less in government run schools and rural background schools.
4. Teachers sometimes show negative attitude towards learning new concepts of digital technology.
5. Certain teachers feel shy to use this modern technology in public, and some are totally unaware of system/computer usage.
6. There is need of continuous updating of innovations in this field, which may not be possible for everyone.
7. This method of teaching is costlier when compared to conventional teaching learning process.
8. Burden on teachers' is too much in this method as teacher should do systematic analysis of every content, standardize and present it to the students according to their ability and level of understanding.

Conclusion

Teacher is now called as a facilitator. The function of teacher is to extend facilities for children to learn and provide a suitable environment for it. The present day is very much relying on technology based education, that is presenting the knowledge to the students using computer/digital technology. It can be any electronic gadget that would make learning a bit different and interesting. It is to make the learning process a more of learner centered one. The task on part of teacher is very much, because teacher has to think different for every content and concept. This provides variety in learning among the students. Overall the responsibility shouldered by present day teachers is too much, it requires active and deliberate thirst for acquiring new knowledge especially in the field of digital technology. This would also be a key to success for one to shine as a successful teacher.

36

Strategies of Flipped classroom in Education

Introduction

A common assumption in the flipped classroom is that new technologies make it easy to convert instructor lectures through digital recordings and place these online for student access outside of face-to-face class time (EDUCAUSE, 2012; Tucker, 2012). As a result, students can review lectures in ad-vance of class, then have class sessions for working together on the assignments that traditionally would have been done as homework. Not only are students seen as gaining through working together on "homework" problems in class, but in-structors are able to more quickly see where students are struggling and provide remedial support which advocates that by using class time for student discussion, collaboration and problem-solving, the traditional lecture-based mode of in-struction can be replaced by a more student-centered learning that is not only more effective but also achieves larger goals of 21st century skills (Bergmann & Sams, 2012). The increased emphasis on higher order thinking, team work, and prob-lem-solving are seen as critical components in modern learn-ing theory (Bransford &

National Research Council, 2000; Pink, 2006; Willingham, 2009). The flipped classroom is gaining support at all levels of education, including in primary, second-ary and post-secondary classes.

Recent advancement in technology and in ideology have unlocked entirely new direction for education. The use of technology is a key component in allowing lectures to be pre-recorded and made available to students outside of the classroom setting. The philosophy behind the flipped class-room teaching methodology is that it allows instructors to teach both content and process. Eric Mazur a professor of physics at Harvard University suggested that "Learning is a two-step process. First, you must have some transfer of in-formation; second you must make sense of that information by connecting it to your own experiences and organizing the information in your brain" (Demski, 2013, p. 34). The flipped classroom is designed to create a classroom experience that inspires lifelong learning and meets the objectives of Mazur's reference to a two-step process. Despite the recent accolades being extolled to the flipped classroom, there are also cautions about the need for both teachers and students to be properly trained in how to use and teach a flipped class.

Flipped Classroom

The term flipped classroom has become a hot topic in higher education. Ideas about and opinions about flipped learning environments vary. Some consider it simply another way of talking about student-centered learning. Others view flipped classrooms as the most cutting-edge approach to learning. Still others see flipping as just another fad that will eventually run its course.

The most widely used description of the flipped class is a learning environment in which the activities traditionally completed outside of class as homework are now completed in class during instruction time. And, the activities traditionally completed in class are now completed on students' own time before class. In many definitions and models, this means students watch a video of prerecorded lectures before class. Then, when they arrive to class, they work through assignments or activities with their peers and the instructor.

While that is probably the most familiar idea of the flipped classroom, flipping can mean more than watching videos of lectures. After all, a video of a lecture is still a lecture. One of the essential goals of the flipped classroom is to move beyond the lecture as the primary way to deliver information and structure class time. A well-developed lecture can be effective, but instructors rely on it too heavily and often to the exclusion of other more meaningful teaching and learning strategies. A flipped classroom allows instructors to introduce new ways of doing things. Yet adding something new generally requires letting go of something old. In the flipped classroom, instructors need to let go of their reliance on the lecture and focus on other ways to enhance learning by introducing active learning strategies that put students in the center of the learning experience.

There are other ways to define the flip. It can be described as moving from an instructor-centered learning environment to a student-centered learning environment. It could also be defined as shifting from individual to collaborative strategies. Although, it is possible to flip a class using individual activities such as quizzes, worksheets, reflective writing prompts, and problem solving assignments. The key is to complete these activities during class time.

Flipping may or may not include technology. Bergmann and Sams (2012) explain, "Ultimately, flipping a classroom involves shifting the energy away from the instructor and toward the students and then leveraging educational tools to enhance the learning environment." Keep in mind that educational tools include but are not limited to technology. While videos and other technological tools can be effective in a flipped classroom, they are not required. The true essence of the flip is really to focus on the student.

Bloom's Taxonomy

Bloom's Taxonomy provides the framework for comparing the lecture-centered class to the flipped class. Instructors focus on higher level learning outcomes during class time and lower level outcomes outside of class. This means the flip could be as simple as watching a video before class and then attending class for more in-depth discussions that involve judging, analyzing, and creating. If students work with the fundamental material before class, they are better prepared to apply the information and engage in higher-level discussions with their peers and the instructor.

Another way to think about the flipped classroom is to focus on involving students in the process of learning during class. Dr. Barbi Honeycutt refers to the FLIP as Focusing on your Learners by involving them in the Process. After all, flipped classrooms really are student-centered learning environments that incorporate active learning strategies during class time. This allows students to spend time problem solving, creating, critiquing, and synthesizing in class with their peers and with their instructor. Students are more active in flipped environments which add a new level of complexity to the classroom.

Regardless of the definition or framework an instructor uses to design the flipped classroom, the end result is a dynamic learning environment. Flipped classrooms are interactive— sometimes even 'messy'—because students are working together and solving problems rather than sitting passively listening to a lecture. Flipped classrooms are also risky. Instructors relinquish a degree of control when the energy in the classroom shifts to the students. And, some flipped strategies may work while others may not. Instructors using any flipped model need to be aware of these challenges when integrating active learning strategies into their classrooms. However, careful planning can mitigate some of these challenges. For example, starting with a flipped lesson plan helps determine the appropriate tools and most effective strategies which can help instructors maintain control of the flipped classroom and ensure learning outcomes are achieved.

Perhaps one of the best places for instructors to begin is by re-thinking their role in the classroom. Sure, there are mini-lectures that need to be presented, but the majority of class time is spent on active learning. Instructors are not simply thinking about teaching in a different way; they are doing it! They are teaching differently using new approaches, tools, and strategies, and as a result, the lesson planning process and the assessment process will also change.

Flipped Lesson

When planning a flipped lesson, an instructor should begin with the question, "What do the students need to DO to achieve the learning outcome?" This change in perspective will immediately flip the focus of the lesson since the question emphasizes the efforts of the learners, not the instructor. Instructors plan learning experiences based on what the students need to do and not what he or she (the instructor) is going to talk about. The instructor may lecture, but any lectures must be designed to help students accomplish what they need to do with the information or material to achieve desired learning outcomes, not just to disseminate information.

Conclusion

Education is one field that is constantly changing and adapting to meet the needs of students. Educators are continually challenged to find new strategies for engaging students in the classroom so as to increase the effectiveness of the learning process. A flipped classroom inverts the normal learning process. It "moves the lectures outside the classrooms and uses learning activities to move practice with concepts inside the classroom" (Strayer, 2012, p. 171). The strategy "flipped classroom" also known as the "inverted classroom" or "reverse instruction" - a method incorporates technology to "flip" or "reverse" what is typically done in class with what is typically done as homework which supports instructional material for students that can be accessed online. At the heart of the flipped classroom which is moving the "delivery" of material outside of formal class time and using formal class time for students to undertake collaborative and interactive activities relevant to that material. This frees up classroom time that had previously been used for lecturing. This paper examines the concept of flipped classroom concept, challenges and its application on a virtual learning environment ahead of class.

37

Relation Between Study Habits and Academic Achievement of Puc students

Introduction

The present study examined the impact of study habits of students in Chitradurga city, Karnataka, India in relation to Academic achievement, Gender and Faculty. The main objectives were to analyze the study habits of PUC students and to compare it in relation to Academic- Achievement, Gender and Faculty. The research design is quantitative. The sample was selected randomly out of 180 students- 90 were boys and 90 were girls. Out of these 180 students-60 were from Arts faculty, 60 from Science and 60 from Commerce Faculty. The questionnaire was administered for collecting data from the students and t-test and Pearson Correlation statistical methods was used for analysis of data. It was found that there is no significant difference in Mean study habit in relation to gender, and faculties such as Arts, Science and Commerce but there is a significant relationship between study habits and academic achievement of PUC students."

Study habits are a well-planned and deliberate pattern of study which has attained a form of consistency on the part of the students toward understanding academic subjects and passing at examination. Study habits determine the academic achievement of students to a great extent. Both study habits and academic achievement are interrelated and dependent on each other. There are students who come from different environment, localities etc. and have different levels of academic achievement i.e., high and low. They also differ in the pattern of study habits. Some students have better study habits while the others have poor. Better the study habits, better is the academic achievement. Academic achievement means how much knowledge the individual has acquired from the school. Academic achievement of the students is determined by their study habits. Study habits and academic achievement are very essential for research worker and educationists to know that every child whether he is gifted, backward etc. should be educated in their own way. But if children possess good study habits they can show performance in academics and in every situation and if children's do not possess good study habits they cannot excel in life. It is the study habits which help the learner in obtaining Meaningful and desirable knowledge. Good study habits act as a strong weapon for the students to excel in life.

Need and Importance of Study

Study habits play a very important role in bringing about the better academic achievement. The study could bring to light the importance of study habits which are the major contributors of academic achievement. The primary aim of this study was to examine the effect of study habit on students' academic achievement. This general aim is expressed in the following specific objectives which are to: Assess the study habit of students in students; Compare the academic achievement of students who have developed a study habit and those who do not have study habit; Examine factors influencing students study habit; Investigate the effect of study habit on student's academic achievement.

Objectives of the Study

1. To study the difference in study habits of arts and science students.

2. To study the difference in study habits of science and commerce students.
3. To study the difference in study habits of arts and commerce students.
4. To study the difference in study habits of male and female students.
5. To study the difference in academic achievement of male and female students.
6. To study the difference in academic achievement of arts and science students.
7. To study the difference in academic achievement of arts and commerce students.
8. To study the difference in academic achievement of science and commerce students.
9. To study the correlation between study habits and academic achievement of students.

Hypothesis of the Study:

1. There is no significant difference in study habits of arts and science students.
2. There is no significant difference in study habits of science and commerce students.
3. There is no significant difference in study habits of arts and commerce students.
4. There is no significant difference in study habits of male and female students.
5. There is no significant difference in academic achievement of male and female students.
6. There is no significant difference in academic achievement of arts and science students.
7. There is no significant difference in academic achievement of arts and commerce students.

8. There is no significant difference in academic achievement of science and commerce Students.
9. There is no significant correlation between study habits and academic achievement of Students.

Variables of the study: The variables considered are study habits, academic achievement, Gender and Faculty (Science, Commerce and Arts).

6. Sampling Technique: For the present study Simple Random Sampling technique was used to select 180 PUC students from different colleges in Chitradurga City, Karnataka State, India. Out of the Sample of 180 students, 90 were Male and 90 were Female and also maintained the equal stream Ratio of students from Arts 60, Science 60 and Commerce 60 students.

Tool: Following tools were used:

a) Study habit inventory developed by *M. Mukhopadhayay and D.N.Sansanwal* (1963)

b) For academic achievement investigator collected the I year PUC examination marks of Graduation students from college records.

Statistical Techniques : In pursuance of objectives of the study and in order to test the research hypothesis set up, the't'- test and Pearson Correlation was used.

09. Analysis Interpretation of Data: The Objectives and Hypothesis wise analysis was done

Objective-1 To study the difference in study habits of Arts and Science students.

Hypothesis-1 "There is no significant difference in study habits of Arts and Science students."

Table I shows Mean, SD, and't' value of Study Habits of Arts and Science students

Group	Sample	Mean	SD	t-value	Significant at 0.05 level
Arts students 'study habits	60	64.66	7.1		
Science students' study habits	60	68.64	7.4	.031	Not significant

The above table reveals that the obtained'-value 0.031 which is less than the theoretical value 1.98.The obtained value of't' is not significant at 0.05 level. Hence the Null Hypothesis is accepted and it is concluded that, "There is no significant difference in study habits of arts and science students."

Objective-2. To study the difference in Study Habits of Science and Commerce students.

Hypothesis-2'There is no significant difference in Study habits of Science and Commerce Students."

Table II shows Mean, SD, and't' value of Study Habits of Science and commerce students

Group	Sample	Mean	SD	t-value	Significant at 0.05 level
Science students 'study habits	60	68.64	7.4		
Commerce students' study habits	60	64.2	6.9	0.40	Not significant

The above table reveals that the obtained 't'-value 0.40 which is less than the theoretical value 1.98.The obtained value of't' is not significant at 0.05 level. Hence the Null Hypothesis is accepted and it is concluded that, "There is no significant difference in study habits of science and commerce students."

Objective-3 To study the difference in study habits of Arts and Commerce students.

Hypothesis-3 "There is no significant difference in study habits of Arts and Commerce Students."

Table III shows Mean, SD, and't' values of study habits of Arts and commerce students

Group	Sample	Mean	SD	t-value	Significant at 0.05 level
Arts students' study habits	60	64.66	7.1		
Commerce students' study habits	60	64.2	6.9	.032	Not significant

The above table reveals that the obtained't'-value .032 which is less than the theoretical value 1.97.The obtained value of 't' is not significant at 0.05 level. Hence the Null Hypothesis is accepted and it is concluded that, "There is no significant difference in study habits of Arts and Commerce students."

Objective-**4** To study the difference in study habits of Male and Female students.

Hypothesis-**4**"There is no significant difference in study habits of Male and Female students.'

Table IV shows Mean, SD, and't' values of study habits of Male and Female students

Group	Sample	Mean	SD	t-value	Significant at 0.05 level
Male students' study habits	90	67.8	8.1		
Female students' study habits	90	66.2	7.6	1.79	Not significant

The above table reveals that the obtained't'-value 1.79 which is less than the theoretical value 1.97.The obtained value of 't' is not significant at 0.05 level. Hence the Null Hypothesis is accepted and it is concluded that, "There is no significant difference in study habits of male and female students.

Objective-**5.**To study the difference in academic achievement of Male and Female students.

Hypothesis -5. "There is no significant difference in academic achievement of Male and Female students."

Table V shows Mean, SD, and't' values of Academic Achievement of Male and Female students

Group	Sample	Mean	SD	t-value	Significant at 0.05 level
Male students' Academic Achievement	90	53.8	14.4		
Female students' Academic Achievement	90	55.2	14.6	0.28	Not significant

The above table reveals that the obtained't'-value 0.28 which is less than the theoretical value 1.97.The obtained value of 't' is not significant at 0.05 level. Hence the Null Hypothesis is accepted and it is concluded that, "There is no significant difference in academic achievement of male and female students."

Objective- 6 To study the difference in academic achievement of Arts and Science students.

Hypothesis-6 There is no significant difference in academic achievement of Arts and Science Students.

Table VI shows Mean, SD, and't' values of academic achievement of Arts and Science Students

Group	Sample	Mean	SD	t-value	Significant at 0.05 level
Arts students' Academic Achievement	60	47.8	13.4		
Science students' Academic Achievement	60	54.2	11.6	3.21**	significant

** Significant at 0.05 level

The above table reveals that the obtained 't'-value 3.21 is greater than the theoretical value of 1.98.The obtained value of't' is significant at 0.05 level. Hence the Null Hypothesis is rejected and it is formulated that "There is a significant difference in academic achievement of arts and science students." It was also found that girls and boys differ significantly in their study habits and academic achievement. (Singh Y.G., 2011). It can be inferred that there may be good co-relation in Study habits and academic achievement.

Objective-7 To study the difference in academic achievement of Arts and Commerce students.

Hypothesis-7 "There is no significant difference in academic achievement of Arts and Commerce students."

Table VII shows Mean, SD, and't' values of academic achievement of Arts and Commerce students

Group	Sample	Mean	SD	t-value	Significant at 0.05 level
Arts students' Academic Achievement	60	47.8	13.4		
Commerce students Academic Achievement	60	53.4	10.4	3.81**	significant

** Significant at 0.05 level

The above table reveals that the obtained't'-value 3.81 is greater than the theoretical value of 1.98.The obtained value of 't' is significant at 0.05 level. Hence the Null Hypothesis is rejected and it is formulated that "There is no significant difference in academic achievement of arts and commerce students." It was also found that girls and boys differ significantly in their study habits and academic achievement. (Singh Y.G., 2011). It can be inferred that there may be good co-relation in Study habits and academic achievement.

Objective-8 To study the difference in academic achievement of Science and Commerce Students.

Hypothesis-8 "There is no significant difference in academic achievement of Science and Commerce students."

Table VIII shows Mean, SD, and't' values of academic achievement of science and commerce students

Group	Sample	Mean	SD	t-value	Significant at 0.05 level
science students' Academic Achievement	60	54.2	11.6		
Commerce students Academic Achievement	60	53.4	10.4	1.81	Not significant

The above table reveals that the obtained't'-value 1.81 which is less than the theoretical value 1.98.The obtained value of 't' is not significant at 0.05 level. Hence the Null Hypothesis is accepted and it is concluded that, "There is no significant difference in academic achievement of science and commerce students."

Objective-9 To study the relationship between Study habits and Academic achievement of Graduation students.

Hypothesis-9 "There is no significant relationship between study habits and academic Achievement of students."

Table IX shows'r' values of study habits and academic achievement of PUC students

Group	Sample	Mean	SD	r-value	Significant at 0.05 level
PUC students' study Habits	180	65.2	9.6		
PUC students' Academic Achievement	180	54.4	13.4	3.42**	significant

**Significant at 0.05 level

The above table shows that the obtained r-value 3.42 is greater than the theoretical value 0.138.The obtained value of't' is significant at 0.05 level. Hence the Null Hypothesis is rejected and stated new hypothesis "There is a significant relationship between study habits and academic achievement of PUC students." There is a positive co-relation between study habits and academic achievement of students. It was also found that there exists relationship between Study Habits and Academic Achievement of Higher Secondary Students (Singh Y.G., 2011).

Conclusion:

The present study has implication for the teacher and parents that they should encourage students particularly boys and girls with poor academic performance have better study habits which is essential for their survival in this competitive world. They should take also special care for the development of the better study habit. This research indicated that students can acquire efficient studying skills by Means of Curriculum for Developing Efficient Studying Skills and they increase their academic achievements thanks to these studying habits. In this sense, if quality of education is desired to be increased, students with high level of academic achievements are intended and growing youth is expected to compete with the young population of other states with the effect of globalization, it is necessary to make students acquire efficient studying skills.

References

1. Bhan, K.S., & Gupta, R. (2010). Study Habits and Academic Achievement among the Students belonging to Scheduled Caste and Non Scheduled Caste Group, *Journal of Applied research in Education,* 15(1), 1-9.
2. Ifshan Bashir, & Nadhia Hussain Mattoo,(2012). A Study on Study Habits and Academic Performance among Adolescents (14-19) years, *International Journal of Social Science Tomorrow, 1 (5).* www.ijsst.com
3. Jagannath. K. Dange., & Girish, T. (2012). A Study on the Relation between Study Habits and Academic Achievement

among Post- Graduation Students in Kuvempu University, *Indian journal of Experimentation and innovation in Education,* 1(6). *http://www.ijeie.in/index.php/articles/current-volume/vol-1—issue-6-nov-2012/104-*

4. Mohd. Ghani Awang., & Suriya Kumar Sinnadurai., (2011). A Study on the Development of Strategic Tools In Study Orientation Skills Towards Achieving Academic Excellence. ISSN 1798-4769 *Journal of Language Teaching and Research,* 2 (1), 60-67.
5. Mawthohiaisan & Deepak kumar. (2011). Study Habit of Post-Students in Relation to Gender, Faculty and Academic Achievement. *Learning Community-An International Journal of Educational and Social Development,* 2(1), 55- 68.
6. Nuthana P., & Ganga Y.,(2007). Gender analysis of academic achievement among high school students, Unpublished M.Ed. Thesis, Karnataka University Dharwad.
7. Omotere Tope., (2011).The effects of study habit on the academic Performance of students: a case study of some Secondary schools in Ogun state, *Published Online By: EgoBooster Books www.omotere.com*
8. Onwuegbuzie A.J, Slate J,R., & Schwartz R,A., (2001), The role of study skills in -level educational research courses. *Journal of Educational Research,* 94, 238-246.
9. Patel & Patel., B.V.,(1976). Study habits inventory. In: *Second Handbook of Psychology and Social Instruments,* Ed. Pestonjee, D.M., Concept Publishing Company, New Delhi.
10. Singh Y.G., (2011). Academic Achievement and Study Habits of Higher Secondary Students, *International Referred Research Journal,* 3(27).

38

The Impact of E-learning on Teaching and Learning Process

Introduction

The Quality of education is an important measure of productivity and prosperity of the nation. Social, political and economic changes and reforms are possible only through education. Today the information arena witnesses an excelling plethora of technological advances, which has to a great extent been responsible for immeasurable enhancement as human knowledge. Technology has also provided the means of managing knowledge through the strengthened capabilities of collecting, strengthened capabilities of collecting, storing, processing, packaging and transmitting information.

The age of the virtual university has arrived a computer technology, specifically the internet, offers increased possibilities for higher education. With computer technology, the education comes to the student; students are freed from time and space constraints of the traditional classroom. The fusion of information science and technology has tremendously augmented storage capacities, accelerated access for updating the processing facility es, refined search strategies and expended access to distant databases network.

E-Learning is a technology which supports teaching and learning via a computer web technology. It bridges the gap between a teacher and a student in different geographical locations. Advancement in internet and multimedia technology is the basic enabler for e-learning. E-learning applications facilitate online access to learning content and administration. Software applications built for planning, delivering and managing learning events has become a crucial need for the corporate training departments of large organizations. Our creative and technical abilities allow us to package the most complex material into a comprehensive and an interactive e-learning application. We work with sophisticated technologies and produce e-learning applications for a variety of situations and deployment methods. The enhanced functionality offers support to existing students and faculty including admissions, events and academics resources. This paper mainly focuses on the impact of E-learning on Teaching and Learning process both from teacher's viewpoint and student's effectiveness in learning. These parameters are analyzed considering some of the important factors related to teaching learning process.

The pressure to expand and democratize educational opportunity have increased enormously, fuelled in part by the population expansion and in part by the need to prepare people for jobs in ever more complex and interdependent societies. Planners are seeking strategies that will not only make education available to greater numbers of people but also an education that will not demand the level of investment and administrative structure customarily associated with the traditional system of education. Understandably the search is on for alternatives to these traditional forms of education so that the benefits of education can be extended beyond the four walls of the schools to embrace a wider spectrum of people, old and young, rural and urban. This paper mainly focuses on the impact of E-learning on Teaching and Learning process both from teacher's viewpoint and student's effectiveness in learning. Its key focus and emphasis is on the changes to teaching and learning that will result from an e-education environment.

1 An analysis of e-learning and its impact on teachers.

2 The changing roles of teachers and the classroom environment with the advent of e-learning

3 How schools can move towards establishing strong pedagogical bases for e-learning.

These parameters are analyzed considering some of the important factors related to teaching learning process.

The Effect of Technology on Students

The implementation of teaching online would extend access for higher education to students who would not otherwise be able to attend classes and would result in increased enrolments. For example, disabled students and students in remote areas would be able to take online courses via computer.

The commonly used teaching tools can be implemented easily through the online system. Instead of oral lectures, professors may send lecture notes to supplement assigned readings. Visual illustrations can be sent via World Wide Web pages or by attaching presentation software files, such as power point, or e-mail messages for students to download and view on their own computers. Students can also be sent prepackaged tutorials that use graphics or CD-ROM software that uses video clips. Many websites act as repositories for lecture notes and course materials they simply modernize the chalk and talk experience. However, on-line lecture notes are not the same as notes delivered in a lecture. Also, although some sites have the ability to exploit video and sound, few do so. Many do not even hyperlink to other academic materials, although news links are sometimes used. One large benefit of on-line delivery comes from instructors being able to disseminate material quickly and upgrade them easily.

Concept of e-learning; e-teachers and e-teaching

The "e" stands for electronic and it relates to the use of the Internet to undertake the wide range of activities. As we become more familiar with the language of the Internet we find just how much it pervades our daily lives in the dot.com age. We readily recognize http://

www......... as an Internet web site and see it plastered on vehicles, billboards, hot air balloons, merchandise and in the screen and print media. Educators are now beginning to hear terms like e- teaching, e-learning and e- education as it subtly becomes part of our regular vocabulary.

E-learning

E-learning is a technology which supports teaching and learning via a computer web technology. E-learning means self teaching. The term "e-learning" implies a new educational technology, based on well-designed computer-based courseware that allows students to teach themselves. *"E-Learning is Internet-enabled learning. E-Learning provides faster learning at reduced costs,* increased access to learning, and clear accountability for all participants in the learning process. In today's fast-paced culture, organizations that implement e-Learning provide their work force with the ability to turn change into an advantage." – *Cisco Systems.*

E-teaching

By comparison, "e-teaching" is the facilitation of live teaching with streaming lectures, whiteboards, downloadable slide sets, and discussion forums. E-teaching is about the automation of an existing teacher-centered educational approach, while e-learning means a new student-centered approach that is more consistent with adult learning theory.

The real action today is in creating content and deployment (learning management) systems that support e-learning. Teacher-centered education is considered obsolete and, within the e-learning industry, "teaching" is almost a bad word and the word "teacher" is not used. People who prepare e-learning programs refer to themselves as "instructional designers" or "educational facilitators," but not as "teachers.

E-teachers

E-teachers are the new generation of teachers who will work in an Internet environment in both regular and virtual classroom situations. They will build new concepts of working in time and space.

E-teachers collaborate, build and discover new learning communities and explore resources as they interact with information, materials and ideas with their students and colleagues.

Review of Research Studies on e-learning

Rosenberg (2001) highlighted the importance of an e-learning strategy and warned that this was not just about utilizing tools:

The people who can help to implement the change according to Rosenberg (2001) are those who are ready and willing to see learning in a much broader context. This is not about reinventing what we do now but about broadening our horizons as we take advantage of new opportunities to enhance what we might do in a classroom that has no traditional walls.

The Web-based Education Commission [WEBC] to the President and Congress of the United States undertook a yearlong study of the potential of the Internet to enhance learning in schools. WEBC issued a statement following publication of the Report on December 19th, 2000. They promoted a nationwide "Call-to-Action To Harness INTERNET'S Power for Learning" and announced the "Broadest Report To Date On E-Learning Recommends Investment, Regulatory Reform". The hard-hitting report urged:

We must immediately put to rest the notion that full development of Web-based technology for education is a choice," Kerrey [Commission Chairperson] said. "The Internet is revolutionizing all parts of society, but its impact on education is just beginning to be understood. We believe that a national mobilization is necessary to ensure that the tremendous potential of this new technology is harnessed to benefit all learners whether in our nation's schoolhouses, college campuses, corporate training rooms, or at their kitchen tables.

The WEBC (2000) found that "the Web is a medium today's kids expect to use for expression and communication—the world into which they were born" while acknowledging "the Internet is not a panacea for every problem in education"

Rutherford and Grana (1995) also focused their research on academic staff fear in the face of technology. They identified nine areas that could prevent staff from making changes that would enable them to integrate technology into their teaching:

1. Fear of change
2. Fear of time commitment
3. Fear of appearing incompetent
4. Fear of techno lingo
5. Fear of techno failure
6. Fear of not knowing where to start
7. Fear of being married to bad choices
8. Fear of having to move backward to go forward
9. Fear of rejection or reprisals

The issues of a lack of knowledge about ICT, a perceived lack of support, and an unwillingness to experiment with innovation all impact on the move to e-teaching.

Impact of e-learning on teaching Learning Process

Due to the large scale innovations in communication system, the society and its economic structure are undergoing a metamorphosis and the information centered society is taking its root very fast in almost all nations of the world. Teacher education is no exception to this development. Computer-based networking system has provided the present day teacher with a choice of modern tools to deliver the goods in the classroom and end the instructional boundaries.

In short we can say that Information and communication Technology in which e-learning's-teaching: e-teachers are built in components has the following impact on teaching learning process:

1. Improves efficiency both in learning and teaching;
2. Increases motivation;
3. Deepens understanding;
4. Promotes collaborate learning;
5. Gives new approach to learning and working;

6. Provides for new ways of interacting;
7. Paves way for personality development;
8. Increases social skills;
9. Creates interest in learning;
10. Helpful for self-evaluation;
11. Wide reach and consistent;
12. User convenient;
13. It is a very flexible and rich medium for students to access learning materials;
14. It is a very useful tool to address students with different learning and cognitive styles;
15. Self-pacing for slow or quick learners reduces stress and increases satisfaction;
16. Confidence that quick reference materials are available reduces burden of responsibility of mastery;
17. Provides a single experience that accommodates the three distinct learning styles of auditory learners, visual learners and kinesthetic learners.
18. Unique opportunities created by the advent and development of e-learning are more efficient training of a globally dispersed audience and reduced publishing and distribution costs as web-based training becomes a standard.

The Shift in the role of the teacher and that of the learner

The instructional methods to be used in socio-constructivists web-based environments no longer position the student as a passive recipient of knowledge and the teacher as the one who will transmit the knowledge. The student becomes an active agent in the teaching and learning process who continuous seeks for new information and experiences under the guidance of the teacher. This paradigm shift also implies in some cases, the loss of authority of the teacher in the classroom and this has been the main reason behind the reluctance of teachers to adopt the innovative methods. Migrating to the online environment does not only have an effect on the learning culture of students but also on the teaching culture and the educational conceptions of teachers.

Teacher education and e-teaching

The institutions that offer teacher education, both pre-service and graduate education, will need to consider their changing roles and the way in which they model good e-teaching practice. For staff working in teacher education to talk about what e-teaching might be like without actually doing it, will leave their students wondering why it might be so difficult. What could even more discouraging for teacher education students is for the institutions to put courses online and assume that this e-teaching. "If teacher education programs do not address this issue at once, we will soon have lost the opportunity to enhance the performance of a whole generation of new teachers and the students they teach"-The Web-Based Education Commission (2000) has warned.

Role of an e-teacher in facilitating e-learning

'e-teacher is not a person who knows all the answers and decides what the question will be', but it is the e-teacher who 'becomes an expert learner 'who can help students solve problems and find answers to their questions'. The teacher therefore becomes as much a part of the learning process as their students as they learn to work in a facilitative and collaborative e-learning environment. Since the teachers are in the dot.com age ,they will have to work in an environment in which they have never been learners and may have had few first-hand experiences.

Hence the e-teacher need to:

1. Look at the course in a new way and re-think and adapt existing course delivery.
2. Move from being a content provider to a content facilitator who has a good knowledge of their subject area.
3. Gain proficiency in using the tools so that there is an understanding of both its strengths and its weaknesses.

4. Learn to teach in absence of face-to-face interaction.
5. Gain an understanding of student's needs and lifestyles in their own communities.
6. Encourage and guide students to set their own objectives and explore their own needs and agendas.
7. Develop positive attitude towards the use of ICT to consider e-teaching.
8. Improve level of internal motivation to utilize ICT and to consider new and challenging teaching options.
9. Teacher educator has to be competent I the methodology to present the concepts effectively utilizing ICT.

Hence the e-teachers should have a vision of their role as e-teachers and what this might mean for them both personally and professionally then the "e"ceases to have any relevance.

Pedagogical bases for e-learning

E-learning depends upon following e-resources:

1. Involving the experiences of students, teachers, strategies and planning schedule and teaching learning content
2. It requires — staff development, technological delivery strategy
3. Teacher's conception of preparation of teaching strategies
4. Students learning interest
5. Software for reading and downloading,saving,printing and transmitting

Conclusion

e – Learning provides lot of opportunities for the students when comparing to other media of learning. The level of participation among students gets improved consistently. Thus, E – Learning enables the students for continuous updating of knowledge, enhances their IT skills and paves way for time management in the teaching-learning process. ICT has important implications for both improving teacher-training methods and more broadly, for ensuring that teachers are in a position to take up new roles suited to education in Knowledge-based societies. We are now sailing into a sea of change made possible by the rapid development and availability of the Internet. These developments have already begun to fundamentally alter the way in which we can utilise ICT in our classrooms. What we can now consider is that the access to the Internet outside of formal classroom settings has opened up possibilities that were inconceivable ten years ago.

39

Blended Learning

Introduction

While teachers have always used a variety of teaching methods and media, blended learning includes the recent availability of digital learning technologies and Internet-based tools that facilitate communication, interaction, and collaborative learning. Neither e-learning nor the traditional classroom are ideal for all types of learning. Blended learning offers the opportunity to incorporate the 'best of both worlds' to improve teaching and learning, to take "advantage of the strengths of both learning environments and be more successful in avoiding their weaknesses." Blended learning has taken many forms since it was first created several years ago. As blended learning evolved, its name and meaning also changed. It has been called hybrid learning, mixed mode learning, and several other names. The second subheading in Chapter One, The many names of Blended Learning, will discuss the countless names of blended learning, review each meaning, and look at how it has evolved into the term we know today.

Blended learning is a term increasingly used to describe the way e-learning is being combined with traditional classroom methods and independent study to create a new, hybrid teaching methodology. It represents a much greater change in basic technique than simply adding computers to classrooms; it represents, in many cases, a fundamental change in the way teachers and students approach the learning experience. It has already produced an offshoot – the flipped classroom – that has quickly become a distinct approach of its own.

No single, reliable definition of blended learning exists, or evens a universal agreement on the term itself. Many use terms like hybrid, mixed, or integrative to describe the same trend. But the trend is significant. In 2000 an estimated 45,000 K-12 students took an online course, but almost a decade later more than 3 million took courses that way, many of them using computers in the schools themselves.

History of the term

The concept of blended learning has been around for a long time, but its terminology was not firmly established until around the beginning of the 21st century. One of the earliest reference to the term appears in a press release in 1999, when the Interactive Learning Centers, an Atlanta-based education business, announced its change of name to EPIC learning. The article mentions that "The Company currently operates 220 on-line courses, but will begin offering its Internet courseware using the company's Blended Learning methodology." The meaning of blended learning widely diverged to encompass a wide variety of synthesis in learning methods until 2006, when the first *Handbook of Blended Learning* by Bonk and Graham was published. In this publication Graham challenged the breadth and ambiguity of the term's definition, and defined 'blended learning systems' as learning systems that "combine face-to-face instruction with computer mediated instruction." Currently, use of the term *blended learning* mostly involves "combining Internet and digital media with established classroom forms that require the physical co-presence of teacher and students."

Why *Flexibility* in Learning?

Today, learners want to have more *say* in

1. WHAT they learn

2. WHEN they learn
3. WHERE they learn, and
4. HOW they learn

Components of Blended Learning

1. *Synchronous* (live) Classroom format
2. *Synchronous* (live) online format
3. *Asynchronous* (not live) self-paced format

1. Synchronous Physical/Face-to-Face Components (not limited to)

1. Face-to-face Tutoring
2. Coaching or Mentoring Sessions
3. Classroom
4. Workshops
5. Conferences
6. Meetings
7. Labs

2. Synchronous Electronic Components (not limited to)

1. Internet conferencing
2. Audio Conferencing (i.e., phone conferencing)
3. Live Video via satellite or Videoconferencing
4. Virtual Online Classroom
5. Instant Messaging

3. Asynchronous Components (not limited to)

1. On-line self-paced Learning Content (Web pages)
2. E-mail, Discussion Forums
3. EPSS (Electronic Support Systems) & Job Aids
4. Web/Computer-Based instruction

5. Books
6. Articles
7. CD-ROM
8. Audio (disc/tape)
9. Video (disc/tape)
10. White papers
11. Archived Live Events

How to develop a rich Blended Learning

Six ways to develop a rich blended learning with your students:

Online Content

Allowing student's the ability to gain access to their module content gives the students a deeper understanding of their subject knowledge. Learning materials such as PowerPoint's, session plans and handout's can be placed on WOLF and PebblePad, giving the student full accessibility 24/7, at the University or at home.

Feedback

Feedback is a vital part of a student's development and allowing regular opportunities to engage with them in feedback will greatly improve a student's experience. Formative online task's allows you to understand a student's learning over a period of time and can be placed outside of the classroom, giving the lecturer more time to focus on the core concepts of the module.

Interactive content

Engaging and interacting with a classroom full of student's is an excellent method of keeping students focused and interested with the content you're presenting. Using anything from interactive whiteboards to post-it notes will help further develop a student's understanding of the content.

Collaborative learning

Collaborative learning can extend out of the classroom. Using collaborative task's in WOLF and in PebblePad, students can manage their learning, while giving and supporting their peers. Collaborative tasks can help students discuss area's they might have misunderstood or help the lecturer be aware of areas that may need to be re-examined.

Personal Development Planning

Personal Development Planning (PDP) allows students to develop and collect evidence on achievements to enhance their employability portfolio. Developing these area's online (ePDP) can allow lecturers to monitor and give feedback on a student's achievements and goals, helping them to be more successful within employment market.

Electronic Submission

Electronic submission allows students to submit anywhere and at anytime (before a deadline.) The student will also obtain their electronic feedback in a similar method, giving them the same accessibility rights as when they submitted their work.

Advantages of Blended Learning

1. Blended learning allows businesses and schools alike to make maximum use of the technologies and other resources that they have available to them. This means that it allows both businesses and schools to take a look at all the technologies and tools that they have and see how it can best be used to bring the greatest benefit to employee/students and the organization even as they spend as little as they possibly can and still maintain effectiveness.
2. The organization offering the course can create his/her own content.
3. The global reach of the blended approach to education and training continues to be one of its greatest advantages. Uses concerning distance are eliminated.
4. The speed with which you can reach thousands of people is unmatched by traditional methods as they can all be reach simultaneously without the restrictions of time and space.

5. Not all content can be properly delivered online. The challenges of using a purely online modality are eliminated when a blended approach is used.
6. Blended learning allows learners the flexibility with their time to do their lessons anytime and anyplace until a meeting with the lecturer becomes compulsory.
7. It can make it easier to deal with educational administration and communication with all students. Virtual office hours make tutors far more accessible than in a strictly face-to-face scenario.
8. Students get their learning needs and styles catered to whether they prefer online or face-to-face because it offers both in a single course.
9. For sessions held online, the communication between teacher and student is open and everyone can benefit from it because everyone can view the responses sent by the teacher.
10. Some lecturers experience an improvement in the quality of students' writing and discussion.

References

1. Seidl, M. (2005). Blended Learning With Moodle: Didactical and Technical Aspects of Blended Learning Scenario with Moodle. Retrieved from http://streaming.fh-stpoelten.ac.at/netties2005/word/Seidl.pdf. On April 28, 2006.
2. www.cybermediacreations.com/elearning/glossary.htm
3. www.teach-nology.com/glossary/terms/b/
4. www.intelera.com/glossary.htm
5. www.itslifejimbutnotasweknowit.org.uk/lt_glossary.htm
6. en.wikipedia.org/wiki/Blended learning
7. http://www.e-learningguru.com/wpapers/blendedbersin.doc.

40

Edu – Digital Skill

Introduction

Youth make up 17 per cent of the world's population and 40 per cent of the world's unemployed, according to the International Labour Organization. It is a crisis with many dimensions. High youth unemployment not only hampers economic growth, for youth it can be a debilitating experience that affects their desire and ability to lead productive and rewarding lives. With the youth bulge swelling the ranks of working age population's worldwide, urgent attention is needed to address the plight of youth and provide them with better opportunities for employment.

Against this backdrop, ongoing advances in information and communication technologies (ICTs) are transforming old sectors and creating new ones. No sector has been untouched, from farming to manufacturing to service industries. This transformation is effectively making digital literacy a prerequisite for both wage employment and creating one's own business. ICT literacy not only qualifies people for jobs in conventional job sectors, but also opens doors to participate in rapidly growing markets such as business process outsourcing and micro work. People with more advanced ICT skills can take advantage of an even wider range of opportunities brought about by the growth of the "app economy," mobile phones, social media, and the game industry.

For today's youth this signals an opportunity, if the right steps are taken. Youth with access to technology are coming of age as digital natives, the early adopters of ICTs and better positioned than their parents to harness the power of ICTs in new and imaginative ways. The premise of this report is that much more needs to be done to realize these opportunities. Youth in developing countries lag their developed world counterparts in experience with ICTs.1 Moreover, even those with access are not being equipped with the ICT skills they need to succeed. There is an overall mismatch between what the market is demanding and what institutions of learning—formal and non-formal—are providing. Schools and other centers of learning are challenged to keep pace with rapid technological changes and many are stuck in old methods of instruction that are ill suited to ways in which ICT skills can be acquired. The knowledge and skills for creating a business are even more lacking in instructional programmes.

Against this gloomy picture there is an explosion of new learning opportunities that employ novel (and often free or inexpensive) ways for people to gain the right skills. The same forces that have unleashed a myriad of new career options are generating new forms of learning. Open courseware, flipped classrooms, mobile learning, and other innovations are redefining the realm of the possible, propelling a learning revolution that has the potential to reach a far greater proportion of the world's youth.

What is needed for youth to acquire ICT and entrepreneurship skills and seize new ICT-enabled career prospects? Is there need for action when the market is creating new opportunities for people with ICT skills, and people can go online and learn these skills? Unquestionably yes. Many opportunities are still largely untapped, and policies and programmes are not aligned to take advantage of the possibilities. The nonstop proliferation of new applications and services makes concerted efforts to prepare youth with the appropriate skills all the more challenging. Accordingly, the primary aim of this report is to spotlight emerging trends, focusing on new work opportunities, new skills, and new ways of acquiring these skills. The hope is that readers will gain a better understanding of a range of new and innovative ways that youth can realize better futures.

In the course of the research for this report, the authors encountered a huge volume of job matching services, employability programs, contests and other programs for entrepreneurs, online learning platforms, and other useful resources. It quickly became apparent that it would be nearly impossible to adequately represent all of these in a report of reasonable length. Accordingly, the project has developed a database that includes the resources and can be continuously updated as new ones become available. It is hoped that this database will provide youth with a valuable asset in their efforts to secure meaningful employment and entrepreneurship opportunities. The database is available at: www.itu.int/ITU-D/youth.

A focus on emerging trends is an inherently risky proposition. Some of the nascent markets and learning programmes will become huge forces that reshape entire industries; others may never gain widespread traction and fizzle. That said, ongoing ICT-driven change is a certainty, and not pursuing new strategies is a far riskier proposition. Fortunately, many of the ideas contained in this report can be pursued with far less expense compared to earlier times. The technology and education sectors (both private and non-profit) are driving many of the changes, generating new opportunities, services, and products. It is possible to pilot a new curriculum, for instance, without having to create one. Doing this requires public-private partnerships, imagination, and openness to taking risks. It is also essential that new initiatives have a system for tracking progress, making mid-course corrections, abandoning strategies that are not working, and identifying and incorporating emerging opportunities. Institutional nimbleness is a key attribute of successful initiatives, and this will become increasingly important in the years ahead.

Youth and unemployment

Around the world youth disproportionately suffer from the malaise of unemployment. The scale of the problem is immense, holding back economic growth while stifling the aspirations of people recently entering the workforce and at the beginnings of their careers. The causes of this situation are multifaceted, and manifest differently in each region. This chapter provides data and context about youth unemployment, and discusses the primary causes of this acute state of affairs.

New employment and entrepreneurship opportunities - Emerging sectors

The increasing adoption of ICTs in everyday life, and the growing marketplace for digital goods and services, are creating opportunities for youth to find employment that transcend traditional paradigms. The way young people find and carry out work is changing. Instead of looking in the local newspaper, youth around the world browse web-based job listings to find work. Those with limited access to the internet carry out their job searches at public venues — telecentres, libraries, cybercafés — and many are even finding and carrying out work via their mobile devices. The very notion of the "work place" now reaches far beyond the local, which has great implications for young people that are challenged to find employment in their own communities. New approaches to outsourcing like crowd sourcing and micro work are providing young people worldwide with task- and project-based work opportunities-many of which are not restricted to highly skilled developers, but can also extend to semi-skilled and low-skilled workers with access to a relatively basic digital infrastructure

The global increase in the use of mobile technologies is playing a key role in expanding employment opportunities for youth. Great potential for employment growth derives from a demand for services enabled by mobile phones.81 Young people can now find and carry out work, launch their entrepreneurial endeavours and even get paid via their cell phones. Young people are doing mobile micro work, and also being contracted to carry out market research in their own communities. Mobile financial services such as M-PESA82 are making it easier for young people to receive payment for services rendered and to launch their own entrepreneurial endeavours.

Given the growth in mobile phones, there is a lot of interest in mobile applications and how the emerging "app economy"83 might generate new employment opportunities for young people around the world. Many young computer programmers are finding jobs working directly for software development firms. In addition there are opportunities for developers with entrepreneurial ambitions to start their own appsbased businesses.

This chapter explores a range of emerging opportunities involving ICTs and youth employment and entrepreneurship. First, the ways in which young people find work through digital job matching services is covered, followed by new opportunities for ICT enabled employment. The chapter then turns to the growing app industry, its potential for employment, and some of the issues related to becoming an appsbased entrepreneur. This includes a need for people with skills to develop accessible software and websites for people with disabilities.

The fields of ICT repair, maintenance, and sales are also explored as they continue to be a source of employment for young people around the world. Lastly opportunities that green jobs may hold for youth are examined.

Apps development

There is speculation regarding how the growing trend of apps development will generate new employment opportunities for young people around the world. The rapid rise of smart phones, tablets, and social media, and the applications-"apps"-that run on them, is one of the biggest economic and technological phenomena today. Since the iPhone was introduced in 2007, the app economy has generated roughly 752 000 app related jobs in the United States alone as of July 2013.92 The figure is 530 000 jobs in the 28 European Union countries.

Apps have inspired a new class of entrepreneurs, spawning a multibillion-dollar industry virtually overnight. The Apple App store eclipsed 1 000 000 apps in October 2013, double the number from two years earlier. The number of apps for Android has risen at roughly the same pace.

Games are still considered to be the most lucrative apps. Young people around the world aspire to cash in by creating the next Angry Birds. Interestingly, winners of Pivot East's recent app competitions for the mobile and developer communities in East Africa have both been games-a Matatu racing game that has been downloaded 150 000 times in over 200 countries and an action game application with an African jungle setting called Tough Jungle.

However, the verdict is out in terms of how sustainable the app economy will be, and whether it will produce enough revenue in emerging markets to support this new generation of entrepreneurs. Vision Mobile research shows that only a select few app developers in more mature markets are managing to make a living as app developers.

Sustaining an app in the market requires much more than developing it, launching it, and waiting for the profits to come in. It requires investment in constant development, upgrades, and new features. App stores are highly competitive and offering new features is essential to maintaining an app's ratings and reviews.

Sizing the number of jobs generated by the app economy is difficult. Any particular app could be created by a single teenage programmer, or by a large team at a big company.

Jobs in the app economy can be categorized as follows:

1. IT-related jobs that use app economy skills—the ability to develop, maintain, or support mobile applications.
2. Non-IT jobs (such as human resources or marketing) which support app developers in the same company.
3. Jobs in the local economies that are supported by app developers.
4. The following is a list of types of app economy employers
5. Large, medium, and small app developers, who may be creating apps for themselves or for clients.
6. Media and software companies that engage in app development for consumer use under their own name.

7. Finance and retail companies that use apps to reach customers.
8. Other large non-tech companies that are developing apps for internal and customer use.
9. Smaller non-tech firms who need a small number of app developers.
10. Non-profit organizations and government agencies, including the military, which require app developers to perform their functions.
11. Support companies to help manage all the new technology.
12. Large companies such as Amazon, Apple, Google, Microsoft, and RIM, who develop and maintain mobile app ecosystems/ platforms,.
13. Large tech companies who develop essential infrastructure and complementary technologies for the app economy.
14. Accounting and IT consulting firms, who provide app development as part of a larger suite of services.

ICT Employability skills

What skills are required to take advantage of the opportunities described in this report? As shown, there is a wide range of ways that ICTs are revolutionizing all sectors of the economy and creating new avenues for starting a business. The popularization of Web 2.0, social media, mobile apps, and other ICT advancements have dramatically changed the playing field. With these changes there has arisen the need to re-think and update the types of ICT and ICT-related skills that are required to succeed in today's world. Being "computer literate" – having the skills to perform basic computer operations – used to be sufficient for most jobs entailing use of computers. While this may still hold true in some cases, basic computer literacy is not sufficient to pursue the majority of new opportunities described in earlier chapters. To respond to these changes, experts have developed new literacy frameworks in order to describe and delineate other types of ICT skills. These go by such names such as digital literacy, information literacy, ICT literacy, media (or multimedia) literacy, and web literacy, among others. New curricula and training programs have emerged to cover the broader set of skills contained within these new frameworks.

This chapter begins with a look at the evolution from computer to digital literacy, the latter widely recognized as a more comprehensive and relevant inventory of the range of ICT-related skills needed for success in career and life. Next, the concept of web literacy is explored, exemplifying new thinking around a variation of ICT skills that is becoming increasingly important for some careers. Finally, the report describes the complementary skills that, in combination with ICT skills, are deemed necessary for employment.

Computer literacy

Computer literacy "refers to the ability to use computers and related technologies, from end-users to ICT professionals. It is generally understood as the knowledge and skills needed to effectively use hardware and software components."

Basic computer skills include (sample):

1. Turning a computer on and off;
2. using a mouse and keyboard;
3. understanding basic computer terminology and concepts;
4. understanding operating system, programmes, and data;
5. Managing files.

Intermediate computer skills (sample):

6. Performing basic functions of common productivity programmes (word processing, spreadsheet, presentation);
7. Using email and web browser;
8. Installing software and hardware.

Advanced computer skills (sample):

9. Programming;
10. Using advanced features of productivity programmes;
11. Fixing simple computer problems.

Computer literacy at the intermediate level is becoming required for almost every job. In the health sector discussed in Chapter 3 for example, hospital employees must be able to use medical records systems, order supplies, manage appointments and perform other routine tasks on a computer that used to be done on paper. Even in many jobs that do not entail contact with a computer employers are screening for basic computer skills as a minimum qualification for employment.117 An increasing number of non-IT positions also expect people to have more advanced skills, such as basic trouble-shooting and using advanced features in productivity programmes, though IT professionals are can still be relied upon for most advanced functions.

Digital Literacy

Most of today's attention around ICT skills is focused on the concept of digital literacy. Being digitally literate refers to the ability to effectively and critically navigate, evaluate and create information using a range of digital technologies. The Institute for Prospective Technological Studies (IPTS), a research centre of the European Commission, has undertaken extensive work around digital literacy. In its 2013 report they propose a comprehensive framework that exemplifies the types of competencies many experts note are required to be digitally literate.

Digital competence framework

Dimension 1 Competence areas	Dimension 2 Competences
1. Information	1.1 Browsing, searching and filtering information
	1.2 Evaluating information
	1.3 Storing and retrieving information1
2. Communication	2.1 Interacting through technologies
	2.2 Sharing information and content
	2.3 Engaging in online citizenship
	2.4 Collaborating through digital channels
	2.5 Netiquette
	2.6 Managing digital identity
3. Content creation	3.1 Developing content
	3.2 Integrating and re-elaborating
	3.3 Copyright and licenses
	3.4 Programming
4. Safety	4.1 Protecting devices
	4.2 Protecting personal data

	4.3 Protecting health 4.4 Protecting the environment
5. Problem solving	5.1 Solving technical problems 5.2 Identifying needs and technological responses 5.3 Innovating and creatively using technology 5.4 Identifying digital competence gaps

As shown above, the framework is divided into five competence areas, each with a set of three to six competences. There are important distinctions between this and other digital literacy frameworks and those focused on computer literacy. First, digital literacy frameworks are typically more explicit about the breadth of life purposes for which being digitally literate is necessary. The IPTS framework, for instance, articulates the following life activities: leisure, social, buying and selling, learning, citizenship, well-being, and employability. The list above illuminates this tendency with the inclusion of such competences as netiquette, engaging in online citizenship, protecting personal data, and so on. In this way digital literacy frameworks adopt a holistic approach, recognizing the deeply embedded nature of technology is all aspects of life.

Second, being digitally literate involves much more than having technical skills. In the IPTS framework, each competence articulates knowledge and attitudes in addition to skills that are required. Table illustrates this with competence.

Collaborating through digital channels

Knowledge examples	Knows that collaborative processes facilitate content creation Knows when content creation can benefit from collaborative processes and when not Understands the dynamics of collaborative work and of giving and receiving feedback
Skills examples	Is able to use the collaborative features of software packages and web-based collaborative services (e.g. track changes, comments on a document or resource, tags, contribution to wikis, etc.)

	Is able to give and receive feedback Can use social media for different collaborative purposes
Attitude examples	Is willing to share and collaborate with others Is ready to function as part of a team Seeks new forms of collaboration that are not necessarily based on a previous face-to-face engagement

Finally, for the purposes of this report, it is important to call attention to the employability purpose. Each of the 21 competences contains examples of its relevance to people in typical work situations. Remaining with the example of *collaborating through digital channels*, a person with advanced skills would have the following ability:

"I have created a draft project document on finance, and put it into an online collaboration tool, so that the others working on it with me can amend it and add to it. The system will alert me to the changes when these are being made, so that I can collaborate with them synchronously if I wish

Web literacy

While digital literacy may be the most established concept, other efforts have also emerged that reflect differing philosophies of how the internet should be maintained, as well as different skillets. The concept of web literacies is worth discussing in this context. Advanced by the Mozilla Foundation in collaboration with global experts, web literacies refers to "not only being able to read the web but also having the ability to 'write' it. Writing the web – creating pages, documents and multimedia assets – means understanding the building blocks of the web. As Mitchell Baker (Chairperson of Mozilla) says, we want to move beyond 'elegant consumption' towards creating a generation of Webmakers. We're not talking about everyone becoming a fully-fledged programmer, but we do believe that everyone should have the skills, competencies and literacies to be able to tinker and make things with and on the web."

Web skills / Competencies / Literacies grid

EXPLORING	CREATING	CONNECTING	PROTECTING
	BEGINNER		
Browser basics *(e.g. URLs, copy/paste)*	**HTML basics** *(e.g. adding images, linking)*	**Participation** *(e.g. etiquette curation)*	**Privacy** *(e.g. cookies, privacy controls)*
Search engine basics *(e.g. keyword search, filtering)*	**CSS basics** *(e.g. fonts, positioning)*	**Collaboration** *(e.g. co-creation, wikis)*	**Security basics** *(e.g. HTTPS, password management)*
Web mechanics *(e.g. view source, hyperlinks)*	**Web design basics** *(e.g. affordances of the web, designing for audiences)*	**Sharing** *(e.g. social networks, embedding)*	**Rights online** *(e.g. copyright, open licensing)*
	INTERMEDIATE		
Browser skills *(e.g. cookie management, addons)*	**Javascript basics** *(e.g. programming basics, javascript syntax)*	**Contributing to web communities** *(e.g. distributed working, collaborative curation)*	**Identity** *(e.g. personal information curation, tracking management)*
Credibility *(e.g. trustworthiness of websites, evaluating information)*	**Advanced web design** *(e.g. responsive design, accessibility)*	**Storytelling** *(e.g. multimedia, augmentation)*	**Security & encryption** *(e.g. data protection, basic encryption)*
Remixing *(e.g. mashups, hackable games)*	**Infrastructure** *(e.g. hosting, domains)*	**Open practices** *(e.g. open standards, open source) agreements)*	**Legalese on the web** *(e.g. privacy policies, terms of service*

To Create New Approaches and Techniques Applying in Education

There are vast opportunities for youth to engage in collaborative (or peer) learning using ICTs. Collaborative learning allows peers to share their knowledge, explore new areas of interest, and benefit from the cumulative knowledge of the group. Collaborative learning relies on positive interdependence with the group, individual accountability for learning and teaching, and clear processes to lead, follow and resolve issues related to project goals or group dynamics. Collaborative learning takes place both inperson and online, with ICTs expanding the range of possibilities. There is evidence that working collaboratively increases productivity, and improves learning outcomes. As a model, collaborative learning undergirds many significant ICT initiatives such as the open source model. In the education sector, students enrolled in MOOCs are found to collaborate through social media and Meetups161 from their own locales across the world. ICTs and social media have brought down the barriers to collaboration and openness.162 with these barriers removed; the possibilities for collaborative learning are open to anyone. Those who participate enrich their knowledge by being exposed to a multitude of viewpoints and experiences of people with whom they otherwise would have been unlikely to connect

In the context of youth employment, it is important to consider the benefits that participating in collaborative learning can offer. Collaborative learning events are opportunities for young people to learn ICTs (basic and advanced) as well as entrepreneurial skills. It can also result in increased connections and contacts with peers and experts in the field of interest; thus collaborative learning offers networking opportunities that may lead to participants learning about jobs as well. The sustainability and success of collaborative learning depends largely on the motivation and commitment of individuals who organize and participate in these events.

As, a growing number of jobs require ICT skills of different levels. Research shows that the best way to perfect or develop skills is to have the opportunity to put them to use, preferably in a job situation. A number of initiatives have been created to help employees get the required ICTs skills on the job. These initiatives are designed to prepare youth for a better and more productive work experience. The initiatives – driven by private sector, civil society and international agencies – offer training opportunities, internships, apprentice programmes, and mentoring. Several reports point to the importance of mentoring in learning and skill development, finding that when youth work alongside more experienced workers they acquire and develop many of the same ICT and soft skills and capacities of their mentors and co-workers.164 This also explains the growing popularity of co-working spaces and technology hubs

Learning and innovation places

The classic notion of the learning place is associated with organized institutions such as schools, universities, and vocational training centres. With the advance of new learning models described above, youth are taking learning to places like technology hubs, co-working spaces, and hacker/maker spaces. The popularity of these places demonstrates the lasting value of face-to-face interaction, which when coupled with interactive online tools, allows these places to offer a rich environment for learning, collaboration and co-creation.

A report prepared for the European Commission in 2008 predicted some of these changes by arguing that the emergence and wide adoption of web 2.0 technologies would give rise to social networking, collaborative content creation and democratized innovation. The technological changes seen in the intervening years have already gone farther than predicted in that report, especially in terms of the widespread impact of social networking and new locales for learning.

Co-working spaces and technology hubs

There are a growing number of co-working spaces and technology hubs that are supporting entrepreneurs and start-ups with training, networking, mentoring, and finding funding. A co-working space is a shared work environment where members have access to facilities such as a desk, meeting space, office equipment, kitchen and other amenities. Beyond the physical infrastructure, co-working spaces host events, offer trainings, and hold social gatherings. A technology hub is a form of co-working space with a greater focus on technology-based innovation. As such, they may offer programmes such as incubation services, hackathons, pitch fests, job boards, and contests that cater directly to the technology community. Tech hubs typically have strong ties with both global and local technology companies as well. In all of these places, it's the community of people that make them thrive. People join for the opportunity to meet like-minded people, share ideas, and learn from other members.

Hacker/maker spaces

Another type of space is the hacker space, or maker space. Hacker/maker spaces have an emphasis on electronics and building physical objects. A core piece of equipment is the 3D printer, allowing one to make three-dimensional solid objects of virtually any shape from a digital model. Laser cutters, vinyl cutters, CNC (computer numerical control) routers and CNC milling machines are often part of the equipment mix as well. Most of these spaces offer classes in how to use the equipment and work with various mediums (wood, metal, fabric) in addition to electronic circuitry. Many innovations have come from hacker/maker spaces, including in areas often targeted by international development efforts.

Social media

Social Media are used extensively for learning as well. Some of the major sites (e.g. Face book and Twitter) became known as platforms for the exchange of personal stories and leisure activities, but more and more people are using these for educational and professional purposes as well. Social networks, blogs, podcasts, video sharing (YouTube, Vimeo), photo sharing (Flickr, Picasa), social bookmarks (Ever note, del.icio.us), presentation sharing (Prezi, slideshare), discussion forums (Google groups), events (Meetup) and thousands of other platforms are being used by individuals and institutions of learning to enrich the learning experience. For example, people who enrol in MOOCs take advantage of both online social media tools and applications such as Meetup to organize face-to-face study sessions at a local coffeehouse, library, or someone's house. Education experts call these connectives, where "knowledge isn't a set of isolated facts to be memorized. Instead, it's actually a large set—or really a network—of connections, and learning is nothing more or less than traversing them. In the same way that you become proficient in a piece of music by playing its notes in order in an expressive way—that is, traversing its connections—you become proficient in a subject by participating in it. You see and appreciate the connections inherent in the subject, even creating new connections based on your experience.

Public-private partnerships

One of the chief complaints from employers is that they cannot find qualified labour to fill the vacancies. This is matched by a similar complaint from young people who say that they cannot find jobs even when they are qualified. This skills mismatch is a leading cause of the youth unemployment crisis.

Establishing channels for dialogue among industry leaders, policymakers, academia, and youth is an important role for government. Such dialogue allows all parties to gain a better understanding of job trends and requirements, which in turn contributes to the formulation of education and labour policies that responds to the needs of the market and spurs innovation. Models of such dialogues can be found in Singapore, Korea, Switzerland, Estonia, and Germany among others, where the national science and technology strategies and curriculum are formulated in dialogue with industry. These policies and investments are designed to attract students into science, technology, engineering and mathematics (STEM) fields. Similar programmes are emerging in developing countries. In Rwanda for example, the government has launched the "National ICT Literacy and Awareness Campaign," a joint initiative of the Ministry of Youth and ICT, Ministry of Local Government, the Ministry of Education, the Rwanda Education Board, Rwanda Development Board, and the Private Sector Federation. An open dialogue between governments and the private sector can help overcome issues related to coordination of investments in skills development and education. Many businesses make public-private partnerships a priority and have dedicated budgets for apprenticeship, job placements, and other programmes. Civil society organizations can be involved as well. In the United Kingdom, the National Apprenticeships Service has developed a three-way partnership with QA Apprenticeships and Cisco Apprenticeship to offer high school graduates three-year apprenticeship opportunities with CISCO.199 In Jordan the Ministry of Social Development is responsible for a programme designed to provide marginalized youth with training and job opportunities in private sector institutions. Youth gain real work experience and on-the-job training through this programme. In Malaysia, the Penang Skills Development Centre,201 created as a joint partnership among government, academia and industry, offers a range of training programmes for youth.

Another area for government-private sector partnership is job placement. In the apprenticeship examples above, participants are remunerated for their work and also have the opportunity to study part-time. After completing the programme, participants are expected to find jobs on their own. Other programmes are limited to training, and businesses use them to identify talent. Often, when businesses offer apprenticeships, internships or any other form of on-the-job-training opportunity, they limit their commitment to the duration of the programme. While students in these programmes in general fare well, this type of initiative could be complemented with a job placement element. Whether the placement is with the companies involved in the partnership, or with the government, or with civil society, the government has a role to play in ensuring that well-trained young professionals find a job. The areas where ICT-savvy professionals can be absorbed are growing as shown in chapters 4 and 5 describing trends and opportunities in macro sectors as health, agriculture, and business process outsourcing, as well as in a vast array of emerging areas from micro work to green jobs to accessibility solutions for persons with disabilities

Sub – Theme : Blended learning

Blended learning is the pedagogical integration of digital and face-to-face instruction. Blended learning encompasses flipped-classroom, mix-mode, hybrid, technology-mediated instruction, and web-enhanced instruction. In flipped classrooms,149 for instance, technologies are intricately integrated in the teaching process. The use of new technologies in learning is more than a mere substitution of the medium of instruction; it is an intentional design that takes advantage of digital tools and technology to enhance learning.

The blended learning process relies on digital environments called Learning Management Systems (LMS). LMS enable the creation of a virtual classroom for the students, complete with lessons plans, discussion for a, grades, quizzes, tests, class calendar and other resources. By having access to the class material, students can learn the concepts at their own pace and use the face-to-face time with the instructor to deepen their knowledge or to explore other issues of interest.

The virtual classroom on LMS is also a space for community building and interaction. Many LMSs integrate web 2.0 tools and applications such as prezi (prezi.com), slideshare (slideshare.net), YouTube (youtube.com), face book (facebook.com), ever note (evernote.com), and drop box (dropbox.com), to name a few – which are readily available through tablets, mobile phones, and personal computers. Blended learning requires active participation and engagement from the students, thereby changing the experience of knowledge acquisition. It is no longer a mere transfer of information, where the student only consumes. The innovative aspect of blended learning rests on the new way it encourages students to learn about the technology while discovering other subjects. Students have the option to present their work using the technology—for example, instead of writing a paper or report, they can make a video, wiki, or podcast. There are some exciting examples of universities organizing contests with PhD students who present their scientific work using video or other technology

Blended learning has gained popularity mostly in European and North American high schools, colleges and universities, especially those equipped with broadband access. The implementation of blended learning is growing slowly in the developing world, where connectivity and infrastructure continue to present challenges. Nonetheless, a number of universities from the South have enhanced their distance education programmes by turning them into blended learning opportunities to reach migrant populations living abroad, mostly in Europe and the United States. These universities operate through satellite offices around the world, and attract working mothers as well as young and older professionals who take advantage of these offerings to complete their academic studies with lower costs, often studying in their native language.

One appeal of the blended model for youth and life-long learners is the flexibility it offers to combine work and study. It is expected that more and more universities and institutions will be using the blended learning model around the world.

ICTs in education

The opportunities for learning and innovating with ICTs are immeasurable, as this report has shown. However, despite significant investments, formal educational systems continue to face challenges in preparing youth with the ICT-related skills they need to succeed. As a recent OECD report on the Outlook of Science, Technology and

Industry points out, traditional models of education are not adequately preparing students to meet the demands of a changing job market.177 The report emphasizes that formal education remains the primary vehicle for improving the supply of skills needed for driving innovation, and that governments need to take measures to address the limitations of their systems.

Many experts have linked the limitations of the educational systems to a lack of real integration of ICTs in education. The lack of integration negatively affects knowledge acquisition using ICTs, in general, and the acquisition of ICT skills, in particular, even when ICTs are available in the classroom. Many factors account for this situation, including: lack of software and technical support; absence of reliable electrical supply; inadequate student-computer ratios; ICT learning restricted to studying basic computer literacy and not for learning other subjects; and importantly, the limited capacity of teachers to make more integrated use of ICTs for teaching and learning.

There are many active regional initiatives. The Latin American Network of Educational Portals (RELPE) gathers ministers of education from 23 countries (25 portals) in the region and Spain with the goal of making ICTs an integral part of education by training and providing resources to increase the ICT capabilities of teachers.

In Africa, School Net Africa and the Pan African Research Agenda on the Pedagogical Integration on ICTs have developed a series of evidence-based policy documents to help educators, administrators, and policy-makers. Other initiatives provide educators and students with practical resources for use in the classroom.

In Asia, some countries have achieved a high degree of integration of ICTs in education while others are still working to provide digital access and basic literacy to large parts of their populations.180 In regional surveys, countries such as Korea, Singapore, Japan, China, and Taiwan rank high for their achievements in ICT in education programmes and support of sciences and technical innovation. In the rest of the region a significant amount of work is still needed. Nonetheless, it should be noted that new national programmes in Afghanistan, Bangladesh, Cambodia, India, Laos, Pakistan, and Viet

Nam designed to support the integration of ICTs in education are starting to show results.

Conclusion

The transformations taking place around youth, ICTs, employment, and entrepreneurship are characterized by rapid change and innovation. Mainstream economic sectors from agriculture to healthcare are witnessing an explosion of new ICT-enabled applications, both raising the bar in terms of the minimum ICT skills needed to perform job tasks, and generating new opportunities for entrepreneurs developing ICT products and services for these sectors. Beyond these sectors, the internet itself is responsible for making possible new opportunities that have generated livelihoods for millions of people. Crowd sourcing, micro work, app development, and other emerging income generating activities owe their existence to global internet expansion that continues to connect more and more of the world's population.

Seizing these opportunities requires the right skills and knowledge. Which skills are needed for which jobs however is not straightforward. As the types of jobs and tasks requiring knowledge of ICTs has multiplied, the range of skills has similarly expanded and diversified into numerous skills subcategories. Whereas basic computer skills and knowledge of productivity applications may still qualify a person for routine office work, such skills are insufficient for many of the new opportunities described in this report. Depending on the area, these new opportunities require one or more of several other abilities in such areas as information seeking, communication, collaboration, content production, multimedia creation, web design, security and privacy, solving technical problems, and programming, among others. Becoming a successful entrepreneur requires business skills as well, such as operations and management, finance, marketing, communications, research, and technology management.

Soft skills such as critical thinking and problem solving, flexibility and adaptability, social and cross-cultural skills, and initiative and self-direction are also essential. Entrepreneurs, more than entry level jobs, will generally require more advanced soft skills, though over time any person's prospects for career advancement will hinge on mastery of these soft skills in addition to ICT skills.

Fortunately, the market has responded with a multitude of new opportunities for people to learn different types of skills, in different ways, using different technologies, accessing different resources, and leading to different types of certifications. Innovations in learning both ICT and soft skills are plentiful and increasing every month. Existing programmes are improving, and new entrants are continuously introducing new products and services. Advances in mobile learning are opening new doors. Moreover, many of the resources are available at little or no cost. Anyone with an internet connection can access open courseware, enrol in a MOOC course, or receive a badge certifying mastery of a subject.

Many programs feature face-to-face interactions. Tech hubs, co-working spaces, hackathons apprenticeships, and networking events represent just a few of the ways people learn, and innovate, together. Indeed, some of the greatest opportunities may be realized by combining online and offline activities.

Youth are ideally suited to take advantage of these opportunities. In general they are naturally comfortable with technology and operating in online environments, adept at absorbing new concepts and skills, and capable of seeing new possibilities. Youth are the heaviest users of most digital technologies, and have driven the explosive expansion of social media and other web 2.0 applications. It is these new applications that have underpinned many of the new job and entrepreneurial opportunities.

How can youth be better prepared and positioned to seize new employment and entrepreneurship opportunities? The report has outlined a number of strategies pertaining to the role of government. Government can lead efforts to incorporate a number of the learning programmes and pedagogical models, such as blended learning and flipped classrooms, into K-12 and higher education. It can also mobilize efforts with the private sector to recognize alternative certification models, such as badges, thereby opening up ways to recognize skills mastery outside of formal education. Government can also lead dialogues with industry, academia, non-profit organizations, and youth to monitor and respond to ongoing changes in job trends. Public-private partnerships can further advance youth employment through training, internships, and job placement programmes. Policies and programmes to support entrepreneurship require another level of dedication. This ranges from creating favourable conditions for start-ups such as ease of business registration and access to low-interest loans, to direct support for such initiatives as innovation spaces and incubators to attract creative talent.

Community organizations also have an important role to play in equipping youth with the relevant skills and connecting them to employment and entrepreneurship opportunities. Telecentres, libraries, community technology centres and other places that offer computer resources, internet connectivity, and space for group activity are ideally positioned to implement programmes that will provide youth with the skills and experience they need to pursue these opportunities. They represent a non-formal channel for learning, and as such they tend to have more flexibility than formal schools to experiment and implement the types of programmes contained in this report. Moreover, many youth require an intermediary to motivate, guide, structure, and otherwise provide an environment that facilitates learning. While self-directed youth can take advantage of online programmes on their own, the majority of youth requires this extra assistance.

All stakeholders in the ecosystem – international organizations, governments, development agencies, private industry, non-profit organizations, and foundations – have important roles to play to realize greater opportunities for youth. Doing so requires that stakeholders embrace the innovative process: be open to experimentation, ensure robust feedback systems are in place to learn from successes and failures, be nimble to change direction as needed and incorporate new technological advances, not seek a one-size-fits-all model (it doesn't exist), and otherwise adopt the same innovative approach that we want to imbue in our youth.

1. Providing authentic tasks and contexts for practice, including digitally-mediated contexts where appropriate.

2. Making explicit community practices of meaning – making.
3. Demonstrating how digital scholarship / professionalism might be expressed in different contexts.
4. Demonstrating how forms of academic communication are constructed and how different media are used to persuade, argue, make claims, and occupy a stance.
5. Helping learners manage conflict between different meaning – making contexts and setting.
6. Recognizing and helping learners to use and extend existing knowledge practices as resources for learning.